The Urbana Free Library

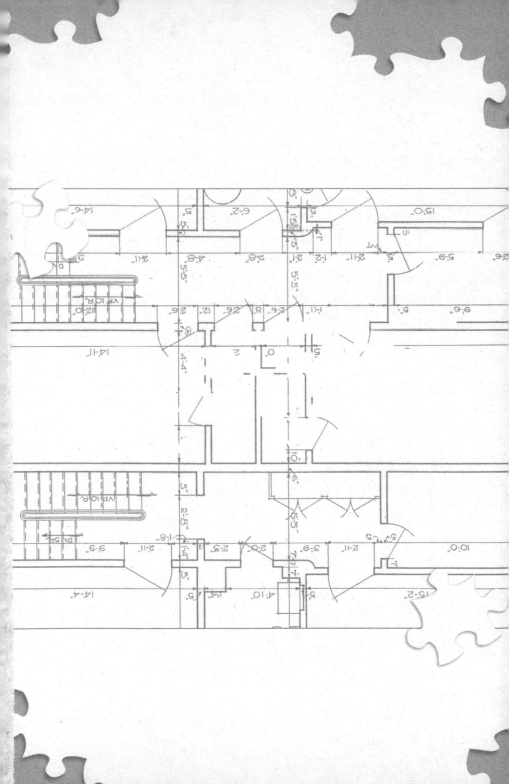

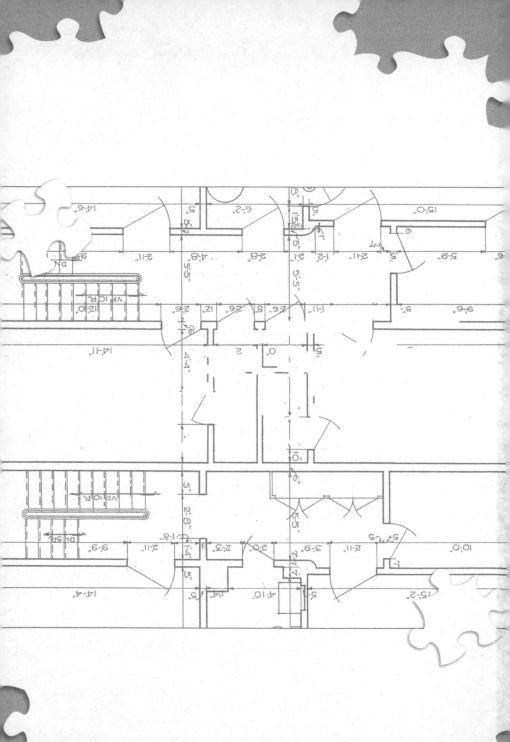

Advance Praise for *Disassembly Required*

"Ostensibly about the break-up of her marriage and loss of her dream house, a four-story Victorian brownstone in Brooklyn's Carroll Gardens neighborhood, Beverly Willett's absorbing memoir is really about finding a home in one's own skin. A delight."

—COURTNEY HARGRAVE, author of *Burden: A Preacher, A Klansman, and a True Story of Redemption in the Modern South*, also a major motion picture starring Forest Whitaker

"Sometimes the best way to find yourself is to lose your husband, your home, your bearings—and start all over again, and that's just what Beverly Willett did in this ebullient memoir about giving up what you thought you wanted to find out what you really need. An enchanting and inspiring look at how less can really be so, so much more."

—CAROLINE LEAVITT, *New York Times* bestselling author of *Pictures of You*

"This is the book Sheryl Sandberg might have written if she hadn't been rich. Beverly Willett had the dream: husband, children, career, and that most important New York achievement, a house in Brooklyn. And then she just had...her kids. She didn't 'lean in,' she sucked it up, moved on, and built a new life. *Disassembly Required: A Memoir of Midlife Resurrection* is more energizing and inspiring than a triple espresso."

—JESSE KORNBLUTH, HeadButler.com

"*Disassembly Required* is Beverly Willett's story of resurrecting her life after a devastating divorce. In it, she reminds us of the sorrow love can bring us as well as that love—of children, of self—really can conquer all. An uplifting and ultimately triumphant story."

—ANN HOOD, *New York Times* bestselling author of *The Knitting Circle* and *The Book That Matters Most*

"In her inspiring debut memoir, Beverly Willett's account of a devastating divorce and its aftermath is both sharpshooting and poignant. Her ability to push through deep despair and reclaim herself while holding on to grace and wit will give hope to anyone starting over in life."

—MELANIE BOWDEN SIMÓN, author of *La Americana* and a 2016 '35 Over 35' Debut Author

DISASSEMBLY REQUIRED

DISASSEMBLY REQUIRED

A MEMOIR OF MIDLIFE RESURRECTION

BEVERLY WILLETT

Post Hill
PRESS

Post Hill Press
New York • Nashville
posthillpress.com

Published in the United States of America

To my daughters—
I love you to infinity and beyond.

"It's just about as poignant to be torn from a house as it is from a person."

—FLANNERY O'CONNOR,
The Habit of Being: Letters of Flannery O'Connor

CONTENTS

1

Les Escaliers

"You should give your house a name," one of my girlfriends said when I told her about the Victorian brownstone my husband and I had bought. "Call it *Les Escaliers*," French for "The Staircases."

There were eight, a total of 120 steps. I finished tallying them sixteen years after we moved in, the day I moved out.

One by one, everyone in my family but me had already left. My daughter Ella had started college in the fall. Nicki, my eldest, had graduated the previous spring, then moved in with her boyfriend. That same summer our beloved family cat Thunder died. It was Jake, my ex-husband, who'd begun the exodus over a decade earlier, after meeting another woman and suing me for divorce.

That left me, alone in our four-story dream house in Brooklyn.

A few months before I left, my aunt and her six-year-old granddaughter Madison came for a visit. That's when I first began counting the stairs.

"You have so many," Madison said, minutes after she arrived. I asked if she wanted to count them, handed her pen and paper, and followed her up the eighteen stairs from the parlor to the second floor where Nicki and Ella had slept in opposite wings, a hallway and double-sinked bathroom in-between their bedrooms. Portraits of the girls as youngsters, taken by official JFK campaign and presidential photographer Jacques Lowe, flanked the hallway. Another of them together graced the foyer and was the first thing that met your eyes after opening the front door. I'd met Lowe at a party in Manhattan, and he'd offered to spend a day photographing my daughters in his Tribeca loft merely for the price of the prints. How innocent the girls had looked through his lens, untouched by time or hardship, prancing about his loft while Jake and I eavesdropped.

My real estate broker's stager told me to remove the photographs before the open house, allowing buyers to envision themselves in my space. But I wouldn't take the portraits off the walls. Anyone buying my house was buying a home. A place where a family had lived, my family, what remained of it.

Madison and I continued counting. Two steps on the second-floor landing, where the staircase swiveled, led to sixteen more stairs and then onto the third floor.

"Where does that go?" Madison asked when we reached the top floor, leaning her neck back as far as she could to stare up at the green spiral staircase in the master bedroom.

"To the roof," I said. The roof deck, a bit rickety now, had been one of the reasons Jake and I fell in love with the house. We needed more space and had started house hunting a year after Ella, our second baby, came along. The house nearly doubled our square footage, but mostly it was all the light, the backyard, and that rooftop, more than practicalities, that drew us to this particular house.

I toured it first, and by the time I'd walked through and gotten to the roof, stood in the brisk winter air and gazed out at the Manhattan skyline, I knew Jake would fall in love as I had. I couldn't wait to rush home and tell him I'd found our dream house. A few months later we moved in; five and a half years after that, after twenty years of marriage, my husband moved out.

What sleep I managed to get after he left had me feeling like someone had punched me in the chest after I woke up. Right after the split-second interval between honest-to-God wondering if Jake's leaving had been a hallucination, and the shock waves that gripped me when I realized my husband was actually gone. *Go lie back down and take a deep breath*, I'd tell myself. *It's real*, I'd say out loud. Sometimes I squinted my eyes shut, gritted my teeth, and shook my head back and forth in an effort to absorb the truth.

I got a prescription for sleeping pills and, on nights when I couldn't sleep, I sat on my bed, poured the contents of the entire bottle into my hand, and stared back. Sometimes I went downstairs to the kitchen and grabbed the others—samples my shrink gave me for depression, medication I took to ward off panic attacks, and leftover painkillers from knee surgeries. Then I'd try to calibrate in my head how many pills would make sure I never woke up.

When I was a kid, my Sunday school teacher taught that people who killed themselves went to hell. After Jake left, hell didn't scare me half as much as continuing to live in such pain.

In my dreams, I stood on our roof deck and leaned slightly over the edge, before spreading my arms, ready for liftoff to the garden four stories below. Only I never jumped. Not even in my dreams. Always, thoughts of my two daughters sleeping one floor below brought me back to life. Jake had left us; I couldn't desert them. Even the thought ripped my heart wide open.

So I'd toss the pills in my nightstand, crawl under the covers, and try and get through one more day, unable to decide if that made me smart or chicken.

~ ~ ~

MADISON WAITED FOR ME in my bedroom while I climbed the staircase to the roof. "Nineteen," I called out when I reached the top. Madison wrote it down on her scrap of paper.

After she and I returned to the parlor floor, we walked down eleven steps to the ground floor where my tenants lived.

"Are there more stairs?" Madison asked, incredulous, watching me walk down the hallway and open the cellar door.

"It's dark down there," she said, peering at the metal handrail, peeling concrete wall, and dankness below.

"It's okay," I said. "You don't have to go down there. Nicki and Ella think it's spooky, too." So did I. Jobs involving the basement had been mostly my ex-husband's domain. After he left, his jobs upstairs and downstairs—draining the boiler, dealing with the occasional repair, carrying things up and down the cellar stairs—also became mine.

"Fourteen stairs," I said, retracing my steps up the cellar staircase.

We had somewhere to go that day so Madison and I had never finished our counting. I came across her notes the morning I left home for good and decided to finish. I opened the kitchen door and counted off eleven steps from the deck down to the garden where Ella had once planted her morning glory seeds. Eleven more steps led from the front stoop to the sidewalk and one of Brooklyn's many grand London plane trees, known for its camouflage bark, which looked in on our picture window. After opening the wrought iron gate at street level, I took two more steps to the ground floor.

I left the wooden spiral staircase descending from Ella's room on the second floor straight down to the kitchen for last. I hadn't meant to; it simply worked out that way. The previous owners had cut a hole in the floor of what later became Ella's bedroom in order to combine the ground, parlor, and second floors into a triplex and turn the top floor into a rental. But Jake and I confiscated the top floor for ourselves, including the roof deck from which we watched the Fourth of July fireworks.

I'd thought of removing Ella's private staircase. She was two when we moved in and I thought the stairs were dangerous. But Jake and I thought the staircase looked cool, and Ella was careful—and I put up numerous child gates—and she never got hurt. We bonked our heads on the staircase many times though, and so did our guests. It ate up a huge chunk of kitchen space where I had visions of a pantry. But the staircase remained.

4

As I descended it my final morning, I suddenly saw what Ella must have seen nearly eleven years to the day earlier, when she'd been only seven. Her mother, me, sitting at the kitchen table below, crying, broken. No wonder she'd been frightened. Hers was a picture of Mom she'd never witnessed before.

"Mommy, what are you doing up already?" Ella had asked, barefoot, standing at the top of the spiral staircase wearing her pink silky nightgown.

"I couldn't sleep, honey," I said.

"Is everything alright?" she asked, rubbing her eyes.

Someone once told me they could stare straight through Ella's big brown eyes and see her soul. That day I felt she was looking directly through to mine.

By the time I moved out, I'd downsized three-quarters of our possessions, giving away expensive antiques and artwork. By then, despite the losses I'd endured, I understood what was important.

And so I kept every single one of the love notes and pictures Ella and Nicki made for me. Many had been taped to the wall above my desk for years, right up until the time I had to box them up to move. "The Wall of Mom," Ella called it.

"I'm fine, honey," I lied to my daughter that long-ago day at the kitchen table. "Get dressed and come down for breakfast." After she headed upstairs, I walked to the vestibule and put my husband's cell phone back into his coat pocket.

The night before I'd worried when Jake hadn't come home until after midnight. I'd phoned the salon where he told me he was going for a massage after work, but they said he'd never shown up. When he got home, he refused to tell me where he'd been. Restless, I awoke early, the house quiet, my husband and children still slumbering. As I walked downstairs, my eyes were drawn to his brown suede jacket in the vestibule. Feeling like a thief, I reached inside the pockets, drew out Jake's cell phone, and carried it into the kitchen, shaking.

I brewed a pot of coffee, conscious to place a moment between what I feared might be on that phone and whatever came next. And then I sat down at the kitchen table, picked up Jake's cell phone, and perked up my ears to hear if my powering it on had woken anybody up.

My husband and I had had problems in our marriage from the start. But we'd worked through so many of them, or so I believed. I hadn't dreamed he was having an affair.

Jake had saved only two numbers—one for his brother, the other for a female lawyer he'd mentioned working with at his new job. No listings for me—his wife—or the children. The other woman held position number one; outgoing and incoming calls and messages corresponded to her number.

He hadn't created password protection so I scrolled to voicemail on my husband's cell phone. Instantly I heard a woman's voice I'd never heard before. The same voice, breathless, caressing, almost panting at times, repeated itself over and over as I paged forward.

"I love you. Call me at home…not sure what time it is," the voice said.

My hand trembled. I grabbed a pen and stray envelope and copied down snippets as fast as I could, writing the words down to keep a heart-beat's distance away from falling apart.

"I love you with all my heart."

"My heart is hurting," panting, "and…wanting," more panting, "to be with you. Bye, Baby."

I inhaled my tears, and stuffed my wails inside so the children, one floor above, wouldn't hear.

"Hey sweetie…me."

"It's five-thirty in the morning and…can't sleep, needless to say."

"Want to come over here tomorrow and have a little time to be private instead of meeting at the office?" the voice continued.

Fear exploded in my chest. I couldn't swallow. I wanted to bolt the doors and keep my family in suspended animation, safe and rolled up in their covers until I could figure out what to do next.

But I pressed the send button to hear more, unable to stop inflicting my own pain.

"Love you so much. Thanks for all your sweet messages...love you dearly."

That's the moment Ella called to me from the top of her stairs, standing where I stood eleven years later, minutes before I left my house forever. Standing where she had stood unexpectedly retriggered the scene that had set in motion the dissolution of our family and the loss of the American dream we'd worked so hard for, right there in our kitchen.

Twice before I'd left home, once for college and then again after law school when I moved to New York City. But this time was different. This time I would be leaving the nest I'd built—the nest that had become the symbol of the most important thing I had ever done and the people I loved more than anyone else and the place where it finally and officially crumbled. Everyone but me had moved on and started a new life. Now it was time for me to leave home too. To exit Brooklyn, pick up where I'd left off over thirty years before, and begin again.

First, though, I had to sell my house.

2

I Got the House

My divorce was final in 2009. I got the house. If anyone had told me how hard and expensive it would be to maintain and fight for, I still wouldn't have listened. The house was our home and that was that.

Jake was in favor of me and the children staying there, initially. Before I learned of his affair, before he moved in with his girlfriend, before he served me with divorce papers. One morning before he left, we were standing in our bedroom when I put my arms around him, buried my face in his starched white shirt, and wept. His grip was looser than mine.

"If we get divorced, I'll be fair and generous," he said. "I'll give you and the kids whatever you need."

"And if I do well at my new job, maybe you won't have to move out of the house," he continued, letting go. "I realize what that will do to the children." And he had done well. He told our therapist he had plenty of money for two households.

Then one night I overheard him talking on the phone to his girlfriend from our bedroom. There was talk of a trip and then my husband's words:

"Unless she goes back to work full-time the house will be divided and sold within the year." I slid to the floor and whimpered.

"Beverly's going back to work or we won't be able to afford the house. My money is my money and I'll spend my money any way I want," he later told our therapist.

"We'll divide things fifty-fifty, but you can't have the house. That has to be sold," he told me. I'd later learn family court also viewed divorce as a business transaction, with zero regard for the reconciliation of families.

How was this fair? I didn't want a divorce. Why should my husband have the right to make decisions about my future after he left? We'd made joint decisions before, including how we'd raise the children and allocate family responsibility. So that's the arrangement I aimed to continue, girlfriend or no girlfriend.

We'd been financial partners too. After putting myself through law school, I moved to New York City and worked for a music company where I'd met Jake. Five years later, I landed a succession of prestigious jobs, first at a major Manhattan law firm, then at a television network, and finally as right-arm to one of the city's top entertainment attorneys. My hours were long and grueling, my husband's hours more regular.

Eight years after we got married Nicki was born, and I became a stay-at-home mom. Five years later, Ella came along. After Nicki was born I had worked at home part-time, those part-time hours turning into frequent fifty hour or more work weeks with regular travel. But we wanted a house, and increased hours meant I could put together a down payment and add substantially to our savings, and so I did. The stress of juggling work, a house, kids, marriage, and travel wore me out. We had bought the house by then and so Jake said he'd bring home the bacon and got a series of plum law partnerships that we mortgaged the house further in order to buy into. Meanwhile, I turned my attention full-time to caring for the kids and house, and building a freelance writing career.

"Why can't we stay in our house?" I begged my husband.

"That's just not happening," Jake said. When I asked about the kids, he said they'd adjust.

Sure, we had problems, but to me this man no longer resembled the one who had broken down crying with me in the bathroom the day we saw the pink dot on the home pregnancy kit. Or the one who shook with tears when Ella came out with her mop of red hair. Before the affair, even during the rough times in our marriage, there were glimmers of the man I thought I knew. Afterwards, I couldn't find him anywhere.

For years I wandered the streets of Brooklyn, perusing real estate boards, making appointments to view condos and apartments, attending open houses while the children were with dad on alternate weekends, one foot in my house, the other out the door.

"Mommy, are we moving?" Ella asked the spring she turned eight. She was scared; I could hear it in the pitch of her voice.

"No, honey," I said.

"Then why are you always looking at the houses?" It was the first time I'd stopped to read the real estate boards with her, though I usually glanced over while walking by. I hadn't realized Ella noticed. Perhaps I should have. Ella rarely missed anything.

"Just looking," I said, at a loss for anything other than a lie.

I'd been scared of leaving too. And frightened of staying. Living the life of a single mother alone in that big house when the kids went to dad's.

A few weeks after Jake left, I collapsed at Barnes & Noble. EMS took me to the emergency room. The panic attacks I'd gotten under control after Jake had been let go from one of his jobs a few years earlier had returned. And I'd quickly dropped nearly forty pounds.

For years, I drifted from day to day, confused, forcing myself through the motions, dragged in and out of court, my daily rhythm off, like teetering in high heels all the time.

"You were in shock," a therapist told me. And perhaps I was. I dreamt of running away, besot with thoughts of escape to remote places I'd never been, where I didn't know the language and had no inclination to learn. My lawyer said the courts wouldn't allow me to leave New York City until the children were grown, more than a decade from when Jake left. I felt caged.

Move on, make a fresh start, some friends said. Better to be liquid than go broke trying to maintain a big, old house.

My final divorce judge (I had seven in total) said she didn't understand me either. She halted the proceedings and ordered me and my lawyer into chambers one day, one of several off-the-record conversations held during trial. Even though I'd been a lawyer for over twenty years, I hadn't realized how so much of the justice system operated in the shadows, out of earshot and in effect beyond the reach of the law.

Why didn't I get myself a nice law job and a condo and find a boyfriend? Judge #7 wanted to know. Only I didn't want a boyfriend or a condo or a law job where I'd barely get to see my children. I loved my husband; I loved my family; I wanted my life back.

My marriage eventually ended and still, I clung to my house, the one tangible thing that anchored me and the children. Our haven and reference point for the family that survived.

"Forget what's going on in court," one of my friends said over tea. "Just believe your husband wants you to stay in the house. Believe that's the truest wish inside his heart even though he may not realize it." To me that was crazy talk. But something in me wanted to believe her. She and a group of girlfriends had organized a chanting meditation retreat at my house the weekend before I'd been due back in court to steel me. And after twenty-four hours of round-the-clock prayer, something negative was purged out of me and got me back on my feet.

Gradually the comfort my house once provided returned, relief settling in whenever I turned the lock and closed the door behind me. Or saw my neighbor Teddy and his ninety-year-old mother, Marie, and wife, Donna, smile when I came up the block. Even the guys in the pizza shop around the corner knew my voice when I called to order. Helen, the Italian woman who lived nearby and had watched the children when I started working from home, had become family, a second grandmother to my daughters and a friend to me. My Brooklyn neighborhood was safe. Shopkeepers knew my kids and me by name. We looked out for each other.

11

Named for the only Roman Catholic signer of the Declaration of Independence, an Irish immigrant named Charles Carroll, my Carroll Gardens Brooklyn neighborhood had been settled by the Irish. Norwegians followed, then Italian-Americans, and next professionals, my husband and I among the first wave. Most recently, there had been an influx of French immigrants.

Public gardens were constructed in the mid-19th century. Many of them later became part of huge front gardens in homes on certain coveted blocks. Most brownstones were built in the 1870s and 1880s as part of an architecturally homogenous plan that is still a hallmark of the neighborhood, along with tree-lined streets and parks. Many of the working-class Italian-American residents who settled in the neighborhood had also worked on the nearby Red Hook docks, which closed in the 1960s, when gentrification began.

Before gentrification, it was the Italians who predominated, the Italians who gave the neighborhood its character—the Sicilians, the Neapolitans, and the Molesi, from a small coastal town in Southern Italy called Mola di Bari. Along with their bakeries, social clubs, and pizzerias, they were known for their annual procession for the Feast of Our Lady of Sorrows through the streets of town, where Molesi men carried a statue of the blessed mother Mary on their shoulders and swung incense from a thurible while men and women sang and played instruments.

I wasn't Catholic and couldn't remember the dates of the feast days. But I'd hear music a block away and run to the front door, stepping out onto the stoop to watch even if I was in my robe and slippers. The solemnity and regularity of this tradition honoring the sacred female grounded me and gripped my heart with joy. I too was a mother.

I know it sounds idyllic, especially in New York City, and maybe it was mostly in my imagination. Still, my little spot in the world seemed a small pocket of comfort in the midst of my turmoil. I refused to willingly leave it, and the stability brought by continuing to live in our home became my mission.

My ex-husband moved many times during the divorce, and the girls schlepped their belongings every other weekend to an ever-changing venue. By the time Ella went to college, she'd lived in nine or so different residences. The average number of residences a person in the U.S. lives in during their entire lifetime is only eleven.

I watched the girls sitting in the foyer beside their suitcases the first time their father picked them up for visitation. To me, they looked like foster children about to be ferried off to the next family willing to take them in. I went into the kitchen and cried silently into my shirt sleeve.

Until they became adults I vowed not to move. And so each time my daughters came home from Dad's or camp or school or church or play rehearsal or countless other places, they walked through the same front door. They laid their heads down on the same pillow, in the same room, in the same house, in the same neighborhood. We cooked in the same kitchen and carried on the same traditions and hung our stockings on the same coatrack.

Did I do the right thing clinging so tightly to my four walls? Was it sensible to spend so much money on a mortgage and home repairs? Sane to fight so hard for stability? How can we know the answers to the decisions we make ahead of time or even in retrospect? *You do the best you can,* my friend Quinnie always says.

You talk as if you were living in a fairy tale, another friend remarked. And perhaps I was. Perhaps my dream world was the only place I could survive during that time, my grief so profound I wasn't capable of letting go of the fantasy that the crumpled floating pieces of my life would magically reattach. Incapable of realizing I deserved better than my husband's betrayal.

Perhaps I was also holding fast to the American dream, a concept that has existed for centuries and one I'd been schooled in and seen reflected in my own family and community, not that I consciously thought about it that way, not then. In the 20th century, this American dream had become a hallmark of achieving middle-class success through a combination of equal opportunity, hard work, and commitment, which was thought to

13

lead to health and happiness. Marriage, family, a good job, and title to a home were the outward markers of this achievement. Today, as the economic gap widens between those at the top and those in the middle and at the bottom, as marriage and family stability decline, as people lose their homes, there is concern this dream is being replaced by the goal of mere survival. For many, the American dream is one divorce, too, can make vanish.

Certainly, those in my family had at one time attained the American dream, though it was by no means easy. "Your father worked hard to send you to college and pay off the mortgage in record time," was the story my mother was most fond of telling. The most hardworking dedicated father and husband I've ever known, he died of a heart attack, but left my mother debt-free, with a modest pension. When I went to college, I had only lived in two houses, and there had never been a divorce in my extended family.

Unlike every other state, when Jake filed his complaint against me New York hadn't yet adopted unilateral no-fault divorce—the kind where both individuals consent to tie the knot, but only one need choose to sever it, even without cause. That meant he had to prove I'd committed some actionable wrong like adultery or cruelty in order to obtain a divorce. I wanted to save my marriage so I elected to defend myself against his wrongful charges. After trial, the court dismissed Jake's divorce complaint.

Even then I caught my breath, hopeful somehow that we would reunite. Only Jake never did come home. He moved to New Jersey where the law would have allowed him to get a divorce without my consent, my marriage all but officially over. Law or not, like it or not, I'd been outsmarted in a game I wasn't even playing.

For me it was impossible to have lived with a person so many years, to have gone through so much, to care as deeply as I did, and accept that the person I'd spent twenty years with could be someone I'd never really known.

Besides, it's easy to see the worst in people. To find the love you've got to dig way deep down and claw your way back to it, past the poison and the pain and the voices calling you a fool because they don't feel inside what you do.

But sadly there was no way to save my marriage. Nothing to do but give in and learn to accept what I couldn't understand, then turn my attention to the fight for my home.

During the divorce litigation, the court ordered real estate appraisers to enter my house several times. Sunlight streamed in through Ella's blinds to wake us up the morning the first appraiser came. It was two years after September 11, and there had been a blackout in New York City the day before. The girls and I were in an office building in Manhattan for Nicki's therapy appointment when the lights went out.

"Mom, what's going on?" Nicki had asked.

"I don't know, honey. I'm sure it's nothing. A power outage somewhere." But there was a sick feeling in my stomach as we joined the procession feeding into the stairwells. All I knew then was I needed to get my children home to safety.

Nicki walked in front of me, while I held Ella's right hand in my left and felt our way down twenty flights of stairs even as thousands of New Yorkers fled their office buildings and took to the streets. Jake met us on the sidewalk; he'd been scheduled to take the girls to dinner. After he spent time with them, I herded the children into the car and fired up the ignition.

We inched along, my Jeep creeping ahead of the throngs of people surrounding our car. I was sweating, but afraid to open the windows, scared somebody might try to climb in even though the crowd was well-behaved. The gas gauge was low so I kept the air-conditioning mostly off, giving us a periodic short blast of cold air while I clenched the steering wheel and kept my foot on the brakes to keep from running over someone. The odometer read five miles an hour.

There could be a bomb strapped underneath, I thought as we ambled across the Brooklyn Bridge. *And nothing you can do to prevent it. Hurry, hurry,* I screamed in my head to prod the car in front of me. Then *breathe.*

"Mommy, when are we going to be home?" Ella asked. The light continued to fade.

"Soon, honey, soon," I said, steadying my voice. Safety waited at home and we were on our way.

Four miles and two and a half hours later, we parked half a block from our house. The street lights were out, but there was a bit of a glow in the sky to guide our path.

"Wait here," I said to the girls in the vestibule, feeling my way to the kitchen and a basket on the counter containing flashlights.

"Hold on to the banister," I said as we walked upstairs to put on our pajamas. After we returned to the kitchen. I found a couple of cold storage packs, and the girls helped me load meat into it from the freezer. By the time we finished it was nearing nine thirty. We hadn't eaten since midday.

"We should eat up whatever is going to spoil," I said.

For the next few hours, we played *Life* and our favorite card games, *Frog Juice* and *Rat-a-Tat Cat*, by candlelight. We ate deli salami and ham and passed around tubs of ice cream. We talked about Abe Lincoln and Laura Ingalls and what life must have been like on the prairie. Nicki and Ella's faces glistened in the flickering flames. Brooklyn was hushed and still. My heart finally stopped fluttering.

"Time for bed," I said after midnight. After tucking Nicki in, I laid a flashlight near her pillow, then guided Ella across the hall. I pulled the covers over her, then slid under the sheet of the twin bed opposite hers.

A few minutes after we woke up the following day, the power went back on. The world hadn't ended. No terrorism this time either, merely a massive blackout across the Northeast. I'd begun unloading food from the coolers back into the freezer when the doorbell rang.

"Who's that?" Nicki asked.

"I don't know, honey," I said, walking to the front door. A woman, fifty-something, medium-build, holding a clipboard, stood on the other side.

"Can I help you?" I asked, puzzled.

"I'm the appraiser. From the court?" I'd forgotten the real estate appraiser ordered by the court to value our house was coming by.

"Who is it, Mommy?" Ella asked, running to the foyer to see.

"Just a lady who has to look at the house for the divorce. It's nothing, sweetie. Go back in the kitchen with Nicki. I'll be there in a minute."

"I'm sorry," the woman said, noticing the tears that had started down my cheeks. "It's pretty routine. It'll only take a minute." I was so tired of putting up a brave front.

"I know you're just doing your job," I said, ushering her in.

I walked her through the house, up and down each floor, silent and standing aside while she measured and photographed, politely answering her questions.

The summer after my husband left I came across a song Elton John wrote with Bernie Taupin in the nineties called "House." It became my anthem, and I'd blast it from the car radio and sing from the liner notes while I looked out from my bedroom window at the tree in front of my stoop. Determined with all my might that my husband would not strip me and my children of our home too.

"I'm sorry," I said to the appraiser, wiping my face. "It's just hard."

"Don't worry," she said, looking into my eyes. "You'll get the house."

Six years later I had.

3

Justice for Moms

Be careful what you ask for, my lawyer warned.
I asked for the house and finally got it in the divorce judgment. Jake had offered it in a settlement proposal intertwined with things we couldn't agree on. The judge said she'd penalize me unless I accepted his offer. I thought she was bluffing; she wasn't.

In addition to the house, I got a hefty mortgage and a six-digit bill for attorneys' fees. Judge #7 ordered me to refinance the house and get my husband off the mortgage, and slashed my alimony, ending it altogether two years after the divorce became final. Luckily, she instructed my ex to pay for college out of his half-a-million-dollar salary, but she cut my child support and imputed income to me as if I had a six-figure job, even though I was unemployed.

The job expert my husband hired testified that plenty of employers would offer me a salary of $180,000 (and some possibly $345,000), despite the fact I hadn't practiced law in a decade and had worked part-time before that. The judge wouldn't allow my lawyer to finish cross-examining the expert, unless I paid to fly him back to New York from California where he lived. I refused. He was my ex-husband's witness, not mine. "We were blackmailed," my attorney told me. "We had the right to cross-examine on their dime. Good appealable issue."

So I appealed. And lost.

The stock market had crashed. Nine million people had lost their jobs. *The New York Times* called the job market one of the ugliest for lawyers in over a quarter of a century. It was the time of the subprime mortgage crisis with banks foreclosing on nearly one million homes in 2008, the year before the divorce court's decision. Before it was over, the housing bubble tore over seven million people from their homes. By 2013, when I sold mine, the rate of U.S. home ownership was approximately 64 percent, its lowest point in two decades.

I was fifty-three, unemployed, and living in a wildly expensive city the children and I couldn't leave because my husband, who immediately remarried, had visitation rights. Judge #7 even asked why my husband didn't have the right to move on with his life. But at what price? What about my rights? I'd labored hard to contribute to the family coffers, raise the children, take care of the household, and support my husband in his career endeavors. The result was to have my marriage dissolved, my family split, and my property taken and divvied up, even though I hadn't been found guilty of any wrongdoing.

In the end, I was in better financial shape compared with many people, although at times an emotional wreck. Thankfully, my house was situated in one of the few areas where there had been a real estate boom. But the injustices were no less bitter pills. In some ways perhaps more so, because my own husband and the justice system I'd promised to serve as a lawyer had both betrayed me. And the person who'd made the final decision about my fate? One of my own kind: A woman, the seventh judge I'd been bounced around to before it was all over.

What I'd once considered normal was turned upside down. But nothing crushed me more than Judge #7's smears against me as a mother.

"What are you doing with your days to be productive?" she asked me on the witness stand. "Did any therapists for your mental health tell you

19

you'd be better off going back to work? Do you believe you're a better role model for your children doing volunteer activities? I haven't heard why you want to stay home and not work." She really said those words. *Stay home and not work.* Like one of five million other apparently lazy stay-at-home parents? Where was respect for my choice? And why had I been made to defend it? This was the 21st century, and women had worked hard for equality and fairness. Why was there a seeming preference for mothers who had decided to "lean in" and continue to work outside the home?

I pleaded with the judge to understand how much I valued my family, how important I considered my job as a stay-at-home mom. For me, no job was more important than raising precious little girls to become loving, strong women.

Some mothers have no financial choice but to work outside the home. Others prefer to. I don't judge them. Why was I judged? As a single mom, every chore, most every decision, was up to me. No wonder I poured pills into my hands before going to sleep. Jake earned a considerable salary. He'd left the marriage, not me.

My contributions to the household allegedly had been included in the judge's final allocation. I felt the numbers didn't add up and that she'd overlooked what I considered other important evidence, the judge's determination no more than lip service to the divorce statute which mandated they be factored in. I appealed; the appeals court rubberstamped Judge #7's decision.

Meanwhile, I strained to keep life as close to normal as possible, at least inside the four walls of our home. I continued cooking dinner most school nights, and the girls and I stopped whatever we were doing and sat down together for a meal. One evening, instead of our usual table games, we made up an original one. We thought up wishes and fun things to do, wrote them on strips of papers cut from pink index cards, and tossed them into a glass jar. Every few days we were going to draw a wish.

"Play hand games," Ella said.

Make spitballs. Play Mother May I. Blow bubbles through straws. Those were some of mine.

"I'll teach you and Ella poker," Nicki suggested. "And we should make up our own recipes and tell scary stories and someone gets a hairdo one night."

"Eat peanut butter!" Ella called out. Nearly every night I packed Ella's lunch and made her favorite sandwich, precisely the way she liked it, a PB&J on whole wheat. As I cut off the crusts, I imagined Ella sitting at the school lunch table with her friends the next day, smiling, because she knew how much love had gone into that sandwich.

The girls and I agreed on a repeat of the dessert night we had one evening and added another pink slip to the jar. Afterwards they went off to finish their homework. Before Ella went to bed, she and I made preparations for the sweet-tooth tasting we'd designed for her science project. We made bowls of regular and diet Jell-O and set out supplies for the friends and neighbors coming over the following day—diet and regular soda, candy with sugar and candy with aspartame, sugar cookies and diet cookies, and scarves for blindfolds.

Nicki became a teenager right after Jake left, but I still babied her on occasion. The summer after she was born, we rented a house with several other couples and while they mixed cocktails, I sat in our bedroom rocking Nicki and singing to her for hours after she fell asleep. Thirteen years later, not much had changed. One night she showed me an essay she'd written for English class about a weekend we spent together while her father was away with Ella.

"As I drifted off to sleep that last night of our wonderful weekend," Nicki wrote, "I heard my mom reading *Huck Finn*. Her perfect imitation of [Huck] almost brought me to tears—I was laughing so hard at it. I closed my eyes and drifted off into a deep sleep wondering how much she would read before she would discover I wasn't listening."

Those were the best days of my life. Even cutting the crust off a PB&J sandwich the way my daughter liked it gave my life meaning and purpose. But my role and job as a mother was apparently a waste of time according to the justice system.

When my lawyer asked my ex's job expert if my being a full-time mom figured into his salary assessment, Judge #7 objected. "This is 2008," she said. "You are on very dangerous ground here."

I wonder if it's even trickier for stay-at-home moms and dads a decade later. My first judge, also female, pounced on me too, after my attorney filed a motion for temporary alimony and child support. "She needs a job," the judge said as I stood before her, emaciated, mere months after being abandoned.

At the conclusion of trial, Judge #7 delivered her final verbal blow to me, off the record, the court reporter's keys silent. I'd prepared a closing statement, but Jake's lawyer only agreed to let me talk if there was no record of my words. The judge concurred.

"I object to Ms. Willett engaging in a soliloquy..." my ex-husband's lawyer said. Those words appear in the transcript. What is missing, however, is my attorney's request I be permitted to speak, the discussion about that, the court's instruction my words not be recorded, my closing statement, and the judge's admonishments to me.

Why conceal my words? Why, purportedly still on the record, had the court reporter failed to record the entire exchange between the judge and my husband's lawyer about going off the record?

I purchased the trial transcripts, despite the expense. When I received the transcript of this final day, I wrote the court reporter's office noting the omissions. I was told I was mistaken about the missing dialogue. But the objection of my ex-husband's attorney had been left in, proof of dialogue that had come after.

Everyone else sat while I stood before the judge that day, like a criminal about to be sentenced. I had barely begun to speak when the judge interrupted me.

You've offended every working parent in the courthouse by becoming a stay-at-home mom, she said. Tears streamed down my face and caught in my throat. I choked on my next few sentences before slumping in my seat, unable to finish. One of my own kind had tried to make me feel like I wasn't a good enough wife or a good enough mother or a good enough woman. You've "shirked your responsibility" to support your children and duty to become self-supporting by retiring as a lawyer and staying at home, she later wrote in her decision. My choice undoubtedly inferior measured against a mother who had continued to work outside the home. She had no harsh words for my husband for anything he'd done or said. But me, the judge admonished.

From the moment I set foot in the family courts, several female judges had tried to silence me, pressuring me to go back to work, reminding me they held my future in their hands, suggesting I relinquish my right to defend myself. Treating me like the wrongdoer. I had ultimately been allowed to contest the wrongful divorce accusations against me, but hadn't the exercise of my rights come at a price? Was I punished for challenging the family court status quo? For speaking up about my rights after I'd been, in essence, told to sit down?

Despite my professional pedigree, I had been naïve about the way the system worked. I entered family court expecting fairness. I exited seven years later with the conviction that family dissolution and my silence were the goals. Not all women were my sisters, and I would have to find the strength to look after myself.

Like other women in history confronted by injustice, I had challenged the status quo. But I hadn't done it only for me. I'd stood up for other parents too poor or scared or beaten down to stand up for themselves. And if I wasn't strong enough to demand fairness for myself, how could I show my own daughters how to be women of principle?

When I began writing about my experiences, I found out I wasn't alone. Critics said I'd brought additional hardship on myself by resisting the divorce. In a sense that was true. But I couldn't face the alternative either; then I'd betray myself.

And still for so long the court's words felt personal, so tangled up with my ex-husband's betrayal. Years of distance have suggested other possibilities. I wonder now if my last judge, rumored to be a mother herself, had felt uncomfortable about her own career path. If so, was maligning me the antidote to her own guilt? Did her advancement in the judicial hierarchy depend on keeping me in line? After all, I was a smart female who had challenged the way the family court did business. Or maybe impugning motherhood attempted to guarantee my silence.

Ironically, in a system historically controlled by men, I had done what good little girls are supposed to by becoming a wife and mother and giving up my own career while supporting my ex in his. So why had I gotten slammed? Were these female judges mere instruments and guardians of a system they believed themselves above?

On the other hand, why no credit to me from women for breaking ranks and standing up to my ex-husband?

In the years that followed, I would learn how being a working mom was becoming the preferred lifestyle in family law. Today some states cap or place other limits on alimony. And permanent alimony is dying out, deemed incompatible with the rise in working women and the clean break idea behind no-fault divorce. The favored legal approach is "rehabilitative" maintenance with a period of time to afford stay-at-home parents—ordinarily moms, although there is a growing trend in stay-at-home dads—the opportunity to brush up on skills, get back to work, and find daycare.

Like other stay-at-home parents, apparently I needed rehabilitating.

In her groundbreaking book, *Mothers and Divorce,* scholar Terry Arendell pointed out the obvious—the same number of women and men divorce. She wrote it's mostly women, however, who are made poor by it. I was not one of them, but over the years I have learned of so many others.

Arendell further observed that the family law system leaves mothers alone to handle the increased responsibilities as well. Indeed, the double shift—women who work outside the home and still spend significantly more time on household chores and childrearing than men—is a well-documented phenomenon.

According to the Pew Research Center, in 2016 there were more than eleven million stay-at-home parents. Another ten-year study by the Center found working full-time had lost some of its appeal, with the majority of working mothers with children under seventeen expressing a preference for either part-time work or not working outside the home at all.

What will their fate be if faced with divorce?

I will never understand everything that happened to me. But back then I had no time to ponder. I'd been legally dubbed a single mother, a role I hadn't chosen. I was reeling. More than six years after the love of my life left, I felt broken all over again. But I needed a plan to save my home, the capstone of my American dream, and that meant finding someone to refinance my jumbo mortgage. Judge #7 gave me only sixty days to find one.

4

Sixty Days and Counting

Traditional banks turned me down for a mortgage, even the bank holding the current mortgage, where I'd done my personal banking for over two decades. The fact I had impeccable credit, a law degree, and had once been a breadwinner seemed to count for nothing. Judge #7 said this was the 21st century, but it sure didn't feel like it. I was an unemployed, middle-aged woman who'd been a full-time stay-at-home mom for over a decade. That's what seemed to count. Against me.

"You need to show three years of prospective alimony," my banker D. said. "Every lender goes by those guidelines."

"But the court only gave me two more years," I said.

"Judges know you've got to have three years to get a mortgage," D. said. "She gave you the house knowing you probably wouldn't be able to get one and would have to sell." Loyalty, whether it was from my husband, the justice system, or my bank, was in short supply.

"Do you know anyone who can help?" I asked my lawyer. He knew a mortgage broker buddy who might be able to. But just when I sensed a loan commitment within my grasp, financing hit a snag. Meanwhile, closing costs and interest rates climbed.

Again, I scrutinized real estate boards. If I couldn't secure a mortgage, the children and I would have to move. But mortgage and maintenance costs for condos and co-ops in my neighborhood, for half the space, were practically as expensive. Plus, I'd have to sell the house first and still qualify for a mortgage, then pass inspection by co-op boards. Rents in safe neighborhoods were also high.

Nicki had started college in the fall, but Ella had four more years of high school. I asked Ella what she wanted to do. "I want to stay in my home," she said. So did I.

~ ~ ~

OUR HOUSE WAS A LATE 19th century four-story Victorian townhouse called a brownstone. Originally built for one family, somewhere in its history it had been converted into an apartment house. Subsequent renovations reconfigured it into a two-family home; we'd used it as a one. For years, wealthy New Yorkers had been scooping up brownstones and renovating them top to bottom. I don't think our house was ever gutted. Jake and I were professionals, but didn't have that level of wealth.

Previous owners had modernized it some with a triangular slanting half wall on the parlor floor and two bathrooms with walls made partially of glass block. I enjoyed the mix of old and new in our otherwise historic home.

Before a lawyer named Clinton, several generations of an Italian family had owned our house. One morning, the year before I put my house on the market, I was upstairs getting dressed when the doorbell rang. By the time I walked downstairs no one was there.

"Did you ring my bell?" I called out to a group of people on the sidewalk talking to my neighbor Teddy.

"Sorry to bother you," a thin, dark-haired woman in her forties said, smiling and looking up. "My sister-in-law and brother-in-law"—she gestured to the older couple standing next to her—"grew up in your house. We're in New York for the weekend and were walking by."

The house was a mess, but I welcomed Diana and her family in for a tour.

"Are you sure?" they asked, dumbfounded.

"Of course," I said. Mary and Anthony became a pair of youngsters once inside, reminiscing about whose bedroom had been where, what walls had been knocked down since they lived there, recounting the many Italian dinners the extended family had enjoyed between my walls.

No one knew why patriarch Lorenzo had decided to board up the fireplaces that once existed on each floor. Jake and I spotted protrusions from the walls and guessed the house had once contained several exposed fireplaces. We gleefully speculated hidden marble treasures existed behind the plaster, too, and talked about excavating one day. We also planned on ripping out the compact 1950s bathroom on the top floor and converting part of that floor into a master bath. We'd taken equity from the house for an inexpensive kitchen upgrade too. But those dreams never came to pass. And kitchen money went to pay lawyer bills.

"Your generosity towards strangers was so refreshing!" Diana said after she returned home, sending me a copy of a trifold poster she had assembled for her mother-in-law's ninety-fifth birthday celebration. The clan matriarch and patriarch stood in the middle. On the left was a photograph of Diana's mother-in-law and Mary and Anthony standing outside my house, circa 1949. To the right was a photo Diana had taken of my home, circa 2012, with the wrought iron railings that at some point had replaced the original balustrades pictured on the left. "Cousin Vinnie" brought news that if there was a perpetual shine to the bottom step of one of the interior staircases it was because this was his time-out spot as a boy.

Ella's time-out spot had been in front of the kitchen door, looking out onto the deck and back garden, Thunder's TV we had called it, hardly a place of contemplation without distraction. We'd had loads of laughter inside those walls, too, but our family had spent more time broken within than whole, more time healing than healed. Decades after they left my house, however, Mary and Anthony were still lighthearted about their family life inside my home.

Thinking on their joy renewed my sorrow when I considered the truncated legacy passed on to my own children and the stories about our family I could not undo.

~ ~ ~

WHILE I WAITED TO HEAR from the broker, I began hauling out years of accumulation in the cellar and ground floor. Before we moved to our house twelve years earlier, Jake and I and the girls had lived in a co-op three and a half blocks away. It had been a Knights of Columbus hall in its prior incarnation, and we often met people in the neighborhood who said, "I once danced in your living room!" We held a few stoop sales before moving, but time got away from us and we dragged most of what we'd stored in one basement directly to the cellar—law school books, children's outgrown clothing and toys, furnishings we imagined one day useful in a beach or country home, mementoes of our journey together, other junk. Jake and I had many things in common and pack-ratting was one of them.

After the divorce was final, I sifted through the boxes in order to hand over what remained of Jake's. His belongings had begun exiting the house in a wave starting seven years earlier, right before Christmas of 2002. Frantic to maintain damage control—Jake had already signed a lease and started buying furniture—I told him to take whatever he wanted when his moving van pulled up, not dreaming that what left the house, including him, would never make its way back.

My lawyer said to make a list of what he took, so I did: The stereo system, a table with two wooden chairs, two leather barstools, a chrome floor lamp, my favorite rug—the red Danish one with black paisley swirls—the TV from the bedroom, the breathing machine for his sleep apnea he refused to use, videotapes, books, including one by our favorite author, Richard Russo. Taking it had seemed like yet another betrayal.

"Why are *you* here?" Jake asked when I followed him to the ground floor on moving day.

"I just want to see what you're taking," I said.

"Well, I don't see why you need to be here. But while you're at it, take this," he said, tossing me the red heart-shaped pillow he'd taken off the sleeper sofa and was about to haul away.

"No, it's yours," I said, flinging the pillow back. "Keep it as a reminder of the hearts you've broken in this house."

While Jake wasn't looking, I removed the Russo book from his suitcase and placed it back on the shelf.

Four months later he came back for more belongings, this time at my insistence. Why he'd left so many clothes I didn't know. But there they were when I went to the closet each day, mocking me.

For years I continued coming across dribs and drabs of my ex-husband's things, evidence of how deeply we'd woven our lives together. More clothes, his deceased mother's menorah, photographs of the children, souvenirs from our travels. I never found his wedding band from Tiffany's, even though I searched high and low. He must have taken it the last time he'd been in the house, on the day he left. I always wondered why he took it. Had he hesitated about the divorce? Or immediately gone to a pawn shop?

Whenever I came across his things, I either hand delivered them or handed them over when he picked up the children for visitation. A few times I included a note—*thought you might want the Father's Day cards the kids made for you one year*—a love offering to the father of my children, hoping it might trigger fond memories or invoke a longing in him that still existed in me. If they did, I never knew.

Once I identified the cellar boxes containing the rest of Jake's things, my handyman's son, Davit, carried them up from the basement so I could sort through them. They were covered in dust, some in mold and mildew, many having stayed in the same spot where we'd placed them when we'd moved in.

My married life flashed before me in photographs, playbills of Broadway shows, and New York Philharmonic concerts at Lincoln Center. Books we'd both read, postcards, and tourist literature from the places we'd visited—Puerto Vallarta, the Isle of Skye, Bath, London, Edinburgh, Paris, Rome, Ravello, five of the seven Hawaiian Islands.

I should have let Jake rummage through this stuff, I thought. *Sparing me instead of him.* But I was fooling no one, not even myself, drawn as I was to own the remnants of my own messy life. And find a way to let them go.

Some things I hadn't seen before. Had I ever really known the man I'd been married to for decades? His betrayal was the last thing I'd have ever guessed him capable of. Was there more I didn't know?

I agonized over that puzzlement for years, and it was at last a mystery I no longer cared to sit on my bedroom floor, sob, and torment myself over. So I tossed the evidence of our joint memories. Jake didn't want them either. I imagined it would be the last of my emotional gut-wrenching and boxed up the mementoes Jake did want, artifacts from the years before I'd met him. Obviously, they pulled on his heart strings in a way I no longer, or perhaps ever, did: Photos and news articles from Jake's childhood, books, vinyl record albums, clippings and programs from my ex's starring roles in college and local community theater productions, his mother's high school diploma. And then Davit carried the boxes to the curb for Jake's pickup.

By then I was almost two months past the court's deadline to secure financing. Jake agreed to an extension, but he'd broken his word before so I was leery.

Once I stopped trying to control the uncontrollable, the mortgage broker called and a couple of afternoons later I sat at the closing table, stunned. I signed papers for three hours, amused when I came to one in which I swore I had sufficient means to pay back my huge jumbo mortgage. How odd it felt to lie. Occasionally I stopped to ask my broker a question or two. But then I picked my pen back up, gulped at his hefty fee, and signed where I was told. I finished as the sun was beginning to set.

Thousands of drivers were headed out-of-town for the long Fourth of July weekend while I drove silently home. I was now a homeowner who held sole title to her own home—my home. The import of my accomplishment and good fortune hit me as I grabbed the steering wheel, recalling how another stroke of luck had brought me a car lease in my own name several years before when the lease on the family car had expired. I'd gone to return our Jeep with no clue whether I'd be able to secure a replacement. To my surprise I'd been easily approved for a lease on a smaller car in my own name. The burden I'd been carrying lifted when the dealer handed me the keys. I got behind the wheel and turned the radio volume all the way up. And then I put the pedal to the metal, slid open the sunroof, and sailed down Manhattan's West Side Highway.

And now I had a house. The gravity of my luck now seemed to require driving in silence. Disasters—financial, natural, and familial—had taken the homes of millions of people, including the great housing collapse that had started in 2007, two years earlier. But me, I'd been allowed to keep mine. At least for now.

5

July Fourth

After I returned home from the closing, I called my handyman Arman, a super in a nearby apartment building. I'd increased the mortgage substantially in order to renovate, bring in tenants, and keep me and the children in our house.

Arman was going to help me. He could fix anything. He'd built houses in Armenia where he'd emigrated from. Before finding him, I'd gone through an ever-changing rotation of plumbers, electricians, roofers, and other handymen. And then Arman came along, and I struck gold.

The first house breakdown occurred a few days after Jake left, during the Christmas holidays. I had crawled under the covers in the middle of the afternoon to escape when the bedroom ceiling began to leak. I stood up, put a bucket under the drip, and climbed back into bed.

"Mom, what's wrong?" Nicki asked with a startled look, after rounding the corner to my bedroom, used to being confronted with the Energizer Bunny.

"Just tired," I said, pointing to the ceiling. My leg was also throbbing from recent knee surgery, and I'd received a legal letter from Jake's attorney demanding to know what I'd done to find a job in the few days since my husband had left. "And now I've got it all to fix alone," I said, filled with self-loathing.

"No, Mom, you don't. We're here. Me and Ella." Minutes later, she and Ella called me downstairs. They'd drawn a bubble bath and laid a plate of Christmas cookies, chocolate espresso beans, and fruit slices on a tray at the side of the tub. I slipped into the bath, and seven-year-old Ella emerged from her room with *Little House on the Prairie* and began to read, somehow knowing how a book that soothed her would also soothe me.

I sloshed water on my face to conceal my tears, grateful for the comfort, guilty my children were the ones guiding me through grief.

Ella's book choice was no coincidence. Years before, Jake and I took turns reading the *Little House* series to Nicki, and then we started the books over again with Ella. Sometimes we'd gather on Nicki's bed to read, the same passage making us all cry. And then we'd huddle in a group hug, all four of us, united like the family out there alone on the prairie.

A year after the first ceiling leak I'd gone to sleep early on New Year's Eve. The girls were with their father, and I was sad. But I vowed to start the New Year afresh. Instead I woke up to a slow but steady drip, drip, drip on my forehead, and my positive mind leapt straight to visions of Chinese water torture. I dialed the roofer I'd found the year before.

The next time the house sprang a leak it occurred four floors below, at night. I'd gone to drain the boiler and found the basement flooded with several inches of water. The cellar was pitch-dark but seemed even eerier at night when I made my final round of chores. I wondered how long before someone found the body if I passed out or got stuck down there, in particular when the kids were away with their dad for days or weeks. The walls were so thick no one could ever have heard me calling for help. You couldn't get a cell phone signal down there either.

Somehow I made it through those years with a combination of meditation classes, listening to poignant sermons at church, nights out with friends cheering me on, cooking with my daughters. Still, the firm grip of despair could suck me down into the pit again where the uniform that divorce had given me shone straight through my cloak of strength and bravery: single, middle-aged, on my own. I could pretend otherwise, but I knew the truth. I was a walking, wallowing cliché. And I hated it.

I hadn't wanted the divorce and had believed reconciliation was possible. Why wouldn't I spare my children hardship if I could? So I fought against what I couldn't accept. Obviously Jake misunderstood my opposition, offering to let me countersue him for cruelty. But not adultery, he said. "I don't want to go around wearing a scarlet A."

The absurdity of that statement astonished more than angered me. Never mind that my husband was having an affair. Never mind that I didn't want to wear a scarlet letter either. Never mind that I wanted to peel off the big bright "A" I'd been slapped with. The "A" that had burrowed its way down deep in my soul, plainly visible to all who knew me or would. An "A" I neither deserved nor prized nor courted. An "A" I abhorred. Alone. Abandoned. Aborted. Jake wanted me to strip off the emblem he'd branded himself with, but who was going to remove mine? For years, it was a label I found impossible to strip from my heart.

~ ~ ~

"IT'S YOUR PIPE TO THE SPIGOT in the garden," Gary the plumber said when he came over the night of the cellar flood. "It burst when the water froze. You probably forgot to shut it off during the winter."

"I didn't know it had to be shut off," I said. There were lots of things I didn't know about a 120-year-old house.

"Well, it's shut off, now," Gary said. "Don't worry about it. I'm a plumber and I forgot once too. It's no big deal. I'll come by in the spring and put in a new pipe."

"But you look good," he said, as we trudged through the water, Gary in his overalls, me in a formless sweatshirt, blue velour sweatpants, and black rubber boots. I was so thin I was wearing hand-me-downs from Nicki's twelve-year-old friend. Drenched in sweat, I wore no makeup and was white as a sheet from a recent prolonged menstrual cycle.

"You look like Sissy Spacek," Gary said. "I always thought you were a sexy, wonderful woman. Your husband's gotta be crazy to leave you." Either that or I was damaged goods, and Gary too lovesick to notice.

"Thanks," I said, following him up the cellar stairs, listless. Ordinarily I'd have had a snappy comeback.

"Hang on and let me get my checkbook," I said when we reached the kitchen.

"Oh, there's no charge," Gary said.

"You can't do that."

"Don't worry about it. Have a good night," he said, before pausing and turning around to take one last look at me. "You know? You really *do* look like Sissy Spacek."

The next time Gary came there was something wrong with one of the toilets; same thing the next time.

And then stranger things began to happen in the house. Squirrels climbed into the crawl space between the roof and my bedroom ceiling and had to be trapped and removed.

A few years later, right before I was about to leave on a four-day trip to Florida with my friend Lola, she called to me from the second-floor bathroom.

"The tub won't shut off," Lola said. It was 4:00 a.m., and Lola had stayed overnight so we could take an early cab to the airport. The spigot had come off in Lola's hands and wouldn't go back on. We tried and tried to turn the water off, but it kept gushing out. There was no shut-off valve for the tub either.

The last thing I wanted to do was disturb my neighbor Teddy. He had asthma and was allergic to my cat. But it was either that or let the house flood and miss my mini-getaway. So, I called Teddy, and he came right over and turned off the main water valve in the cellar—I had no idea where it was—happy as pie to help me out.

Soon after, bird mites invaded my bedroom.

I'd been going back and forth to the dermatologist for a rash unrecep- tive to any of the creams she'd prescribed. Each night I'd shower and lotion up, don fresh pajamas, change the sheets and blankets, and vacuum the mattress and bedroom rug. Initially I'd feel relief when I crawled under the covers, until the creepy crawler sensations began again and I'd start itching uncontrollably.

One night I told Ella I was too tired to read and went upstairs to begin my nighttime ritual. I'd just gotten under the covers when Ella came upstairs to give me another hug.

"What's that, Mommy?" she asked as we snuggled.

"What's what, honey?"

"The black line on the wall," she said, pointing to a two foot scrawl of what appeared to be black soot. We got up to make a closer inspection and realized the line started at the window, spilling onto the ledge and across the molding before continuing along the wall and onto the floor, where it reached my bed and ultimately me. The whole thing was moving. We screamed and danced up and down, afraid for our feet to touch the floor for too long. I shooed Ella out of the room, repeated my bath and lotion ritual, and went downstairs to sleep.

The following morning I called an exterminator listed in the yellow pages.

"I've never seen anything like this," the young man who came said, before he started howling and slapping his arms. The more he tried to wipe the creatures off, the more they clung. "I don't know what these are. But I'm getting out of here!" he said, fleeing down the staircase and out the door. The guy from the next company I called didn't know what they were either. His boss coached his moves from his cell phone the whole time. First, he removed the air-conditioner from the window, wrapped it in towels, and carried it down to the garden. Next, he removed the birds' nests which had been lying underneath and sprayed the window ledge. Finally, he swiped my credit card for $800 and guaranteed whatever had invaded my house was permanently gone. A few nights later I woke up digging the life out of fresh sores. The final exterminator—a local guy from down the street—knew exactly what to do.

"Bird mites," he said immediately. Birds had built nests in the gap between the window ledge and air-conditioner, allowing mites to breed, infest the air-conditioner, and crawl through to my bedroom. Mites are generally naked to the human eye without magnification, but they had multiplied so much that Ella and I had finally been able to see them.

Years later I still came across them in boxes of legal papers. A few were still alive! As I wiped each piece of paper down by hand and set it aside to dry I couldn't help wondering if God had sent me one of the ten deadly plagues and how many more were in store.

After the bird mite infestation, the ground floor ceiling began to leak. I was getting ready for the annual church auction when I discovered the ceiling had buckled and was wet and soft to the touch. By then I had found Arman, and he came right over, even though it was a Saturday night.

"Go on, get dressed," he said. I watched Arman pierce the bubble and water gush out, gulping as I walked upstairs. When I came back down, there was a gaping hole in the ceiling with black gunk oozing out, like the bowels of the house were about to swallow me up. Sweat soaked straight through my cocktail dress and poured down my face.

Arman gazed down at me from the ladder and laughed. A short, slight man, he nonetheless wielded such power with his hammer and saw.

"What you worried about, Beverly?" he asked. "Go to your party. Have a good time. I can fix this. No big deal. You worry too much." He had caught on to me quick.

A few years before my marriage broke up, I had started going to meditation classes and put my whole heart into trying to worry less. And then I found out about the affair and my life collapsed and toppled over and took me along with it. I lived on the edge, vigilant for the next shoe to drop.

But I never saw Arman unhappy or depressed. A gulf existed between our economic and educational worlds, but I loved talking with him. He valued family more than anything else, too, and worked harder than anyone I knew, and thrived on it. I'd been raised with the same ethic and worked summers and school breaks from when I was sixteen. Even as a kid, I picked strawberries from my grandmother's garden to sell at a roadside stand. Somehow Arman and I were kindred souls.

When I returned from the auction, Arman had already let himself out. He had repaired the pipe connected to the dishwasher one floor above that had sprung a leak, plastered the ceiling, and cleaned up the gunk. I sat there and sobbed at how much his kindness hurt. I'd gone so long without anyone having my back except the children, who I felt guilty asking for help. And now I had Arman.

Later in the week he came by to paint the ceiling.

"How much do I owe you?" I asked.

"How much you want to pay, boss?" he said. He always called me boss, knowing I'd laugh. And he always dodged my question, uncomfortable talking about money, perhaps not wanting that to get in the way of our friendship.

"How much will make you happy?" I asked, as usual, no clue how much was enough and underpaying him was the last thing I ever wanted to do. Arman was already happy of course, and occasionally refused to let me pay him anything if the repair was minor.

He'd suggest a price only after I insisted. And then I'd hand him more, knowing it was insufficient to match his kindness.

"What you rich or something?" he would say. And then we'd shake hands and laugh some more.

~ ~ ~

BIRD MITES, ROOF LEAKS, basement floods aside, I wanted our home. After the closing, I spent the Fourth of July holidays with Arman and his sons and son-in-law at Lowe's home store.

Rather than hire a contractor, I commandeered the role myself, with Arman's team ready to execute my vision for turning the ground floor into a rental. There was already a separate gated entrance, but Arman would have to seal off the half wall upstairs connecting the parlor and ground floors, then add a locked door in-between. The downstairs layout was near perfect, a railroad style configuration with two rooms on either side of a beautiful blue-tiled bathroom with a full-sized soaking tub and two sinks. The front room had two closets and would serve as the tenants' bedroom. Jake and I had used it as a guestroom/sitting room; after he left, I'd used it for storage. The large open room facing the back garden would serve as a loft-style living and dining space. It had once been the children's playroom, and I'd outfitted one whole wall with built-in cabinets where the girls stored books, games, art materials, dress-up clothes, and toys. An adjacent double-doored closet held more toys and a balance beam, gymnastics mat, tent, art easel, and chalkboard. We'd had loads of birthday and slumber parties in the playroom, had hung piñatas, and staged impromptu fashion shows.

With Jake gone, the girls and I often had what Ella called our "Girls' Night Out." We cooked, played games, and sang Broadway show tunes around my grandmother's out-of-tune upright piano. There was so much sadness inside those walls after Jake left. But so much magic happened there too. I saw to it the best I could.

In addition to contractor, I assumed the role of architect. I can't draw but have a discerning eye. Arman understood my chicken scratch and gesticulations. Two crucial decisions had to be made before starting the renovations—where to install a kitchen and how to provide me with access to the cellar, since the door to it would now be inside the tenant's apartment. Arman and I debated the merits of here versus there without arriving at a solution.

It was easy to imagine a living area around the kitchen. But where to place the kitchen so as not to overtake the space? I eyed the playroom closet.

"If we tear it down, will the kitchen fit inside?" I asked Arman. He measured and it would, down to the inch. The spot lined up perfectly, too, with the plumbing and electrical lines Arman needed to access in the cellar, leaving only the problem of entry to the cellar.

I considered including a term in the lease allowing me to enter the tenant's apartment, but that seemed intrusive. Arman suggested cutting another door to the cellar from the hallway, underneath the staircase leading to the ground floor. The height couldn't exceed five feet though and would have to be at a right angle to the stairway leading to the basement. I pictured a series of tumbles—mine.

As a single mother, I often found myself in a series of dichotomous situations. I needed solutions to problems that seemingly had none. It was the realization of this irreconcilability and often the letting go of resistance—like when the house financing finally came through—that permitted options to reveal themselves or occasionally for problems to simply disappear.

Since I couldn't move an immovable wall I decided to build another one, further down the hallway, on the other side of the cellar door, thus creating a new entrance to the playroom before the entry door to the tenant's apartment. This had the bonus of providing the tenants with a place to hang their coats, take off their shoes, and store things. In essence, a mudroom.

"I can do that," Arman said when I presented my proposal.

At Lowe's we bought three doors (one a custom sliding glass patio door), two windows, and molding for door and window frames. We bought sheetrock, plaster, paint, lighting fixtures, switch plate covers, a ceiling fan, electrical outlets and outlet covers, bathroom fixtures, five brushed metal silver-plate doorknobs (three sets with locks and keys), a robe hook for the bathroom, shelving for closets, light bulbs, polyurethane for the floors, grout for the bathroom, lumber, tools, cleaning supplies, drop cloths, baseboard molding, a toilet seat, pipes, and a bunch of other hardware foreign to me. A few weeks later I picked out a stove, refrigerator, kitchen cabinets, kitchen tile, and granite for the countertops.

When we arrived at Lowe's, Davit grabbed a dolly and began selecting lumber. I watched as he held up each 2 x 4 to check for warping, laying a few aside and discarding others. I inhaled the intoxicating smell of fresh cut wood.

"Show me how to do it," I said.

41

"Hold it up like this and look down," Davit said, placing the end of a board on his cheek, right below his eye, then closing the other eye and looking straight down the plank.

"Now you try it," he said, handing me the wood.

I did as Davit instructed and continued with several dozen more. Davit double-checked each of my selections and rejects and gave me a perfect score.

Until you try it for yourself, it's hard to describe the rush that occurs when the eye glides effortlessly down a slice of sawed wood. With warped pieces, the eye stops along the way. After mastering lumber, I poked out my chest as we moved on to sheetrock, molding, and nails, finally loading it all onto the back of a flatbed truck I insisted on driving home myself.

My maternal grandfather was a jack-of-all-trades. During his many careers, he was a carpenter, made false teeth, and founded two Southern Baptist churches. He even made my aunt's wedding veil. People called him in an emergency because he knew what to do. When I was a teenager, he built my grandmother a red cottage with his own hands. And then he added a matching wishing well on the front lawn. They were love birds until the day they died.

My dad's father worked as an engineer on board ships, circumnavigating the world before settling down to grow tobacco and fish from the Potomac River, fish my grandmother sold from a nearby icehouse. Their son, my uncle, was self-taught, too, and a sought-after homebuilder in the county. He also built the brick house my family and I moved into when I was twelve. Another self-taught uncle built his home too.

Quinnie, a friend from the South now living in the North like me, said she thought it was a custom for Southerners to build their own homes because she had seen it often in her own community. Is this true? I have no idea, though I never knew anyone in New York—except for Arman, who was from Armenia—who had built their own house.

Growing up, I was considered an intellectual, along with another cousin my age. We were both first off to college, and as youngsters sat in a far-off corner and played chess at my grandmother's while other cousins fooled around with their food and made farting noises under their armpits. My mother used to joke she found me in a wicker basket on her doorstep because I was unusual.

And yet I had some of the do-it-yourself in me too. As a teenager I made most of my clothes. I loved to knit and cook. As an adult, I had a flair for decorating. And the summer after Jake left I took the kids to the beach, where I showed them how to crack open crabs like a real Maryland girl. Until I stood at Lowe's picking out lumber with Davit, I had forgotten how much I enjoyed working with my hands.

Six years to the day earlier, on July 4, 2003, I had been alone in the house while Nicki and Ella went to sleepaway camp for a month. Nicki had been going for several years, but Ella was the baby, and there weren't going to be any more babies, and the truth was I wanted Ella home with me as long as possible. Before he left, however, my husband had begged me to let Ella go too.

"If you sign her up, it'll be like it used to," he'd said. "Before kids. Maybe we'll go to Europe. Just the two of us." A second honeymoon. Happy tears ran down my cheeks as I mailed Ella's camp application. And then my husband had an affair and left.

My mother phoned that July Fourth to find out how I was managing home alone.

"Somehow you ought to make this your Independence Day, Bev," she said.

"That's sweet, Mom," I said. "But I'm not ready for my independence." Independence is something you fight for, yearn for, not something thrust upon you. I wasn't ready for mine, not then, not the following year, or the one after that. Even the summer Arman began renovations I wasn't set on liberation, though that summer was a turning point. I did not know it then, but even as Arman sawed and drilled, I too was beginning to rebuild inside.

6

Reconstructive Surgery

Renovations took less than three months. Each night after the girls went to sleep, I checked on Arman's progress. He was often still downstairs and explained the stages of his work.

Before he began hammering and drilling, I had to rid the area of our belongings. I carved out a space for a family room in the midst of the parlor floor and squished the red velvet couch and TV from the playroom in-between the living room, dining room, and kitchen.

Downstairs, the girls weeded out toys and games. Together we sorted through hundreds of books, culling out ones for storage in the cellar and others for letting go. In all our purges, parting with our precious books was one of the hardest tasks. My private fantasy had been to one day have a real library à la Henry Higgins in *My Fair Lady*. But that wasn't going to happen, at least not in this house.

I'd grown up in rural Maryland, and the bookmobile making pit stops at the post office across from my house every Saturday provided my main access to books as a child. Saturday mornings I'd sprawl on the floor of the bookmobile until it closed, checking out as many books as I could carry home.

The summer of our renovation we gave up so many books, and hundreds more four years later. Brooklynites love books and per neighborhood custom we left them on our stoop, no sooner deposited than snatched up. At least I knew they were bound for fine homes.

Unfortunately, my grandmother's piano had to go too. She left it to me after she died, and I'd lugged it around for over thirty years.

During my childhood, my family often went to my paternal grandparents' house for Sunday supper after church, where I'd play her piano.

"What did you eat?" Ella asked me once, while I was showing her how to pop string beans like my grandmother taught me.

"Probably chicken or ham, MaMaw's homemade buttermilk biscuits, and one of her coconut and jelly cakes." Ella licked her lips.

After supper, the family would sit on my grandmother's plastic-covered furniture in the parlor. My grandfather, Pop-Pop Frank, reclined on his BarcaLounger smoking a cigar while I played hymns. When I cleaned out the piano bench before selling it, I found a notebook where MaMaw had scribbled phone numbers alongside fish orders. Three and a half decades later I still recognized her handwriting. The notebook was crumbling and of absolutely no use, but I could not toss it—I had watched her hold it in her precious hands, rough from working in the garden and scaling fish.

But the piano had to go. After law school, I moved it from three apartments in New York City before it landed in the playroom. Its first home had been in the three-hundred-square-foot Manhattan studio with a fifth-floor walk-up I'd been thrilled to snag, such was the competition for housing in the early 1980s. Jake and I had only dated a couple of months when he and my dad shared a U-Haul to cart the piano from Maryland. When the men I'd hired to carry the piano upstairs saw it, they had a conniption, shaking their heads and talking in Spanish. I thought they'd known about the piano. But Jake settled them down with extra cash, and the piano finally made its way up five flights of stairs.

Jake whispered to me that he thought my father hated him because Dad hardly said a word the whole trip. Minutes later, Dad pulled me aside and said what a great time he'd had listening to Jake's stories. Seven months later Jake and I got married, and the piano made its way back down those five flights to our apartment in Brooklyn, then to our co-op, and finally to our house in Brooklyn. With the renovations, there was no room for it. So, I sold it to a happy new owner on Craigslist.

I had an equal pang of regret selling our kitchen table and chairs—they had been the locus of life for me and the girls. I believed in having family meals together no matter what else was on our plates. After he started working for law firms, though, my ex-husband usually came home late, where I'd have dinner for one waiting. Still, the girls and I maintained our ritual.

After Nicki went to college, what Ella had christened Girls' Night Out dwindled to just me and her. We forged our own tradition, once a month Fridays at Buddy's Burrito, followed by a movie at the local cinema.

Nicki watched the piano leave home, but I sold the table and chairs after she went back to college. There was no room for them either with a desk and computer now in the kitchen. Nicki noticed their absence first thing when she returned from college. Was that sadness crossing her face? If so, she said nothing other than to ask where they'd gone.

By then I'd bought a new stove, and Nicki baked pies all summer. Blueberry, strawberry, strawberry and rhubarb, strawberry and blueberry, and apple. And so our kitchen became the site of family life once again. Unable to forgive myself, I'd hoped the stove we needed would be sufficient consolation.

After the split, friends encouraged me to redecorate. But I couldn't bring myself to, not at first. I couldn't afford it either. I thought rearranging things might upset the kids, too, though I admit I had no desire to shuffle furnishings around—I wanted my family back, and would the couch swapping places with the living room chair change the fact of my husband's leaving? And so the house pretty much remained a shrine for a long time.

It took nine months for my first minor alteration. The girls and I had made our annual fall trek to pick apples in upstate New York. We drank cider, ate donuts, and climbed trees, and on the way back stopped at a diner, where Ella ordered her first cheeseburger. Up until then she had been the original chicken nugget girl, but she smiled when she bit into the cheeseburger and I tucked the sweet moment away.

After lunch, we pulled off at a garden center. Bedraggled pansies were on sale, along with pumpkins and jams.

"You can pick out five honey sticks each," I said.

While the children were busy with their selections, I walked outside and saw a white cement urn trimmed with rosettes. Our broken ceramic filigreed one had stood guard on the stoop throughout the spring and summer, a testament to my allowing divorce to be the hub of our lives. The pot had cracked beyond repair the winter before, and I'd wrapped a cord around it to hold the pieces together, instead of tossing it. The blue and yellow pansies I'd planted the previous summer had given me a lift. Now the pot held only dirt.

"Have you considered a new portrait of yourself and the girls?" my best friend from high school emailed from his military base in Iraq. "Paint, move the furniture around, get rid of things."

Walt's words stirred in me as I meandered through the graveled lot. Summer was over, and there was a chill in the air no longer warmed by the midday sun. Wooden bins encircled what was left of the harvest. I walked back inside and paid for the flower pot, and the girls and I filled it with soil when we got home and lowered in the last purple pansies of summer.

Another Saturday my daughters and I recovered the kitchen chairs I would later sell. They were beaten up, but the seat cushions came off. The screws were in there deep, and it was tougher physical work than I anticipated, but Nicki gave me a hand. She and Ella picked a different pattern for each seat from remnants I had collected.

"This is going to look cool, Mom," Nicki said, as we folded the fabric around each seat and screwed the cushions back on. Our family project gave me another lift when I cooked dinner and glanced over at them.

Gradually I embraced the possibility of replanting roots where some had been pulled up. Our everyday dishes broke; I replaced them with one-of-a-kind flea market finds. A friend was selling her wrought iron votive stand that had once adorned a church; I bought it and inserted one hundred candles. I became proficient at fixing minor stuff like loose doorknobs and cabinet hinges. Ella and I spray-painted a wicker mirror frame purple and glued on sparkly doo-dads and buttons. I redecorated Nicki and Ella's rooms. I bought Nicki a desk for doing homework and bookshelves for storing books.

I splurged on a mattress and bedroom set for myself. Jake had scoffed at so-called feminine colors for our bedroom, but I was now free to choose what I wanted without pushback. So I bought a bright pink silk blanket. I'd planned on getting rid of the bedroom set my ex and I had used for most of our marriage, further exorcising Jake's ghost from the room where I slept each night. But when Ella learned of my plan, she claimed the furniture as a replacement for her own. So when I tucked her in at night I continued sitting on the bed where her father and I had created her. No matter how hard I tried it seemed my ex-husband continued to occupy space.

The following Christmas I finally threw away Jake's stocking. For years I'd stood over the garbage bin with it while the girls were in the other room decorating the tree, hesitating before returning the extra stocking to the storage bin. I bought the stockings while the girls were young, four matching red velvet stockings on which I'd embroidered each of our names in green. I knew throwing out Jake's stocking would signal some measure of finality, and for years I couldn't give it up. Now I was ready. Ready to throw out the old pills I'd been hoarding too. I made a list of what I wanted in a mate, something friends had been urging me to do for years. At the top I wrote the words "kind, honest, and generous."

After I bought new bedroom furniture, I asked Arman to paint my bedroom walls. But I took my own brush to them first. Over my bed I painted a heart and within it, my name and the names of my two daughters with lines connecting each of us to the other. On the opposite wall

48

I painted the words "GOOD-BYE JAKE" in bold block letters. Arman glided his paint-filled roller over my sketches, sealing my words forever within the walls of my home. And hopefully within my heart.

~ ~ ~

ARMAN BEGAN CONSTRUCTION in July of 2009; in mid-September, tenants moved in. Every year we lived in the house I had measured the children's heights and marked them with a pen on the wall outside the bathroom in the playroom. I toyed with placing a panel of Lucite over the markings to preserve them, telling prospective tenants it was an art installation. Eventually I painted over it. But I asked Arman to paint that strip last, running my hands over it one final time.

I posted the apartment listing on Craigslist and scheduled staggered appointments for prospective tenants. I researched landlord-tenant law, downloaded a standard form of lease, amended it with terms of my own, and compiled a two-page application. I instructed apartment hunters to bring identification and copies of bank records. The application required them to provide employment verification, two references, and the names of current landlords.

"How you like it?" Arman asked, going behind me with a brush while I pointed out places needing touch-ups, minutes before the first applicant showed up. I scrubbed the apartment the night before and was installing fresh light bulbs.

"It's beautiful," I said. And it was. The floors gleamed from sanding and two coats of polyurethane. We'd never had the upstairs floors done— and the parlor floor needed it—although we had sanded the floors in our earlier co-op.

"It looks like a bowling alley," my mom said when she visited.

I can't believe you did this all by yourself, my girlfriends said when I invited them over to see the rental. The vision was mine, but Arman and his family had executed it beautifully.

"We want to live here!" my friends said.

"I want to live here!" I said. Indeed, it was the kind of place I imagined having one day after the children had families of their own. The girls were already teenagers, but imagining them as adults, living on their own, seemed so far off, even though Nicki was nineteen and Ella fourteen.

Half a dozen or more couples viewed the apartment; several more emailed. A few couples were already living together, but this was to be the first cohabitation for some. I wondered what might happen if they broke up and decided to select a couple each of whom qualified to pay the rent on their own. I knew from research that cohabitation had increased fourteen-fold, with cohabitating couples far more likely than married ones to break up. I called landlords and references, poured over applications and financial papers, and asked each applicant to write something about why they wanted to live in my house. I read their answers carefully, nervous and a tad scared. I hadn't even known the father of my own children; now strangers would be living one floor below me and my daughters. One couple backed out, saying they couldn't wait for my decision.

I narrowed my choice to Kim and Nate, and they stayed three years. They both had first-rate jobs. Nate could have listed many people to recommend him. But he gave his mother as a recommendation.

"He's a fine boy," she said when I called. "And his girlfriend is a fine girl." I chose them. Their rent allowed me to continue to keep my home, and I was grateful.

7

House for Sale

Four years after it became mine, I put my house up for sale. It was time. I had gone back to practicing law or so they called it, a series of glorified temp jobs, the only work I could find. My tenants had gotten married and moved. Although I found another wonderful couple through Craigslist, there was a shortfall when it came to paying the bills.

People ask why I became a lawyer in the first place. I'm not sure. I was reared in a modest, hardworking family, before the era of career makeovers, second acts, and reinventions. Perhaps I lacked the microchip to take risks, at least where paychecks were concerned. No one talked about finding and pursuing your passion back then. The truest answer I can offer is that I majored in political science, and law seemed the next logical step for many of us during the late 1970s. I was part of the first surge of women into law school too, also prestigious. Growing up with the Civil Rights Movement as I did, the thought of serving justice inspired me. And the law was supposedly designed to accomplish justice.

I stumbled into entertainment law, too, by the sheer coincidence of sitting next to the general counsel of NPR on a flight on the legendary

Eastern Air Lines Shuttle from New York City to Washington, D.C. He put me in touch with my first boss, who considered songwriters the underdogs of the music industry—I suppose that's where the justice part came in—and offered me, a small-town girl from the sticks, a job in New York City. I saw stars, hopped on a plane, and soon fell in love with a dreamy-eyed guy in the legal department. Life carried me along and then came Nicki and Ella. But the four walls of my offices never glittered in the middle of the night like my daughters did, and frankly it was a relief to leave the long hours required to practice law. The children grew, I discovered a love of writing, and Jake told me he was all for it. Until he got a girlfriend and lost interest in my dreams. In our dreams.

Divorce is about money, my attorney had said. I hadn't believed him. How could I? I'd been brought up to believe in marriage and motherhood, in family and community, in trust and loyalty. I'd been taught about the connection between hard work and achievement of the American dream. I'd chosen a career grounded on the principle of justice.

After more than a decade as a full-time stay-at-home mom, I reentered the job market in my fifties. The divorce decree stated I could be highly compensated, but well-paying jobs in the legal profession no longer existed for me. Droves of recent law school graduates with crushing tuition debt couldn't find steady, well-paying employment either. Nor could middle-aged lawyers who, unlike me, had continued in the field and been laid off well before retirement age. Hourly, sporadic assembly-line temp work, reviewing documents at all hours with no guarantee of pay from one day to the next, was the only kind of legal employment so many of us could find. And there was stiff competition for that.

Interest rates declined though, so I tried to refinance again. I filed papers with my bank and waited. And when I called to find out the status of my application the bank officer said they were missing papers I had already sent, so I faxed them again. And waited. This process continued until the bank rejected my application even though I had excellent credit, never missed a mortgage payment, and always paid by the due date. I could not qualify for a mortgage to pay the same lender less per month than I'd been paying without fail for years.

Meanwhile, I temped. I wrote this in my journal one day:

"Temping straight since December. An hour and a half to get to work on subway today and I'm not there yet. NYC has become unlivable unless you are well off. It is bone and soul crushing. The F train is a cattle car uninhabitable for humans or animals. I wear boots, a jacket over a dress because it's cold where I temp. I have a scarf, hat, down coat on over it. It is so crowded sweat pours down my armpits, legs, feet, back of neck, hat, hair…. I feel I may overheat and die. I feel panic coming on. No seat, strain to hold on so I don't fall down and sway backwards. Knees hurt from sciatica. It's all in my head or is it? How much I make after taxes, subway fare, lunch, clothes, coffee? Is it worth it?"

Considering the level at which I had once practiced law, it was humiliating when one of my supervisors, a lawyer who could easily have been my son and hadn't practiced in the big leagues like I had, chastised me for asking too many questions. My fellow temps advised me the best way to keep our piddling jobs was to fly under the radar and pretend to know what we were doing. I tried to disable my brain and switch off my conscience, but it was impossible, so I sat in my chair, hour after hour, churning inside. "Chimpees" and "chimpettes," one of my cohorts, who dubbed himself "Coco," called us. A perfect description. We were monkeys in a cage, pretending to practice law.

Still, that's what they called it and that meant taking regular, continuing legal education classes for the privilege. At one class I glanced behind me and spotted Judge #7 in the next row staring at me. I glared back, cold sweat oozing down my collar. After class was over, I hurried home even though I'd also gone to schmooze and explore work opportunities. She showed up at another class too, this time to introduce the speakers on the dais. Again, I fled home after the seminar instead of networking.

"What's this I hear about you stalking Judge #7?" my former divorce lawyer Paul asked when he called. Another judge had corralled him in the courthouse hallway one day, he said, to tell him my judge said I was stalking her. *Stalking her!* Who else had she allegedly spoken to? Other judges I might someday find myself in front of? Colleagues? Lawyers I sent résumés to asking for a job? Paul laughed it off and told me not to get so worked up; it was probably said in jest. I wasn't amused, so Paul said he'd talk to them. I'd filed a motion for increased child support after a clerk in the family court recommended I do so but withdrew it when Jake's lawyer moved to have the hearing transferred to Judge #7. I vowed to stay as far away from her as possible, believing she wouldn't dispense justice.

~ ~ ~

SHORTLY AFTER MY MARRIAGE BROKE UP, I had an appointment with my psychiatrist, Doctor Goldman, to refill my panic medication. A tall, slim, mid-sixty-something psychiatrist with thinning grey hair, Doctor Goldman, normally the picture of calm, was aghast at how much weight I'd lost—a five-foot seven-and-a-half-inch, medium-framed woman, down twenty-three pounds to 120 in a few months. (I would go on to lose more.)

"I'm very concerned about you," he said, handing me a prescription for antidepressants, alarm in his eyes. "In all my years, this is one of the worst cases of divorce abuse I've ever seen."

"I'm not taking any more pills," I said, returning his hand.

"With the pressure you're under, there's nothing wrong with a little something extra to get you through." A little mother's helper.

"I have my meditation class and I'll be fine," I said, baffled why my weight loss had him so worked up. Doctor Goldman arched his eyebrows.

"I'll be fine," I repeated. Some days I even managed, more or less.

"Well, you've got to start eating more. I want you to go to the drug-store and get this," he said, handing me another slip of paper on which he'd written the word "ENSURE." "It will help you put on weight." I took the paper to appease him. I already ate. And I didn't purge. No laxatives either. No matter how many calories I ingested weight poured off, all by itself. Flesh eaten up by loss.

Examining my naked body in front of the bathroom mirror became a ritual after showering. Day after day, I shriveled from a size 12 to a 10, then from 10 to 8. Fascinated. Slipping easily into a size 6. I loved swinging my arms. They felt so light. Shrunken, stick straight and seeming to go on forever. And my buttocks, which had once resembled a round peach, now had hardly any meat on them. Neither breast filled a palm. Front and rearview, you could see the outline of each rib, count vertebrae. And I'd acquired those model-worthy cheekbones: Prominent, chiseled, hollow, with the flesh scooped out.

Clothes fit, snapped, and zippered effortlessly. A walking, talking skeleton underneath it all, with each ounce lost purging each part of me my husband didn't love, exterminating each cell he'd rejected and trickling down to my essence.

There was no one to comfort me so I consoled myself. When I stepped out of the shower, I crossed my arms in front, one on top of the other, and wrapped them around my torso until they almost touched in back. And then I squeezed and held myself. Jake said no one would ever love me, but if I stayed thin enough maybe I could love myself. My body was emaciated, gaunt, perhaps even breakable. And yet I was never so in awe of it. In time I slipped easily into a size 2.

Years passed and I struggled with menopause and my body morphed from waif to middle-aged spread. One day I woke up and realized I no longer loved Jake, years after people said I should have. But time had taken time. I began to fantasize about finding a companion to share my home with. But no one came along.

Nicki and Ella helped with housework when they could. Once I hired a kid walking down the block with a shovel looking for work. I found my first tenant's girlfriend outside at 6:00 a.m. one morning shoveling snow—the job I hated most—because she said it was good exercise. Bless her! Mostly, the job fell to me, beginning before Jake left.

He'd gone on a business trip after I learned of his affair, right when the next immense snowfall blanketed New York City. I dropped Ella off at school and stared at the mess in front of our house when I returned and kept on walking up the stoop. *Not my frigging job*, I thought. Only it was my frigging job because Jake was gone and eventually would be, forever.

Reluctantly, I retraced my steps, found a shovel, and started hauling snow away, cutting into the ice with the sharp end of the spade and watching as big chunks split apart on the sidewalk. I scooped them up and threw them over my shoulder in a frenzy and laughed with my passersby, scoring a few near misses into oncoming foot traffic. My back hurt and my legs ached from so many knee surgeries and I intended on making only a tiny path, enough for me and the kids to get in and out of the house and for people to walk by. But the more I shoveled, the more I couldn't stop.

This one is Jake's girlfriend, I said, picking up the next load and chucking it into the street, watching a car go by and crunch it. A heaping pile of Jake's lies got tossed next and flattened when another car drove by and squished what I'd flung. I pitched Jake's curses, and feeling guilty, lobbed some of my anger and jealousy into the mix.

When I finished, I unlocked the cubby under our stoop and pulled out the ten-pound bag of salt, sprinkled it around, and then went inside my warm house and cried.

Eleven years later the toll had crept up on me, the house too physically demanding and expensive. No helpmate had come along either, even though my friend Billy, an astrologer, had assured me one day he would.

"You've got a second marriage line," he'd said, pointing to a faint line in a fold beneath my left thumb. "About five years between them."

I asked Billy where I'd meet this single, employed, kind, forty to sixty-something male with no baggage who didn't have a gaggle of children he wanted help raising.

"In a bank on a rainy day," Billy said, cackling. I could seldom tell whether he was serious or joking.

The divorce decree was stamped March 2009 so, according to Billy's calculations, I'd be married again sometime in 2014. It was now 2013, not much time left to meet my husband-to-be. For several years I occasionally trudged to the ATM when it rained, even if I didn't need to go. One Saturday, during the winter of 2013, I headed there again.

While I filled out a deposit slip, an attractive forty-something man said hello and asked me to join him for coffee at the sandwich shop next door after we both finished at the bank. I inspected him up and down. He smiled. Trim and attractive and he was in a bank, probably employed, no ring on his finger. I said yes. When we reached the sandwich shop, however, I learned he had a toddler-aged son and had recently separated because he wasn't feeling in love with his wife anymore. I found myself telling him about Elizabeth Marquardt's *Between Two Worlds,* a heart-breaking book based on interviews with children of divorce. I wrote the name of the book on a napkin, handed it to him, and recommended he reconsider his decision. I was happy I had planted a seed of hope and sent him unspoken good wishes as I watched him walk toward the subway.

I'd had a few dates since the divorce, but nothing serious, no partner material. The decent ones seemed taken already, and why wouldn't they be? I knew no relationship, whether casual or not, could heal the holes of loss in my heart. That was for me alone to face. And still, in a perfect world, I yearned for a partner. So I had a mini pity party for myself on the way home from the sandwich shop, feeling not good enough.

It wasn't merely age and expenses that convinced me it was time to sell my house; even the neighborhood had changed. Celebrities were frequently spotted in local restaurants or in the park where my kids had once twirled on the tire swings. Twenty years before, Jake and I couldn't persuade friends to cross the Brooklyn Bridge for dinner. Now Brooklyn was trendier than ever, and the real estate market, thankfully for me, hot. Sometimes I missed the old grit. Before there were too few restaurants; now there were too many.

Stroller congestion clogged the sidewalks, and I felt more affinity with the original settlers, the "leftovers" as some of the newcomers called them, the Italian families who had built the neighborhood and become my friends and neighbors. They'd accepted me and my family into their neighborhood and we assimilated, not the other way around, expecting them to. But the tide had turned. And one by one I watched long-standing businesses close and stores I couldn't afford to shop in replace them. Young people flooded the town, and my family had grown.

One day I was out running errands when an elderly Italian woman called to me from her stoop.

"Look," she said, waving at the condo monstrosity being erected across the street, sadness in her eyes. "They're taking my view of the sky." Many generations of Italian families had lived in the same houses for generations, and this woman had probably sat on that stoop her entire life. As a young professional entering the neighborhood once myself, I undoubtedly played some role in the transition taking her view of the sky away, even though I'd been unaware of it. But I lamented the changes in my own life I'd been powerless to control so I understood. I sat with her on the stoop and nodded.

A block away the local senior citizens center, which had been edged out in favor of a children's boutique and pricey classes for toddlers, had reopened. While their new quarters were being renovated, the old folks were shuttled from one temporary venue to the next with no guarantee the daily place where they once gathered for lunch, bingo, and birthdays would reopen. Finally, though, the banner had been cut. Their new space was a smaller windowless room, beneath ground, below the prancing toes of dropped-off toddlers, the leftovers one step closer to the earth in which many of them would soon find themselves.

Maybe my days as a homeowner had simply run their course, my exodus as normal as everyone else's, standard operating procedure for the matriarch to exit last when the rest of the family had been taken care of, when that part of my life's work was done. Maybe life waited for me on the other side—love and career possibilities I found harder to envision the longer I stayed.

One morning during my last winter in Brooklyn I came inside after shoveling and began spontaneously laughing and singing, "I ain't gonna shovel snow no more."

"You'll have a delicious hot meal when you get home," Ella texted later while I was at the office temping. It had been hectic for her too with college applications and senior year of high school. She was about to leave the home she'd lived in since age two, when we were an even headcount. After dark, I wearily rode the subway home, but when I turned the key and walked in, there she was, standing in the kitchen to greet me, smiling as she presented me with the plate of food she'd prepared.

Martin Luther King Jr. taught that only love could drive out hate. And at times it took every fiber of my being to push away the anger bubbling up in my throat instead of allowing it to pull me down.

But there Ella was, standing in the kitchen, love in all its purest glory, reminding me to do just that.

8

The War Room

A house is merely a house, right? Four walls and a bit of brick and mortar. Millions of people sell their homes and move. After a seven-year slump, approximately 4.8 million homes were sold in 2013, the year I sold mine. According to the U.S. Census Bureau, between 2012 and 2013, approximately thirty-seven million U.S. residents, about 12 percent of Americans, moved. About half of movers separated from their spouses said "family-related" reasons accounted for their relocation, with change in marital status the primary cause, which isn't surprising. The family home is generally the largest marital asset to split in a divorce and, unless couples have sufficient assets for one party to keep the house, refinance, or otherwise buy the other spouse out, the family home is often sold. Sometimes the sale is delayed if there are young children and the custodial parent receives exclusive occupancy of the home for a specified period.

After Diana and her relatives, the previous owners of my home, left, I treasured my house all the more, feeling lucky to have learned some of its origins and add to its history myself. I had limited cash for renovations, but I nurtured the house, preserving what I could.

Once I resigned myself to sell, some friends wondered if I should. *Where will you go?* they asked. *What will become of you?* My mother wanted to know. *Why not renovate and condo the building, sell three units and keep one for yourself? Or move to the ground floor and rent out the upstairs? Take in boarders.* They sounded so scared, and their concern for my future so bleak. And yet relocation is often cited as the third most stressful life event, behind death and divorce. Death, divorce, relocation: I would eventually face them all.

For months I waffled again. But the condo project would have taken years and money I didn't have. Nor did I feel comfortable renting Ella's room to a stranger. And the estimated income from renting the top three floors would barely have covered the overhead. What if the real estate market tanked? Forecasters predicted by 2020 there would be another substantial housing crisis as the number of Baby Boomers selling their homes far exceeded demand, with the result that America's aging population would be stuck in homes they could no longer afford or physically take care of. I didn't want to be one of them.

I still had excellent credit and hoped to keep it that way. In short, selling my house was the most judicious option. I needed to believe letting it go would be best.

Some friends said unloading the house would allow me to reclaim my life. I wasn't sure what they meant. Most of my life was surely behind me. And who knew what challenges aging might bring.

Mom, daughter, wife. I had a strong sense of myself in those roles even though I occasionally had misgivings about my effectiveness. But I was no longer a wife and while I'd always be a mother and daughter, those roles steadily consumed less of my time, first when I left my mother's home and now as my own children exited mine. Who was the other girl, the one before I became a wife and mother? If I was to reclaim myself, at what point? Before kids? Before my marriage? After my husband left and I'd been bogged down with litigation and being a single mother? Start over at a point where I had veered off on some misguided trajectory?

Despite the hardship, I didn't regret marrying Jake—my kids wouldn't be here otherwise—or relinquishing an unsatisfying law career.

My children knew part of that other woman. In second grade, Ella wrote a profile about me. Her insight took my breath away, and I posted it on my bulletin board to remind me, though often I failed to look.

"You are raspberries, Venice, and green," Ella wrote, listing some of my favorite things. At seven she even knew Richard Russo was my favorite author.

"And you are the sound of me and my sister laughing," she continued. That Ella heard me in the sound of Nicki's laughter as well as her own was almost too much to take in, the roots binding us embedded in our DNA and understood by a second-grader.

"You are all these things and more," Ella said. "Strong, brave, that's where you're from. That's where I'm from too."

The same school year Nicki wrote a piece entitled "My Mom." She said many people knew me but didn't know my soul like she did. *Kind, loving, comforting, cool.* Always jumping to help her, she said, going well beyond the call of duty, enjoying nothing more than making her and Ella happy. But she acknowledged I nagged and yelled sometimes, like all moms. At twelve, she even identified my profession as "writer," something the family court hadn't countenanced.

In the upper right-hand corner of my bulletin board, I had also tacked a scrap of paper bearing the word "Resiliency." Doctor Goldman had handed that paper to me after I shook my head no when he asked if I knew my main attribute. He meant it as a compliment, but at times I'd rather have slashed and burned that two-inch piece of paper, tired of the thankless task of being strong. Years passed, and I grew evermore concerned that being resilient for so long through so much had dampened my lightheartedness. "Funniest mom on the block," Nicki had written, but it seemed I laughed less and less and that keeping my spirits up required me to pump myself up more and more.

Despite my physical age I have almost always felt young inside. Perhaps that's true for everyone as they age. In her eighties, my grandmother still wanted to dance, ever the giggly girl we watched on the 8mm home movies until the day she died. But her walker and her children's apprehension she would fall and break her hip restrained her, and it saddened me to think how caged up her mind was inside her body. After I sold the house, I visited my own mother and bought her a walker and realized, only then, I was next in line.

It was with these thoughts and questions, paired with my penchant for perfectionism, that I began the process of collapsing the contents of my four-story, nearly 3,500-square-foot house and cellar, belongings I'd amassed over more than five decades.

Starting at the top and working my way down seemed sensible. I began in the war room, the name I dubbed the middle section of the top floor in-between my bedroom and the laundry room. It contained most of the papers relating to the divorce lawsuit, and the largest concentration of paper generally, along with my desk, several bookcases and filing cabinets, a closet system, and other assorted furnishings. A multitude of papers filled cabinets, while the rest occupied boxes or were stacked haphazardly in corners alongside the edges of the room.

My friend Pat had gone through a divorce and was in the midst of selling her own house. Until her house sold, she was broke, so I paid her what I could to help me. On our first day, we headed to the war room. Pat walked straight to the laundry room, situated in the corner, stood on the step stool, and started opening cabinets.

"This goes, right?" she said, a handful of junk in her hands and already on its way to the garbage bag.

"I've got to look at everything first!" I said, freaking out.

Pat looked at me quizzically. How would anything get done if I couldn't even make a quick decision about junk? Although we'd begun, I hadn't absorbed what was happening. But I understood shielding myself from the process would keep me crippled. I wanted to soak it all in. Yet I protested beginning in the laundry room.

"We can't start here," I said.

"Why?" Pat asked, a fair question. It made sense to begin in the corner, make quick progress clearing out a small space, and work our way across the rest of the floor.

"I want to start out here," I said, pointing to the grand-sized war room and deflecting Pat's question. I had panicked when Pat began opening cupboards in the laundry room and hadn't known why, but proceeded no further with my thoughts, not then. Besides, there was so much to corral in the war room, the locus of the divorce paperwork that had precipitated the selling of my home. Starting there made sense too.

Pat and I pulled out papers from filing cabinets and spread them on a folding table for sorting through. During the lawsuit, divorce papers had even infiltrated my bedroom, crawling over my dreams like those bird mites. So I banished them from my bedchamber. Still, they lodged close by on the other side of double French doors.

Early on, when the children were with their father, I often cloistered myself upstairs, surrounded by those papers. Most of the documents relating to our marriage resided in the house and so the bulk of the burden to find, organize, copy, and hand them over to Jake's lawyers—and the considerable cost of doing so—fell to me. Motions and other divorce paperwork flew back and forth for years. My lawyer said Jake's attorneys were trying to wear me down, and, if true, they succeeded at times. No wonder I became emaciated and in shock. I referred to this upstairs space as the war room because that's how it felt to inhabit it.

One weekend my friend Maggie drove in from New Jersey and stayed overnight.

"I'm a fast typist, Bev," she said, sitting at my desk for several days while I sat on the hardwood floor dictating an affidavit. Right before the computer crashed and I dissolved into wails. I sat on the floor a lot those days; it was the only place that felt solid.

Before Pat and I began hauling out, I walked up and down and in and out of every room and made a list of chores. What needed to be cleaned or cleared out, repaired, replaced, organized. Hire an attorney, retain a real estate broker, enlist Arman's help, find movers. I scribbled down cost projections and phoned my accountant to discuss tax implications. I added "find a place to live," way down on the agenda. What to throw out, keep, donate, or sell and where. I spent days on the computer researching.

How hard could it be to create an eBay business and make quick, easy money? I got sidetracked for several days reading the fine print on eBay's website about how to establish an account, set prices, stage and upload photos, commence and track an auction, and then ship goods. Trying to figure my cost, eBay's take, my risk and ultimate return. The history of the objects I researched fascinated—and distracted—me. As a test, I scurried about the house grabbing items I thought might be worth something given their age or original cost—a Steuben bowl, Green Hornet and Batman pins, an Italian leather briefcase, a pair of marble bookends, other doodads. I cleared off space on countertops, floors, my bed, anything that might serve as a suitable neutral backdrop, and flashed pictures. Sunlight glare obtruded. Other objects appeared lifeless or out of focus. I'm not particularly proficient with a camera or calculator, and quality photos are essential for selling, so I scrapped the idea, unable to get beyond step one.

My mind raced at the enormity of my task, easily the biggest to-do list I had ever made, requiring completion in the shortest amount of time. Was this a test and of what, my patience? Hadn't I already proven myself or was selling my house the final and most important test of my strength and ability to let go? And who was testing me?

My goal was to move by the time Ella left for college, about eight months from when I started. A master juggler, but a decade later and a decade older after Jake left, I was afraid the process would take me down. I hurried off to my temp job in the morning, and rushed home at night to make dinner and catch up with Ella. The house was more disorganized than ever. Items I set on the countertop or tables or floor to deal with continued to lay there from one day to the next, constant visual reminders of how much there was left to accomplish.

One moment I was in the war room and the next, like an octopus, multitasking in a frenzy all over the house, putting away laundry or lured into another room, spying an inevitable house-selling project and I'd think, *I'll just do this one tiny thing and I'll be that much more ahead.*

Paralysis often settled in when I confronted the sheer magnitude of my to-do list paired with the growing barriers of stacks throughout the house. *I'll just take off one evening and watch television and play Pac-Man on the computer.* Some evenings too tired and immobilized for anything else.

Early on in the divorce, I hopped the subway one day to Manhattan to ask my Buddhist meditation teacher Anders for advice.

"How wonderful," Anders said when I told him about the latest divorce happenings, beaming like a cherub, then swathing me in a hug. A tall, handsome, unshakable man of faith.

"You've been presented with the most incredible opportunity for transforming difficulties," Anders said. "The greatest opportunity we can ever hope to encounter for swift spiritual growth."

"But I'm in so much pain."

"It's your attachment, and all you know. A habit created over countless lifetimes." I had heard Anders teach about this often. People, things, worldly pleasures, all of them letting us down. Yet, I traveled back to the well. As Simone Weil said, "Attachment is the great fabricator of illusions."

"What do I do?" I asked Anders.

"Mix your emotions with wisdom. And concentrate on what's important. Try letting the rest go."

I went straight home and walked through the house, up and down each staircase, like I had with my friend Quinnie several months before, right after Thanksgiving. The girls and I had planned to go away for the weekend while Jake searched for an apartment, and the Brooklyn divorce lawyer I consulted told me not to leave the house without compiling a record of our possessions.

"Some wives make that mistake," he warned. "And find things missing when they come back."

My heart pounded, gripped by fear, and I phoned Quinnie, who realized even faster than I did how to inventory my entire life on such short notice. Within the hour, she'd taken the subway from Manhattan to

Brooklyn and stood on my doorstep, two slices of hot pizza in hand with a video camera dangling from her left arm. For two hours, I played tour guide to my life as Quinnie and I floated from room to room, cataloging a lifetime of memories.

"Those are the masks my husband and I collected over the years," I said, pointing in response to Quinnie's cues, syncopating my words to suppress the horror bubbling up inside me, and push it back down. "We got this one on our first anniversary on a remote island off the coast of Mexico called Yelapa." Jake and I had loved that one, a fierce looking mask with real animal whiskers.

"The leather mask came from Venice, the year I was pregnant with Nicki," I told Quinnie. "And this is the bowl my mother bought us for our tenth anniversary. We picked it out together in Hawaii where we planned to retire." Each item had a story behind it. And the house was filled with them.

"Girl, you've gotta slow down," Quinnie said after we finished, giving me a kiss and a hug and heading off. "You're doing too much." True, as usual.

The second time I strode through the house, after talking with Anders, my purpose was not to take inventory, but to pare down, watching in my mind's eye as one great fire engulfed my worldly possessions. I walked slowly through each room, considered what was important, and then poof, visualized the nonessentials disappearing. The furniture was easy, even though I had a few favorites, like the gleaming polished aluminum French Art Deco hall tree where we hung our Christmas stockings. After pausing over a few pieces of my favorite jewelry, sensing the pull, I tossed them into the blaze. Sunlight slanted through the back door lighting up my computer, my writing, and the chair where I spent much of my time. Poof. Downstairs I pondered the family photo albums and children's stuffed animals. The more I stalled the more nervous I became, like time was running out. Pangs of grief released their sting. I whittled everything down, chased Thunder and the girls out the door, and then watched, surprisingly peaceful as my house of cards crumbled, holding on for one last second, and nearly forgetting to flee myself.

More than ten years came and went and my visualizations became reality. How foolish to think when the time came for letting go it would be as simple. Waves and waves and more waves of loss and letting go and so much more to come. Everyone else walked away, but I was left cleaning up—and confronting my resentment.

Quinnie and I had taken a cursory inventory of my possessions. And then I had a momentary taste of freedom watching them disappear. But selling my home would require taking inventory of my life. And entering the laundry room, and dealing with what it held.

9

Hoarders

Growing up I usually ate home-cooked suppers at the kitchen table with my mom, dad, and brother. But there were also evenings during my childhood when we dined on tray tables in front of the television. Between temping and Ella's late rehearsals at school, she and I often ate dinner on trays in front of the television too. One evening Ella suggested tuning in to *Hoarders*, a reality series about sufferers of compulsive hoarding. From then on we were hooked by the residents that occupied Dante's fourth circle of hell.

No matter how far removed the resemblance between the clutter and filth on-screen and our living quarters, the show gave me the heebie-jeebies. Try as I might the house had never been as clean and tidy as when Jake had lived there, when I had regular help. Jake had hired help, even as a bachelor, and it seemed *de rigueur* for professionals in New York City. After Ella's birth, Jake suggested our cleaning lady come every week instead of every other, and with my bad back and multiple knee surgeries, I was grateful. After Jake left, except for a brief time and occasional splurges, my ability to pay for help dwindled from sporadic to nonexistent.

On my way to bed one night after watching *Hoarders*, the two-foot-high stack of magazines in the vestibule caught my eye. Nearby baseboards that hadn't been scrubbed in over a year, or more, grew tentacles and reached out to me. The prospect of scrubbing dingy baseboards after a long day, baseboards that rose three stories and curled up banisters, dredged up my resentment. No matter how I tried to extinguish my anger, the flames rose.

Several years after Jake left, he bought cats for each of the girls. Ella said his girlfriend was allergic though, and asked if I would take them in—the cats that is. To this day residual guilt washes over me whenever I remember turning down my daughter's request. Moms are supposed to fix things—and there was so much I had not been able to fix but tried to. I explained the expense to Ella along with the fact that our elderly cat Thunder undoubtedly would have thrown a fit. Prone to stress, Thunder mewed and pawed at Jake's pillow for months after he left, obviously taking him for dead. Jake's reappearance at the front door one day, where he called to her, sent Thunder into a peeing frenzy on the Oriental rug. The most potent potentiality I kept to myself. I hadn't yet seen an episode of *Hoarders*, but I already pictured the crazy Cat Lady in my dreams. Visions of an elderly woman with untamed hair and nails surrounded by mewing felines pawing at her feet as she shuffled along, alone, in a dark, dilapidated house. The Cat Lady, of course, was me.

My mom laughed when I complained about the size of my task. She had postponed her own hauling out even longer, having lived in the same house for forty-four years, my second home in life, a house that had been there for me to return to every day after school and come back to after college, after law school, after Daddy died, and even now. We moved a mile down the road when I turned twelve, from a small green shingled house in the middle of nowhere with a backyard and swing set, to a brick house with a basement. Squirrels, deer, and chipmunks roamed the front yard. The town boasted a post office, a few general stores, a gas station, an auto repair shop, a firehouse, one honky-tonk, and a fair number of churches.

In the fall and winter, I built snow forts and played football. In the summers, I picked strawberries, pedaled my bike to the general store for penny candy, and hauled tobacco from the field to the barn with my grandfather. Jake joked about my humble beginnings and called my hometown a "flyspeck," which was fairly accurate.

"I've saved every letter you wrote me from college"—and I wrote so many—"and every card you've ever given me," Mom said. In her eighties, Mom said my brother and I would have to sort through it all after she passed. It was not a task I welcomed, but she'd become too frail to undertake it herself.

After Jake left, I made a rule with the children nothing new could enter the house unless something else exited. It worked for awhile, until I became the perpetrator. Like many families, we expanded our space with each subsequent residence and then began filling it up. We had far less practice whittling down.

But I was on a tight schedule to place the house on the market by spring. Cleaning would come later; clutter was my initial focus. What to keep and what to discard? And what was an appropriate benchmark? Need, utility, aesthetics? Should my test be the same for all categories of objects or did it depend, and on what? If need, how to define need because how much does anyone really *need*? Yet why acquire something to cavalierly throw it away? How much use was sufficient before tossing? One friend renewed her wardrobe each season while another kept hers for decades. Should I aim for the middle, and would I ameliorate guilt if I sold or donated items?

Clutter experts say if you haven't used something in a year you should err on the side of throwing it out. I could have filled truckloads using that litmus test, but it seemed wasteful.

Besides, what if I plain loved something, even if I barely or never used it? Keep the things I liked best? Some clutter experts maintain you should keep the objects that bring you joy. But don't inanimate objects merely provide temporary pleasure? Maybe choose the thing with the most useful life left instead. Or the one costing the most or the more sophisticated or refined purchase. Perhaps the one best assimilating with my future, a future I could not envision.

How had I accumulated so much stuff anyway?

Did guilt plague me because of my modest upbringing, the daughter of parents from a small rural town who had sacrificed to put me through college? Had years of being called upon to justify my every move and expense during the divorce hard-wired me to defend myself even to me? Was it my deep-seated perfectionism at play? Or a combination of all three? Of course, I'd also been meticulously trained as a lawyer, schooled in the art of cross-examination and purportedly divining the truth. So what *was* the truth?

These mental machinations drove me crazy, my own mind my harshest and most unnecessary enemy. The standard of perfection I measured myself against guaranteed failure before I'd begun.

I've often wondered why these sorts of thoughts occupied space in my brain, especially when no one was looking over my shoulder but me. But the process of selling my house called up my relationship to everything and everyone, the growing chaos around me nothing compared with the chaos emerging within.

Certain things lent themselves to easier disposal than others, duplicates and items clearly beyond their expiration date. Manuals and accessories for cell phones and computers twice and thrice removed. Torn pajamas. Swimsuits with zero elasticity. Twenty-year-old tax returns. One glass left over from a set. Cheap giveaways. Coffee mugs whose mold felt awkward in my hands. A frog for a flower arrangement I would never construct.

But those fake lilac eyelashes I wore in the summer of 1980 when I'd gone dancing at the long defunct Mudd Club and Danceteria? Tossing them provided pause.

One night I couldn't sleep, rose at 3:36 a.m., and filled three large black Hefty bags with garbage before going off to temp. On February 25,

I bagged up three more sacks and dumped them in the trash. The following day, Ella and I lined the trunk and back car seat with eight more large bags and dropped them off at the Salvation Army. Over the next five days, I stuffed thirteen more Hefty black bags with rubbish, and left stacks of books on the stoop for neighbors along with a white bookcase and wooden shoe rack from Ikea. All were snatched up overnight.

Although I'd thrown out dozens of bags, you couldn't tell I'd begun. If anything, the house looked like I'd taken garbage in. In paring down, I pulled items out first to examine them, emptying out the contents of drawers, cupboards, cabinets, cardboard boxes, and all sorts of other containers, closets, wall units, bookshelves. I was amazed at how much more I owned than I'd thought; at how much a drawer or well-designed container could hold, creating the illusion of orderliness and control, while making room for more stuff. I wasn't surprised when I learned The Container Store, a chain of retail stores devoted to products for storing and organizing stuff, doubled its opening price its first day trading on the New York Stock Exchange. The stores were often a madhouse of shoppers in desperate pursuit of controlling their clutter.

I used to chuckle when my magazine subscriptions arrived in the mail because there was often a story line about clutter on the cover, second only to the latest advice about happiness. Why the never-ending coverage if these problems were solvable? Or was the advice flawed?

A real estate friend dropped off a book about clutter for me one day. She thought it might help. Her gesture was thoughtful, but I laughed whenever I saw the book, unopened, on my nightstand.

Sometimes I placed objects on another surface in the course of cleaning out. A weigh station to allow my psyche to absorb the reality of what I was doing before making a decision. This middle step created the illusion of progress, though perhaps it was.

Maybe I will regret tossing this, I thought, standing over bags destined for debris or donation, feeling a momentary pang. An actual physical reaction in my chest or stomach. Some objects I hadn't used more than once or perhaps ever, but in phase one—staging the house for sale—I often wavered.

Am I packing up too much to keep? Deep-sixing too much?

With drawers emptied, I made space and slid other objects back in. I knew from the get-go there would be a second stage of hauling out, a time for reexamination once the house sold. Again, was this delay the perfectionist in me? The girl afraid of making a mistake, of having to replace what she tossed and thus creating double work and expense? The girl frightened to face the future and postponing it as long as she could?

Four unused single-serving-sized crockpots with lids and handles had occupied a second shelf kitchen cupboard since 1997 when we moved in and before that, shelves in previous kitchens. The soup bowls had been a gift, but from whom? I couldn't ever remember using those miniature tureens designed to hold French onion soup either. But I loved eyeing them whenever I opened the cupboard. I'd never made French onion soup either. All sorts of other soups, butternut squash, watercress, cucumber. I served those in the white bowls, the crocks reserved for my someday-to-be French onion.

I began to wonder if whenever I gave up something I rarely or never used, especially something I was drawn to, whether that meant parting with a little dream for the future. A tiny dream like serving French onion soup in those cute crocks at an imaginary dinner party with friends and perhaps a new partner from a yet unimagined life. Perhaps I thought by holding onto all the little dreams, ones I could control, like the serving French onion soup in sweet little bowl ones, they would develop into something more substantial by virtue of keeping the collection of so many little dreams intact. I'd been obliged to give up so many big dreams already. The cumulative effect of relinquishing so many smaller ones scared me.

Of course, the opposite might occur. Years of pining away for lost dreams might grow so large in my imagination that disappointment could crowd out joy, with hope sliding toward resignation and regret. Intellectually, I knew a happy future depended on halting the slide. Still,

I closed the cupboards, leaving the crocks in the space where they'd been for years.

Pat broke down one day while helping me clean out. Her house closing had fallen through and she was broke. She had raised three kids practically alone and her ex (considerably better off than she was *and* on wife number three she said) was pressuring her about his share of the house sale money. She sobbed and shook like I'd never seen anyone sob and shake. I hugged her while she cried on my shoulder.

"What am I going to do?" she asked. She was much further along in the selling process than I was so I knew what to look forward to. And this was a place I did not want to go, let alone venture beyond. My pulse already thumped in my throat. The year before I'd gone through extensive tests and had worn a heart monitor for twenty-four hours after experiencing the same sort of thumps. After the results came back, I was given a mostly green light, but warned continued stress could impact my heart.

"It's going to be okay," I said, comforting Pat as much as reassuring myself. "You've done so much. You'll get through this too. Don't let him get to you," I said. Spouting the same platitudes others had well-meaningly mollified me with for over a decade. It had been at least that long for Pat.

Nora Ephron said divorce was forever. It was true. You had to get used to falling into the pit every now and then and clawing your way back out.

Perhaps that's why mantras had become such a powerful presence in my life. *Om Tare Tuttare Ture Soha.* Liberation from fear and suffering by going for refuge to the Buddhist mother of compassion, Tara, the great protector and manifestation of wisdom. Recitations of this ancient mantra, along with Psalm 23, became a practice in which I endeavored to evoke pure lands in the midst of the daily inferno of divorce.

Years ago I asked a fellow practitioner at my Saturday morning meditation class how he coped with walking through the doors of the psychiatric hospital where he worked each day.

"I imagine I'm entering a pure land when I open the door," he said. In Buddhist parlance, a pure land is an uncontaminated, blissful abode, where suffering does not exist and fear has no place.

Still, as I held Pat, my mind entered the circle of indecision I'd spun around in months earlier. Maybe I shouldn't sell the house after all. It was early yet in the process, and I was overdue for a spring cleaning. But my options hadn't shifted. Neither had my obstacles. I walked home late from the subway one night, on my way home from temping, and my phone lit up with a message from my tenants. The lights had gone out on our block. But how was I supposed to fix it?

I had to simplify my life somehow.

One day I ventured into the laundry room. I avoided the cabinets, however, and dragged two large cardboard chests from the floor into the war room. Each held a dozen smaller cardboard boxes into which I'd organized the girls' schoolwork from preschool through high school. Storage for some of my best memories. I needed to wallow in them.

I'd periodically thrown out some of the girls' papers, but not many, saving most every test taken, portrait painted, and paper and poem written. Every draft of the play Ella penned in seventh grade. Construction paper and plastic plates with pipe cleaners and buttons and fake jewels stuck together with globs of Elmer's glue. Dried glitter drifted to the floor when I unfolded artwork. Broken pieces from pasta necklaces lined the bottoms of boxes. At four, Nicki drew rainbows, hearts, flowers, and girls with smiles. Ella sketched manga and girls with straws on their cheeks for smiles. All happy pictures. Sometimes Nicki and Ella titled their pictures, and I wrote the titles and dates on the backs.

Except for the broken pasta, I returned items to their respective boxes so the girls could sort through them. An excuse or hoarding? I decided to find out.

Compulsive hoarding is a form of OCD. The website for the International OCD Foundation states allowing items to clutter living areas to the extent they are no longer usable as intended and cause distress elevates "collecting" to the level of compulsive hoarding. Hoarders also seldom put their possessions on display while collectors keep collections well-organized and display them with pride.

People don't think they'll become compulsive hoarders, but I suppose you can say the same thing about most people with other addictions.

Like addictions, compulsions can give rise to a host of problems impacting the health and welfare, not only of hoarders, but also their family members. Hoarding involves attachment to items one finds it difficult to part with, so in essence we're all hoarders of one form or another, although compulsive hoarding takes attachment to a higher level.

And I was attached to things—and people. I had difficulty disposing of items and felt overwhelmed by my household possessions, although they hadn't overtaken me. Instead, I kept my files, including the children's memories—schoolwork, photos, baby clothes—meticulously organized, probably stemming from my Alpha tendencies.

I fell into grey areas on other hoarding factors. Occasionally I lost things and purchased bargains. Haven't we all? But I loved to entertain and the house was relatively easy to navigate, except for the growing obstacle course occasioned by packing.

No, I wasn't a compulsive hoarder, not that I seriously thought I was. But the reassurance I was normal by hoarding standards provided scant comfort. I was deeply attached to certain things. *Hoarders* both fascinated and saddened me. I certainly felt the same pull as the woman with the three thousand purses when I examined a few of mine. My heart broke for the woman dying of colon cancer, so overpowered by life that she'd become a compulsive hoarder. And the woman who kept her dead baby's clothes for years? I understood her more than all the others. The fear, the inability to let go, and the need to have control, the fear of not having enough, along with the burden of having plenty. These susceptibilities dwell inside each of us, and I recognized them in me. Was I also hiding pain behind my stuff?

I had also begun noticing something else at the other end of the spectrum—a trend toward disposability. People so dissatisfied on all levels—with their bodies, homes, acquisitions, food, lifestyles—that when they fell short, when they outgrew their presumed usefulness, they chucked them and found replacements. No wonder there was growing concern we were destroying the planet. We were even ditching each other.

On March 10, I weeded through the top drawer of one of my filing cabinets, where I'd placed important papers for safekeeping—school information relating to the children, medical insurance documents, tear sheets of articles I had written, folders with drafts and ideas for writing projects.

Midway through sifting I lifted out a white manila folder more than three decades old. It was my wedding preparation folder with my original to-do lists, right there among my "important" papers. I no longer yearned for my ex-husband romantically, but the familiar tug of attachment grabbed me when I opened the folder. The contract for the piano player; my wedding registry at Bloomingdale's; orders for the florist, caterer, and limousine drivers; swatches from my bridesmaids' dresses—I'd stuffed them into pink and periwinkle organza. Even a letter from my grandfather, the Southern Baptist minister who married us, along with a copy of our wedding vows, and my grandfather's own commentary.

"Truly, then, these words are most serious," my grandfather had said near the close of the ceremony. "Not knowing what is before you, you take each other for better or for worse, for richer or for poorer, in sickness and in health, until death. And because these words involve such solemn obligations, it is most fitting you rest the security of your wedded life upon the great principle of self-sacrifice. Sacrifice is usually difficult and irksome. Only love can make it easy. We are willing to give in proportion as we love."

The years of fighting for my marriage had been difficult and irksome. But my love for my family had no bounds.

"How many do you love me?" my daughter Ella used to ask.

"I love you so much there's no number big enough," I would say. "And how much do you love me?" It was one of our games.

"A million, billion, trillion."

Nicki and I played the game too. "To infinity and beyond," she might say. Or "googolplex." And I would answer her as I had Ella.

"He's just angry, Beverly," Quinnie said, when I broke down sobbing at lunch, on my birthday. I'd just received my husband's divorce complaint over the fax machine, threatening to seek sole custody of the children.

"You know how much I love them," I said. Jake had promised to make them hate me too.

"Your girls are never going to hate you," Quinnie said. Oh how I wanted that to be true. But my husband's love had changed, something I'd never dreamed possible, why not theirs? What a terrible admission for a mother to make. But betrayal makes you doubt everything you thought you ever knew about everyone. The thought I might lose the love of my children haunted me, each time I said no, or enforced a curfew existing in our house but not in my ex-husband's, or asked my children for help with housework. I'd never raised teenagers or been through divorce, so what did I know when my teen screamed "I hate you"?

"They're my little girls, Quinnie," I said.

"I know, honey," she said, patting my hand. "You're going to get through this, Beverly. But you've got to be strong." And so I was for so long, and so tired of trying to be.

Many years later, though, I stuck my wedding folder back in its drawer. Something in me still clung, not ready to let go.

10

Emptying Nicki's Nest

Nicki, my firstborn, was second to leave home. She left for college six months before the divorce became final, then for good several years later when she started working and moved in with her boyfriend. When she came to clean out her room, I asked her to separate belongings into four categories—garbage, storage, charitable donations, and items to carry to her new apartment. We sorted through the contents of her bookshelves, drawers, desk, and walk-in closet. Clothes, makeup, jewelry, knick-knacks, stuffed animals, books, mementoes, papers, gadgets, electronics, photos, accessories, girl gatherings from twenty-three years.

She paused briefly to read a card, letter, or school paper, but otherwise made her selections decisively, quickly distinguishing between articles without any visible sign of longing. I sat on the bed next to her, peering over her shoulder while my heart raced, periodically impeding her progress to ask, "Are you sure you want to toss that?" or "Can I see it for a second first?"

"Do you want me to do this or not? They're my things," she said.

Affirmative to both.

"I just want to see it before you throw it out," I said, straining to get a look at the item in Nicki's hand before she disposed of it and working hard to restrain myself from any outward display of anxiety, a full-blown breakdown destined to make matters worse.

"I can't believe you made these invitations for my birthday," Nicki said, smiling as she unfolded an invitation to Peter's Ice Cream Parlor adorned with glitter, stars, and hand-traced stenciled letters. How had so much time passed between then and now?

I watched, relieved as Nicki laid the invite in her stack of keepsakes, hoping she'd recognized one among many tokens of my undying love.

While Nicki's things were her things they had also been the most important part of my world. Proof of my existence. Proof that being a mother was how I had spent most of my time. Evidence of what truly mattered.

Nicki turned next to her bookshelves. The top shelves were chock-full of trophies and plaques from speech and debate tournaments. She handed me one of each to bubble wrap and said to toss the rest.

"Are you sure?" I asked.

"Yes," she said. "I saved the most important ones. I don't need the others." I gagged at the thought of throwing them away.

Why was the task seemingly easy for Nicki, yet so hard for me? Could the difference be reduced to youth, since I'd had two or three times as long in life to grow attached? Because most of Nicki's life was before her, while the majority of mine had passed?

Maybe it was also the process of letting Nicki go all over again, reminding me how often I had let go of her in the past and the reality she would never be home again, certainly not in this home. In 2012, a record 21.6 million millennials, 36 percent of young adults aged eighteen to thirty-one flocked back home. What if Nicki lost her job or broke up with her boyfriend? Once I sold the house, where would I be and would there be an option for Nicki to return to?

I don't recall feeling sad when I left home for college or law school or when I moved to New York City. I was excited about the worlds opening

81

up before me. That my parents had my back was a given. The stability of the home and family that had formed the foundation of my life undoubtedly gave me the self-confidence to leave.

Now, though, I was no longer the young daughter leaving home; I was now my mother. And I felt guilty there would be no childhood home for my children to come back to, even on holidays, especially for Ella during her first year in college. I took for granted that my own mother, then eighty-two, lived in the house I'd grown up in and still stored some of my school things in her attic and garage. Wasn't maintaining the nest something mothers were supposed to do? And here I was disassembling mine!

In 1968, children's book author and illustrator P.D. Eastman, a protégé of Dr. Seuss, wrote a well-known book called *The Best Nest* about a discontented mom-to-be bird who flies off in search of a new home. No other nest is quite right, however, not the mailbox or the church bell tower or the already-occupied boot. Mr. Bird goes off in pursuit of Mrs. Bird. Unable to find her, he flies home, weary in the mistaken belief Mrs. Bird has been eaten by a cat during her excursions. He finds Mrs. Bird at home, though, where she has just laid a baby blue egg. The two happily reunite as they conclude their old nest is the best nest after all. To me, Eastman's final words echoed Dorothy's from decades earlier in *The Wizard of Oz*. Indeed, could anywhere compare with home? And once it was gone, it was gone.

When the girls and I pared down our mountain of books, there was no question *The Best Nest* was a keeper, perhaps mostly for me. I choked up when I read it to my girls. Ella ended my recitations with a hug.

Over time, I had of course reached the usual milestones parents practice for letting go of their children—sending kids to school and sleepaway camp, allowing them to stay out late with teenage friends. Mini empty nests, I called them. I even encouraged my daughters to experience another part of the country when they applied to college and had already seen Nicki off. Like all parents, the more my children grew, the less I saw them.

If anything, divorce should have primed me even more for losing my home and time with my children. Made the transition easier. After all, my children and I led partially separate lives for more than a decade. But, in addition to the usual parent-child partings, divorce brought a steady stream of forced goodbyes and a never-ending exodus of new ones. And therein lodged the problem.

After my husband left, the children toted their clothing back and forth. They packed and unpacked until I could no longer stand it and suggested my husband buy the kids clothes to leave at his apartment.

When Ella was ten she brought home a bag of clothing she could no longer fit into. For years I had shipped her outgrown clothing to old friends who had unexpected twins; somehow Jake must have gotten wind of my recycling project. After Ella returned to her father's, I sat in the dining room, alone, in the dark, weeding through her clothes, unfolding each piece, then holding it, arms outstretched against the stream of light filtering in through the picture window, before refolding and moving on to the next item. With growing children, sorting through clothes is a regular task. This time, though, I felt like I was performing some forbidden act, best done in secret. Better done before Ella came home the following day.

I realized I hadn't seen Ella wear most of these clothes, thus reaping the karmic retribution for suggesting the whole matter of separate clothes for our residences in the first place. With divorce, whole chunks of time went unaccounted for in my memory, producing an amnesia-like hole in my brain that threw me off kilter. Divorce sped up the natural progression of time, my children and I spending less time together than we would have, thus rendering their eventual departure all the more seemingly premature.

Divorce created new zones of privacy too, all ripe to be invaded.

"How was your weekend at Dad's?" I asked Ella one evening after she'd spent the weekend with her father.

"Fine," she said.

"Does his girlfriend treat you alright?"

"Uh-huh."

"So, what did you do?" I asked.

83

"Nothing much," was Ella's response the weekend she saw *West Side Story.*

Was it okay to even ask these questions? Were certain parts of my children's lives off-limits to me once the family broke up? A whole code of political correctness to figure out and follow on my own?

The clothes I looked through that day permitted peeks into the nooks and crannies of my daughters' secret lives, an attempt to fill in the missing pieces of our family jigsaw. Holding onto those nooks became scraps of shelter in the vast wasteland of places gone, smiles posed, bikes ridden, sleep slept, meals eaten, and laughter laughed—all without me. One night I woke up in cold, sweat-soaked sheets, wondering if the web of silence that had begun to spin around us would one day break apart. Minutes before, Ella had danced in the moonlight in my dreams. Nicki had stood shyly beside her prom date while bulbs flashed and people laughed and chattered in the background. Only I wasn't there.

The truth is I never got used to their absence. Sure, I grew to enjoy evenings spent with friends during my weekends "off." But I never welcomed Friday nights when the law required me to send my children away.

"It's a negotiation. That's all," Jake explained, when I asked him why his divorce complaint sought sole custody of the children. "I don't want sole custody. I don't have the strength or will or power or smarts to raise the kids the way a woman needs to raise them."

But the harrowing divorce tales I heard petrified me. After Jake's betrayals, how could I trust him? Pounding headaches and diarrhea wracked me in daylight. Nightmares wrecked my sleep. Dreams I had of killing myself turned to my husband and his girlfriend. I imagined my children torn from my womb. In one dream I ran into Jake and his girlfriend at Ella's dance recital.

"Ella's coming to live with us," my husband said in a dream, marching off with his girlfriend to find Ella. Again and again, I woke up in a cold sweat, immersed in either guilt or terror, for an instant unable to discern fact from fiction.

My fear ebbed, but the undercurrent lingered beneath the surface, a steady reminder loved ones can disappear overnight. Admittedly, my girls returned, but it wasn't enough to undo the sorrow.

Eventually my nightmares subsided, and Nicki started high school in downtown Manhattan. The September before a little yellow school bus had picked her up in front of our house. I stood on the stoop, teary-eyed as I watched her walk to the corner, pause for the light to turn, and head to the New York City subway, alone. She was a full-fledged city kid at last, and it was a natural rite of passage for me to let her go. Yet after I closed the door that day, the familiar sense of loss gripped me again. My daughter would be attending high school in the fallen shadows of the Twin Towers, but it was more than that. Mine was a potent, deep-down anguish, like the panic from my dreams and the one that struck the instant I realized my father wasn't going to rise from his coma after he had a heart attack in his fifties. A feeling of unquenchable loss that followed me for years.

Nicki won the plaques and trophies she asked me to throw away during high school speech and debate tournaments. I remember the exact day she won her most prestigious award, February 4, 2006, a Saturday afternoon. I'd waited to hear from her before finally going out to run errands. While I was gone, Nicki phoned and left a message.

"Hi, Mom. It's Nicki," she said, excited. "I just had my final round and it was excellent! I love you!" I replayed her message over and over. *I love you more*, I cried in my head. Nicki had been the first one to rebound those words back to me after her father left. "I love you," I'd said. "I love you more," she'd replied. Stunned, I didn't see how that was possible, and my heart swelled and leapt and danced, alive with hope that no matter what loss I'd suffered, or still faced, losing our relationship would not be one of them.

I puttered around my empty house that day, doing laundry, cleaning, our cat Thunder at my heels, waiting for the phone to ring again. Nothing in the freezer appealed to me so I ordered take-out and while picking up my food, missed Nicki's call again. Talking to her had been the one thing I'd waited for all day.

"Hi, Mom. It's Nicki. Just thought I'd tell you I won! It's kinda crazy. Anyway, I love you," she said in her voicemail. And then she giggled, bless that wonderful child of mine, before closing with the most wonderful words of all, "Bye, Mommy."

Congratulations, baby girl, I echoed back in the silence, plopping down in my office chair to let it sink in. I yearned to hug her, but I'd have to wait; it wasn't my weekend.

I poured myself a glass of wine, ate my cheeseburger and onion rings, and bided my time to phone my ex's apartment. Nicki said they'd be going out to dinner. After waiting for what I knew wasn't long enough, I phoned anyway and left a message for Nicki. Anything to satisfy my longing to connect with my daughter.

Despite Nicki's ability to part with her trophies and other mementoes, she was not unsentimental. I watched her gather up important keepsakes from her childhood. A miniature silver frame in which I'd placed a few bits of pile from the pink carpet from her nursery, cards from her grandmother, her geodes, a fragment of wallpaper from her nursery.

Jake and I had even named the bears on that wallpaper. And even now I can picture Nicki and Ella standing in their cribs wide-eyed while their father and I pointed to the wallpaper as we made up stories about the skateboarding bears named Fritz, Willie, and Goober.

I asked Nicki if there was anything else in the house she wanted me to save.

"You're not getting rid of the Jacques Lowe photos, are you?" she asked with a catch in her throat. Moments like this I wanted to bottle up her innocence and preserve it. Those photographs were as dear to me as they were to her. Didn't she know that?

"You should have sold the house after Dad left," Nicki said. "Ella and I didn't need to stay in this big house." But how could she have known that in foresight? How could I have known how a move might have affected her and Ella given everything else we were going through? Certainly, a lot of things might have changed. Their schools, their friends, our neighbors, our neighborhood. We had lost so much already, and I wasn't game to gamble on making our lives worse, not if I had the strength to save our house.

I had done what I assumed best, and Nicki's words irritated me at first, particularly after what I'd given up financially and personally, until I realized she was probably letting me off the hook for the future and telling me she would have let me off the hook for the past. Jake had split the family, but my daughters loved their father. And hard as it had been for me being a single mother I'm sure it had been challenging at times for them to live with one. Could I have asked for better-hearted children?

The following weekend Nicki packed up more things and then she and I and her boyfriend drove to Ikea to buy items for her apartment. Jake had given them a couch and tables from his former apartment; I bought Nicki a table and chairs and other odds and ends. I winced when she served me dinner at her apartment using the plates and silverware Jake and his girlfriend had once used to feed themselves while we sat at the table I had purchased, the experience more than surreal.

The week after our trip to Ikea, I hired Moving Man, a local mover I had used for years, to tote the items Nicki wanted for her apartment including the red wool Belgian rug from my bedroom.

"Store my chair if you can," Nicki said, even though the green velvet chair and ottoman in her room where she'd curled up so often were badly worn.

"How about your bed?" I asked.

"My bedroom is too small for it," she said. "And I have to buy a dresser." Her new bedroom was too small for her wooden dresser too. I remember when we bought it, the year after we moved into our house, the year Jake lost his job. The antique furniture warehouse we traveled to in Queens was having a special sales event, and a guy dressed as a swami greeted customers at the entrance and offered free tarot card readings. Jake turned up his eyebrows at these sorts of things. The Ouija board and Magic 8 Ball, however, were two of my favorite toys as a kid, the spirit world having fascinated me. I told Jake I wanted to have my cards read before we left and was dumbfounded he was also eager to have his cards read. But I said nothing, too blown away to ask why.

The fortuneteller knew Jake had lost his job and about my worries concerning paying the mortgage.

"But everything's going to be fine," the soothsayer told us. He predicted we would live in the house for many years to come and fix it up and that Jake would find another job. We hadn't done much fixing up, but Jake found another job, an outstanding one, and at least I'd lived in the house with the kids for years to come. The fortuneteller also told us Jake would soon head off on an important trip, the most intriguing prophecy of all. Jake and I used to talk about that what it meant because the guy said it wasn't going to be a family vacation or in the United States or take Jake anywhere he'd been before.

A year or so later my cell phone rang at the dental office. Jake was on the other end of the line, crying.

"Remember what that guy said about me going on an important trip?" he asked, struggling to get the words out as I, too, became overcome. Jake's company was sending him to the Holy Land for a conference and although my husband hadn't practiced Judaism since I'd known him, and regularly railed against religion, something about that prediction coming true held significance for both of us.

Not long after, I was walking along Smith Street in Brooklyn one morning when a decrepit woman wearing a silk turban and parched skin called to me from her screened-in porch. She sat before a round table covered with faded white lace; a neon sign flashed "Special Reading $5." Seconds later her long sinewy arm held my palm.

She predicted Jake and I would separate, but added we'd reunite after I started to cry.

Looking at Nicki's dresser brought back memories of the day we bought it and what came after, and my visit with the old gypsy. She'd been spot-on about Jake leaving, but off the mark about him coming home.

"Where are you going to live?" Nicki asked me the day we sat on her bed cleaning out.

"I don't know," I said. I didn't want to leave New York. I didn't want to leave my house either. I suppose everyone else who left home had wanted to. Jake, obviously. And it had been natural for Nicki to move on, as it would be for Ella. They had new futures to embrace.

Ever since I mentioned selling the house friends had been needling me with the same question Nicki had asked. *Where are you going, Beverly? What are you going to do?*

I didn't know, but eventually I would have to answer.

11

Aging, Sickness, and Death

Cleaning out a house and a lifetime of what's in it is hard, backbreaking work. My entire body ached.

Pat and I broke for lunch one day when she dropped by, but otherwise spent the day in the war room, sorting through the contents of a tall, metal filing cabinet crammed with papers. I pulled out batches, thumbed through them, then handed the papers off to Pat in piles—save versus shred—before going on to the next set. I stood in one spot while Pat periodically got up to use the shredder. She kept telling me to get off my feet, and I kept meaning to, after I finished the next stack and the one after that.

But the day wore on and when I sank into the couch by evening, the pain grabbed my back and shot searing throbs down my legs.

"What's wrong?" Pat asked when she saw my face crumple. I was unable to answer her at first.

After multiple visits to the chiropractor, the pain eased off. But I resumed my stubborn ways. After filling bags, I'd carry a few at a time down the main staircase and through the front hall, then descend the

AGING, SICKNESS, AND DEATH

stoop before continuing out to the garbage cans inside the wrought iron gate. When I ran out of thirteen-gallon bags, I opened a box of thirty-gallon-sized ones. An audible groan escaped when I stooped to pick up the first loaded bag.

This is too heavy for you. Put it down, my brain screamed. I ignored the warning, carried on, and lugged the sack to the next landing, where another voice chimed in.

Look around. Do you see anyone here to help you? Doesn't the garbage man come tomorrow? If you want to get the trash out, don't you have to do this now? That voice had connived with great success for years to convince me my body was invincible. But you can't know what it's like for your body to betray you until it does. Even then, it's hard to listen because your mind reverts to its younger self.

So, I hoisted the thirty-gallon bag, descended the stairs, crossed the foyer, and made my way out the door and down the stoop, where I thrust the bag into the garbage pail.

And then I missed several days of temping. The second day Ella had a college orientation. I doubled up on Advil, wore flats, and somehow hobbled back and forth to the subway and into Manhattan with her.

A third voice—the well-oiled problem solver—had tried to intervene before I injured myself. *You don't need to carry the bag out this second,* she said. *You can go to the store and buy more small bags. You can wait for Ella to come home and help you. You can leave the bag where it is until next week.*

I'm not exaggerating when I say that's pretty much how loud and clear I heard the voices. But I'd grown weary of hearing the fixer. Besides, the voice who conjured Superwoman had far more practice asserting herself and demanding control. And when the voice of reason attempted to overtake her, she jumped in with guilt to clinch the deal. *What if Ella's late or too tired? Do you want to burden her with one more thing? Don't you need to sell the house and get going?*

"You're going to have a heart attack from stress if you don't leave town and get away from your ex," my doctor had warned several years earlier.

But that would have meant leaving my children, something I couldn't do. My doctor said the girls would understand and forgive me. How was that possible? It was a terrifying prospect I refused to consider.

Besides, if the past was any indication, I knew there would be occasion for my body to process the shocks once the crisis had passed, once I sold the house, once I landed wherever I landed. Through counseling, I had recognized that instead of processing calamity in the moment at times I had delayed reactions. When they hit, hopefully I could cope.

After missing several days of work, I jumped on the subway, returned to temping, and resumed my pretense of invincibility. The train swayed me, but I hung on, sandwiched between a throng of stressed-out New Yorkers struggling to reach Manhattan. Exiting the train, I prayed, yearning for the office chair awaiting me, only to discover my discomfort unbearable whether upright, sedentary or—later in bed—prone.

So I quit my temp job. The pay was lousy anyway, downright embarrassing for a person of my skill. By then, only one voice demanded to be obeyed.

I wondered if the roots of my physical discomfort reached far deeper than I imagined, to the very dilemma faced by every human being—the fear of death and the corresponding need, and reluctance, to confront it. Ernest Becker said in his Pulitzer-Prize winning book *The Denial of Death* that man's "deepest need is to be free of the anxiety of death and annihilation, but it is life itself which awakens it, and so we must shrink from being fully alive."

He explained that the fear of death underlies all our activities and other fears, in service of our need for self-preservation. If our conscious mind continually focused on death, we could not function. Therefore, we repress coming to grips with our nature because it is too frightening to fathom. Instead, we succumb to busyness and constantly map out our lives.

In dissecting Soren Kierkegaard, roundly regarded as the father of existentialism, Becker explained this basic psychology of humans:

"That man is a union of opposites, of self-consciousness and of physical body...He was given a consciousness of his individuality and his part-divinity in creation, the beauty and uniqueness of his face and his name. At the same time he was given the consciousness of the terror of the world and of his own death and decay."

Becker concluded that freedom, true health or peace of mind, transcendence, however you want to phrase it, is achieved when humans realize this impossible paradox and yet manage to break through their armor of self-delusion.

One of the most powerful tools for breaking through this delusion is the Buddhist meditation on death. I heard my first teaching on it decades ago.

Before then, church had been the focal point of my upbringing. My family went to church on Sunday morning and Sunday night, and to prayer meeting on Wednesdays. Every summer as a child, I attended Vacation Bible School. As a teen, I often spent weekends with the youth group. Except for holidays, I rarely attended church during my marriage, however, and felt a bit guilty, especially where the kids were concerned. Too weak to stand up for myself in the face of my ex-husband's distaste for religion? Tired of defending myself? Embarrassed to acknowledge my beliefs in the intellectual world we hobnobbed in, where admitting my Southern Baptist background might have brought snickers? In a hectic New York life spent juggling work, two kids, a husband, a house, and a cat, church was one more thing to interfere with weekend sleep, errands, and family time—and if it was going to cause friction, well, easier to let church slide. I hadn't rejected God or the conviction there was more to this world than existed on the surface. But I put my spiritual life on the back burner.

Three and a half years before Jake left, I began attending Buddhist meditation classes. A year later, I returned to church. And my spiritual practice guided me through the worst days of my divorce.

93

Through my meditation classes I became sensitive to the endless tasks of daily life and how becoming absorbed in them inevitably drew my focus away from the reality of death. And how, once death arrived, hindsight would reflect back on the pointlessness of all my busyness. By then, however, it would be too late.

In contrast, by remaining focused on death's eventuality—along with the unpredictability of when—individuals could die peacefully, and avoid living a life of regret.

The first time I heard these teachings I thought *how frightening.* But they began to shake lose my habitual mode of thinking when I investigated them more deeply.

Indeed, Becker wrote that the shocks experienced in our lives can dislodge our repression of death. Shocks perhaps like my father's death in his prime and my husband's abandonment or the day my body failed me in the midst of selling my home.

Several years after Jake left, I drove to upstate New York for a four-day silent meditation retreat. I was juggling two kids, in and out of divorce court, and needed to get away. During the retreat, my daily schedule consisted of four self-guided meditations of one to two hours each while sitting on the floor of my modest room. I ate my meals in silence, and spent the interludes hiking, reciting mantras, and sleeping. Initially I was energized and peaceful, and then I crashed and slept like a baby for ten hours. I woke up the next day raging with hunger and exhaustion. Midafternoon I broke down in sobs, desperate for speech and human contact.

French mathematician and philosopher Blaise Pascal once said: "I have discovered that all human evil comes from this, man's being unable to sit still in a room."

Later that day, the chatter in my mind melted away. When I thought about the experience years later, I understood I'd been going through some kind of withdrawal. The moment my mind latched onto fear, my worries had come rushing back, as if to stop me from examining what lay beneath the surface which had been nibbling at me for years. Over and over I intoned, "I shall certainly die." And in the clearing of my mind I perceived unresolved anguish over my father's death twenty years earlier and my ex-husband's abrupt departure. Letting go was the fear I had smelled, my mind yet again wanting to run from the truth of my aloneness, the false security underlying my deepest attachments, and the inevitability of my demise.

Days later I drove home with a smile on my face.

And yet my mind ran away again and again. Until I scheduled the next silent retreat. Or drove myself to the mental and physical breaking point. My hold on my mind was so strong it fed my deluded belief I must shield myself from the very things that could relieve my load.

Even my infrequent requests to friends and neighbors for help—necessary as it was for my ability to cope—was itself a form of denial, a way to avoid recognition of both my mortality and imperfection. Buddhists might sum it up this way: By all means, ask for help if you need it, but don't think by receiving help you've addressed the root problem, because the next crisis is already on the horizon.

After the divorce, my ex-husband's aunt told me how pretty I was while we were having lunch one day.

"You should find someone else while you've still got your looks," she said. But years passed and I never found anyone. For so long, I hadn't really looked. It was only while selling my house I realized I hadn't stared squarely in the mirror at myself either for a long while. I washed my face and brushed my teeth without a mirror. And when I applied makeup, I had trained my eyes to focus intently, in succession, on each subsequent discreet spot of application, not stepping back to view the finished product.

Once this astounding realization struck me, I vowed to overcome it, marching into the bathroom over and over resolving to look myself in the eye. Only I couldn't do it, so powerful was my aversion to aging. After many attempts, I steeled myself. And didn't like what I saw.

Aging had arrived and my body was well on its way toward sickness. Only one thing was left and that, too, was inevitable.

When I said I held on for dear life riding the subway, I meant it. For more than a year my father's sudden death from a heart attack had haunted me. I was approaching the same age at which he'd died and somehow got it in my head I wasn't going to outlive him.

The last time I saw him, he was in the emergency room lying in a coma. I took his hand, told him how much I loved him, and watched as tears streamed out of the corners of his eyes, shocked he'd heard me. He died that same day and never woke again.

I could go for months without thinking about him, then out of the blue I could be parking the car and suddenly collapse over the steering wheel and cry out. And then I'd go on as before until the thought of never seeing him struck again without warning.

For me the "D" word had meant divorce for so long. Now it was trumped by the other "D" word. The "D" word to trump all "D" words: Death. To finish hauling out I would have to focus on that word more and more. And let the other D word I'd clung onto for so long finally go.

12

Stuff

The self-storage business is a multi-billion-dollar industry, fueled by the rise in American consumerism. Today, approximately one in ten U.S. households rents storage space for overflow. Twenty-five years after the birth of the storage industry in the 1960s, the average American family had doubled the amount of its possessions. Our family had done the same thing.

In 2010, A&E Network debuted *Storage Wars,* a reality show in which the contents of storage lockers, whose owners are in default, are auctioned off. By its second season, the show had become the most watched program in the cable network's then twenty-seven-year history.

Despite downturns in the economy, there seems scant letup in the American thirst for stuff. I suppose we're all trying to fill one hole or another inside.

Landfills in the United States are at capacity. We consume, we toss, we waste. The majority of our landfills are leaking. Hazardous substances leach into the ground and saturate the air. In the last fifty years

Americans have tripled the amount of waste they generate. There's been a corresponding trend in family breakup.

Clutter fills not only physical space; it pervades our psyches. Americans spend nine million hours per day searching for misplaced items. Each year employee disorganization costs U.S. businesses substantial lost profits, proving time *is* money. And compulsive hoarding, often caused by grief and depression, affects approximately 5 percent of the population.

As I prepared my house for sale, my own stuff gnawed at me. The girls and I curbed our spending habits after the divorce, but still owned more than our fair share of stuff.

By then I had survived the age at which my father had died, a huge relief. I'd grown increasingly cognizant of my own mortality, but that did not solve the short-term, practical reality of disassembling my four-story house.

Once I quit my temp job, my back improved. I was fine one moment, though, and drained the next. After sleeping for ten hours, I woke up one morning, drank coffee, and hurried upstairs to sort through files when a surge of exhaustion flattened me. Was it my heart? A panic attack? A delayed reaction to the fear of not outliving my father?

At a lecture several years before, I had heard a self-proclaimed expert expound about the path to happiness through endeavors like cleaning closets and getting more sleep. I was uninspired. During the Q&A, the speaker admitted meditation hadn't worked for her. I was aghast at the audacity of extolling the virtues of decluttering while pooh-poohing the wisdom of Buddha. I gazed at the other female faces in the audience, all intelligent, professional women, and no one else appeared shocked. Instead they seemed to hang on every commonsensical Heloise-like hint promising the antidote to their stressful lives.

Spending even one minute reading about clutter was to me, by definition, a shallow pursuit. Books on clutter fell into the category of new age-y happiness bunk for folks with too much time on their hands. My bedside table boasted books by Pema Chodron and Thomas Merton, a copy of *The Bible* and *The Tibetan Book of the Dead,* thank you very much.

Perhaps lightening one's physical load could help provide favorable conditions for developing inner peace. But I believed true spiritual progress required something far deeper than organizing one's physical surroundings. And for me, and most men and women at midlife, or at any other time, it's not realistic to eat, pray, and love on the other side of the world either.

While studying Buddhism, I had been fascinated by the story of a Buddhist monk named Lam Chung. He had scarce aptitude for the rigors of dharma study and became discouraged by his inability to memorize scripture. So Buddha gave him a simple two-word mantra to repeat while sweeping the temple. (No one seems to know what the mantra was, but that's not the point.) In one lifetime, through this simple practice alone, Lam Chung purified his negative karma and literally swept his way to enlightenment.

In moments of frustration, I channeled my own inner Lam Chang, picking up the broom and dustbin and going outside to sweep the endless Brooklyn sidewalk dirt, leaves, and debris.

One night I grabbed the decluttering book that had been lying at my bedside. I told myself I was merely looking for pointers to speed up the process of hauling out.

But this book was different. More than a simple how-to, the author advocated a holistic approach that integrated the mental, emotional, and spiritual with the practical. My fascination embarrassed me. I covered the book jacket when I read it on the subway.

But research shows that being organized and crossing items off a to-do list can boost one's sense of well-being. A poll conducted by a leading household goods and furniture chain found about one-third of those surveyed reported a greater sense of satisfaction from cleaning out closets than having sex. I was overdue for both so this possibility intrigued me! Could there be some merit to this decluttering nonsense? (I can now report back that cleaning out closets felt pretty darn fabulous.)

The voice of William Wordsworth, one of my favorite poets, spoke to me as I bustled about the house. "The world is too much with us; late and soon," he said. "Getting and spending, we lay waste our powers." Kierke-gaard and now Wordsworth. No flesh and blood man had come into my life, but I had a knack for carrying the torch for dead 18th and 19th century poets and philosophers. Now if I could only find their reincarnations!

On my way downstairs to the kitchen one day, I eyed the trophies and plaques Nicki had discarded the previous month. They'd been lying on her green chair ever since; I'd been unable to bring myself to toss them.

"Do you think your dad might want one?" I had asked Nicki.

"Please, Mom, I'm an adult," she'd said. "Throw them out." And still I couldn't.

Finally, I grabbed a black Hefty bag and began filling it. When the bag split, I divided the contents between two bags. Even with the weight evenly distributed, the awards weighed the bags down. I lugged them to the bathroom and placed them on the scales: twenty-six pounds. Once I carried the bags down the staircase and outside, I heaved them into the garbage bin. And I swear as I did, weight left my body and a lightness entered my mind.

I'd had my first taste of this physical sensation more than twenty years earlier. I had been working long hours at a prominent Manhattan law firm, usually eating my dinner, often a greasy cheeseburger and fries, after midnight and put on thirty-five pounds. I wanted to lose it before I became pregnant, so I joined WeightWatchers.

"Go to the grocery store and pick up a ten-pound bag of potatoes and see what it feels like to carry that around," the session leader suggested during one of my weight-loss meetings. So I went to the supermarket and lugged a ten-pound bag of potatoes through the aisles. It was pure dead weight, what the dictionary calls a heavy or oppressive burden, and I'd been carrying three-and-a-half bags of potatoes around on my body every day for years. After I connected my instructor's analogy with my own physical sensations, I lost weight steadily.

Years later I carried my babies around effortlessly, though. They were pure joy. My grandfather was right. Love makes sacrifice easy.

How many ten-pound bags of potatoes had I already thrown out while cleaning and how many hundreds more were to come? Scientific evidence exists that physical activity can supply mental health benefits. But does the connection go deeper? As I shed the contents of my house, might the weight pour off me too, emotionally, in a way it had once done physically?

I pictured Atlas as I had seen him depicted, hunched over, ordered by Zeus to bear the responsibility of the world on his back and shoulders. That was me for so long. Abandoned, divorced, over-the-hill, unemployed, single. How might Atlas have looked and felt if someone had given him a reprieve? If he'd given himself one?

Ever since I'd arrived in New York more than thirty years earlier, I'd gone from one residence to the next, accumulating more. Jake and I had also brought baggage that had plagued us from our first anniversary straight on through to the divorce. For years those marital difficulties weighed me down, and in the last decade, so had my anger over the lifestyle of a single mother I hadn't chosen.

By refusing to remove Nicki's trophies perhaps I held on even tighter to the past. To the image of my daughter as she had once existed. Not unlike the comedic image of the six-foot adult male whose feet stick out beyond the edge of the twin bed in his childhood bedroom preserved by his mother.

Nicki's trophies pulled on my heart strings. I suppose I thought holding on would keep me happy, only the tighter I clutched the more uncomfortable I became. Attachment is intoxicating, but it's still a delusion. When I pried my hands loose from her memorabilia and the impossibility of maintaining things the way they once were, the discomfort that lodged in my mind began to lift. After I passed the moment of wavering and moved to the other side of indecision, the energy that letting go released fed on itself. It was a fresh sensation, this link between my mind and my body. An intoxicating one, more so than the previous sense of attachment.

That same day I filled up one garbage bag with paper, another two with miscellaneous trash, and eight bags with donations for the Salvation Army. I marched to the kitchen and vowed to tackle something more substantial, a piece of furniture perhaps. I washed down an old library card catalogue I had restored and used for cutlery. Perhaps I'd sell it. I pulled out drawers and started cleaning them out. *One, two, three, four, five, six.* Why did we own six bottle openers? Why had I saved dozens of wooden chopsticks from Chinese food deliveries? And fifty or more miniature erasers the girls got in party bags during elementary school? Or the odds and ends from miscellaneous cheap cutlery sets predating my marriage?

To my left I eyed five years' worth of phone books on top of the refrigerator along with three fly swatters. I hadn't opened the phone books in equally as long, and I shooed flies and bees and bugs out the back door. Why hadn't I tossed the whole lot whenever I wiped down the top of the refrigerator instead of moving them to the counter, then putting them back in place? No time like the present.

Books held a place of honor in our home. Still, why had I kept so many cookbooks and stray recipes, lined two rows deep on the kitchen counter? Some I'd never used, others rarely. I cooked frequently, but mostly made up my own simple concoctions or consulted recipes from the batter-stained *Good Housekeeping Cookbook*, circa 1973, or the handful I'd taped inside a blue spiral notebook.

I suppose I'd kept all those other books and recipes just in case I'd finally use them. And while I loved the idea of experimenting more, something told me I wouldn't. That there wasn't time.

Wouldn't keeping all these cookbooks and untried recipes allow regret to grow stronger? To serve as a constant visual reminder of remorse? On the other hand, perhaps I wouldn't regret getting rid of them, the fear of doing so more of the driving force behind my keeping them for so long.

What more did I need than our trusty *Good Housekeeping Cookbook* and the handful of recipes the girls and I consulted over and over at Christmas and Hanukkah—our stuffed mushroom recipe, the notes for our portobello mushrooms and latkes, the recipe for butternut squash soup we'd gotten from the Mondavis during a trip to the Napa vineyards. And Pino Luongo's *A Tuscan in the Kitchen*, the cookbook that had opened my eyes to the freedom of cooking without any strict recipes.

I felt freed to cook even more or not at all when I placed the cookbooks I didn't need or use in bags destined for donation. Let those recipes be tried out by families in other Brooklyn kitchens.

Next up, the kitchen spices. Two spice racks, plus a dozen or more unopened dried spice jars that occupied the ledge about the kitchen sink. Without one drop of hesitation, I kept the nine or ten we used and threw out the rest. Things I wouldn't have tossed even two weeks before.

I'd been wasteful, Jake and I had been wasteful, friends who had given us gifts we didn't use or need had been wasteful, although the gifts had been tendered with kindness. Saving them would continue to be a hedge against acknowledging none of us had known any better how insignificant stuff would become in our lives. How burdensome it had become to clean and store and organize and maintain. How much of life it stole.

I opened the cupboard to the left of the sink. Two of my three ice buckets occupied the top shelf. I'd purchased one in law school; the other was a gift. The third, a metal ice bucket in the shape of an apple, was on top of the wall unit in the other room. That's the one I loved. The others diminished the beauty of the one. So I grabbed the surplus and placed them in the donation bag.

From another cupboard I pulled out miscellaneous glasses. And my ex-husband's mother's bowls. Everyday chipped serving bowls, four big ones and eight small. Why had I kept them in the cupboard for more than a decade since Jake left? He didn't want them. The kids didn't want them. And I hadn't used them in years. I lifted them down from their shelves and put them in bags bound for other homes.

As I moved about the kitchen, my possessions began to irritate me. During the first phase of my cleaning out, I'd been disturbed by all the clutter. Now well-ordered stuff I'd felt an affinity for began to feel sticky, like some gravitational pull was coming from them, an actual visceral aversion. Allergic almost. The more I thought about holding on to something, and hemmed and hawed about letting it go, the stickier my possessions became.

My eyes continued down the shelves where I had removed the ice buckets and landed on the crocks reserved for my French onion soup to-be. I counted out all eight and laid them in a large paper bag for delivery to the Salvation Army.

My brief moment of discomfort letting them go transformed into relief, lightness, and lightheartedness. Into the possibility of making French onion soup in the future—or not. Perhaps a fresh way of looking at my possessions too. And the items I might acquire in the future, because that future might be a whole lot different from the present beyond which I had had a hard time envisioning.

How little can I live with? How much can I get away with tossing or giving away? Can I pare down to next to nothing? I had done so in my mind once, years before, after Jake left, when I had imagined all my possessions consumed by flames. These were my ruminations as I cleared out, and they excited me. No judgment, no guilt, purely playing with my thoughts. Early in my marriage I'd read home decorating magazines religiously, and the more sparse the interiors, the better. Something in me admired minimalists. I figured photographers and decorators staged those settings for wealthy individuals who had the cash to carefully orchestrate and maintain the illusion of less while having more. Still, something drew me to those photos. Couldn't I achieve something similar for myself, but more authentic?

Along with the card catalogue, I identified other furniture to sell. One antique dealer walked throughout my entire house, filled with things our friends oohed and aahed over, and other than the hall tree where the girls and I hung our stockings—which I wasn't selling—he said nothing was worth buying, even the silver Art Deco martini glasses. I pointed to one of my favorite chairs—I'd seen the guy eye it twice—and asked: "What about that?"

He shrugged and said, "I can only offer you seventy-five dollars for it."

"Yes," I said without hesitation. I loved that pink chair and I'd picked it out by myself, without Jake. But the urge to create space and resist the word "no" took charge.

Other antique dealers either weren't interested or never answered my calls or emails. I placed a few items on local classifieds and a parenting listserv. Photos and descriptions of my card catalogue, a beautiful grey velvet Art Deco bar with a lacquered bottom and two matching barstools, bedroom furniture, marble bookends, and other odds and ends. A man answered the ad for the bar and made an appointment to stop by one evening. Jake and I had bought the set shortly after marrying and used to joke that even though we needed a dining room table and other basics, we'd purchased a bar. And we weren't even big drinkers, mostly using the set for added seating or as a showpiece. Later it held our CD player and then after Jake left, the shelves stored the games the girls and I played—*Clue, Monopoly, Life, Scrabble, Connect Four, Mancala*, and so many more.

Ella was at Jake's and I was nervous about a male stranger coming inside so my friend Dirk from church stopped by to keep me company.

"I'll pretend I'm your husband," he said, taking off his jacket and making himself comfortable, as if he lived there. But the purchaser was lovely and brought his wife. They loved the bar, too, but already had stools, and requested a discount off my rock bottom price.

"Sold," I said, practicing the word "yes."

"The kids are growing up," Dirk said, getting into character as he helped me lift games off the shelves. I nearly spit on myself when my gay friend called me "hon" and "dear," his delivery so natural he might have used those words for me every day.

"That book you gave me on decluttering was a lifesaver," I told my real estate friend when I saw her in the neighborhood.

"Really?" she said. "I thought you would never open it."

Me too.

After I finished it, I reached for another book that had been on my nightstand for over a month: *The Metamorphosis* by Franz Kafka.

Nicki had two copies and had given me the extra when we cleaned out her bookshelves. The title of Kafka's masterpiece piqued my interest. I figured I could knock off the slim volume in a night or two.

Walt, my best friend from high school who had watched over me from afar during those first rough years of divorce, had used that word about me.

"It's good to hear your voice," he'd said during one of our long-distance calls. He had remembered that December 14, 2003, was the one-year anniversary of Jake's leaving, and called from his post in Iraq to check on me. "I've noticed a change in your emails, like you are metamorphosing. At first, I felt you were in shock, but it sounds like you have your wits about you now."

I *had* been in shock. There were days I thought I'd lose my mind and days I thought I had. Walt's call caught me in one of my better moments. But the years dragged on and my metamorphosis slackened.

"People sometimes experience many Good Fridays in their life," Walt later wrote from Iraq, wishing me a Happy Easter. "But all of them eventually experience their Easter Sunday, when all is well after the total darkness. You will eventually experience your Easter Sunday."

Intellectually, I knew Walt was right. A decade later my heart was finally beginning to sense it.

I headed back to Nicki's room that March day when I had discarded her trophies, and began packing up her special childhood books for safekeeping, including her complete set of the *Little House* series. I'd forever felt our family at its essence had been that loving family from *Little House*. But in that brief moment, while sitting on the floor of Nicki's room, packing up her special books, I wondered whether my image had been an illusion. Whether I'd tried so long to fix a past that never was. And if that's why the breakup had hurt so much.

Before children, my reference point had been me and Jake. And after, kids and family, and then just the girls once Jake had left. But my reference point was changing again. With Ella gone, the reference point of my life would soon be me.

13

Not Worth the Paper

accumulated more paper in all its varieties than probably anything else. Reams of research materials, drafts of articles, and books. Journals, notepads, stationary, envelopes in various colors, Post-its, calling cards, letters, greeting cards, photos, books, newspaper clippings, drawing pads, stray quotes and affirmations on scraps of paper pinned to my bulletin board, calendars and desk planners, my daughters' schoolwork and art projects made with paper plates, fortune cookie fortunes, postcards, magazines, playbills, programs, recipes, phone directories. Divorce papers. The Wall of Mom.

Paper on every floor, visible on nearly every surface, covered in a light coating of Brooklyn dust.

Except for books, most of my paper fell into the 8½ x 11 category. After getting sidetracked elsewhere in the house, I headed back to the war room to tackle the paper. Pat and I carried about a dozen heavy boxes up four flights of stairs from the cellar. Over the next month, I paged through each sheet, initially wanting to count, then weigh them all.

For someone who loves paper so it's bewildering how often I can't find a handy notepad when an epiphanic thought strikes me in the middle of the night. Or, as it often does, during church. Hesitant to let the thought go, I'll reach for anything—an unused tissue or the back of a Hall's cough drop wrapper, the margins of my church bulletin. Words burst from my brain at a rapid rate—writing them down on paper helps tame them.

A famous Hollywood songwriter I used to dine with when he came to New York City regularly made notes during dinner. Having worked in the music business I recalled the tale about Johnny Mercer writing "One for my Baby" on a napkin in New York City's P.J. Clarke's, where I hung out with friends when I first moved to New York.

I guess I figured one of my doodles might turn to fairy dust too, but most were illegible when I got around to deciphering them. In elementary school my handwriting had been impeccable. And each day my second grade teacher called me to the chalkboard to copy "Dear Diary," her daily recitation of the day's activities, so my classmates could practice their penmanship.

Pat, Sandra—another friend from church—and I fed thousands of pieces of paper through the shredder that spring. Decades of my life flashed before me. No more than three pages in slow succession seemed to be the magic formula, even though the shredder advertised itself as double that capacity. Even then, the shredder—which Pat dubbed "The Bitch"—constantly conked out.

Paper multiplies exponentially when you shred it—my shredder yielded about 350 shreds per page according to the product specifications. The shredder stalled whenever it reached capacity and often before. Errant shards clung to my hands and clothes like packing peanuts.

After I filled bags, I stacked them outside next to the garbage cans. One night someone punctured one of the bags and scattered the confetti-like strips over the sidewalk. After that, the vestibule became a way station until recycling day, and Ella and I navigated getting in and out of the front door.

Not all paper required shredding. But unless it was a catalogue or magazine or junk mail I examined it first for my social security number, credit card data, or other private information, then segregated the paper into piles based on its relative sensitivity—tear, shred, or simply bag and toss. My hands swelled. My cuticles became jagged. I hoped the feeling would return to the numb patches on my thumbs.

To pass the time my mind drifted off to calculations of how many trees I'd destroyed. These wacky ideas often leapt into my jangled thoughts. Paper yield per tree depends on the tree used, and the height, width, and age of the tree—I looked it up. Pine trees account for the production of most paper. No way I could gauge the tree source for my paper or obtain an accurate tally, but I figured I'd killed more trees than the ones on my mother's mostly wooded two-and-a-half-acre plot. But I used recycled paper for printing, and recycled my paper. Did that make a difference?

The majority of paper evidenced the troth Jake and I had once plighted. Tax returns, insurance policies, bank and investment statements, health insurance plans and receipts, credit card and utility bills, car leases, and so on. Those same papers became legal proof employed for our disunion, augmented by complaints, answers, motions, exhibits, affidavits, briefs, and subpoenas. Every staple I eliminated pricked my heart with reminders of my harrowing divorce. Every accusation, lie, court appearance, and sleepless night. Every harsh word two people once head-over-heels in love had exchanged. The hard-earned cash so easily confiscated by divorce bills. The evenings I stood at copy machines, and the days I dragged boxes of documents down to court, then back again, unopened, the court limiting the evidence I could produce and the questions my lawyer could ask. And the weight, always the weight of it all.

Each bit of paper provided a window into my life, and the assemblage an image of before, during, and after the divorce, from beginning to end. Evidence of how Jake and I spent our earnings, when, where, and on what. Proof of our priorities, where we ate, what we wore, the choices we made, and the choices divorce took away.

Aloha Airlines. Pepe Viola Restaurant. Lands' End. The New York Philharmonic. The Musician's General Store. Storybook Heirlooms. Book Court. KC Art Supplies. Barnes & Noble. Costco. Macy's. Bayside Fuel. Amazon. Johnnie's Bootery. Gracious Homes. Manhattan Jeep. St. Paul's Church. The Cobble Hill Animal Clinic. Nu Look. Bella Nails. Exxon. Yankees MVP Service. Brooklyn Heights Montessori School. D'Amico's Coffee. The Linen Source. AOL.

No more than a word or two conjured up the memory of a moment. Historical records of an era, a time, and place in history. My history. Of businesses that had opened and closed. Of a family come and gone. All of it ephemeral. Which was also partially promising news, knowing nothing was permanent. Not even the pain. And still, the pain.

And then records of the aftermath, my separate life without Jake and Jake's without me. Credit card statements reflecting meals with *her*, trips with *her*, the couples' counseling he'd attended with *her* and quickly abandoned with *me*. The shame, the enduring disbelief, the unanswerable whys. Rage rose up again. I held up page after page. Pat gasped.

One day Pat fed papers to The Bitch while I perched on a stepstool at the other end of the room, sorting through legal papers that had mildewed in the basement.

"Look at all these papers!" I yelled, sobbing. "All so worthless!"

"Just throw this shit away!" Pat said, jumping up from her chair. "You're torturing yourself. Get rid of it."

"I can't," I said, grabbing back the papers that Pat had snatched from me. "I need to look at them first."

"Why do you need to keep any of it?" she asked. The litigation was over, true. But would tossing them strip me of my memories, or was it only processing that could relieve me of the pain?

Once I guarded those papers so carefully. As if they had the power to protect me from so many fears. Fear of failing in my quest to save my marriage. Of losing my children. Fear of being alone and not recovering from the shock. Fear of dying, and not being understood. These fears called out to me from the pages while I reexamined them.

But while paging through, I also saw the meticulous, detail-oriented person the girl behind those papers had been, the careful and complete way she had assembled them. The beautiful orderliness of her mind. The strength she had harnessed not to waiver in her convictions when she had every reason in the world to shrink away. But I felt sorry for her too, beaten down by fear and anguish, surrounded by the false security of paper she thought would protect her.

In the midst of this, I had tried to remain the lighthearted mom I'd once been, who made Eyeball Soup for Halloween with peeled green grapes floating in a bowl of vanilla custard. And now the children were grown, and Ella would soon be gone.

How to leave resentment at the threshold when I left and make a reasoned, business decision about which legal papers to keep and which to throw out? Letting go did not require returning to my naïveté. Nor could I discern the future.

It took weeks to cross-reference and weed through duplicates. I phoned my accountant for advice about financial documents. I used my lawyer head to make prudent decisions about others, retaining documents I'd advise any client to keep. With a mind of wood, I organized, packed, and sealed the documents selected for storage.

I tore and shred the others for transportation to the dump. Did that reinforce the split? Tear asunder in my mind the crazy pieces of the broken jigsaw I'd desperately tried to reassemble? I don't know, but power resided in the ritual of making and executing decisions with non-attachment.

But what to do about the duplicates of my ex-husband's separate tax returns, bank statements, credit card bills and other documents? Jake hadn't been my husband for a long while, and even before the official split, the justice system didn't seem to think he was my responsibility. So tear, toss, or shred? Did I have an obligation to protect my ex-husband from identity theft? He was the ultimate reason I had come to this fork in the road; shredding his documents would cost me more money and energy. Do unto my ex as I suspected he'd do unto me? The decision was easy using that yardstick—stand on the street corner and hand the documents out.

I could never have done that. But my ex-husband was a stranger now, and had been for a long time, a man perhaps I hadn't really known. So I decided to treat him like the stranger he had become, like any other stranger whose documents happened to be in my house, doing what I believed to be right in the case of any human being. I shredded the most sensitive information and tore the rest into bits. In this way I was able to distance myself, my decision no longer about him or me or the two of us.

The size of a thirty-gallon Hefty garbage bag filled with shredding is deceptive. It looks heavy. But even filled with pain, it's so very light.

I stacked the culled boxes of paper in the laundry room, allowing purchasers to view the wide expanse of the top floor, ready for them and their stuff.

After I finished sorting my legal files, I returned to my black filing cabinet where I still had a couple of drawers of important papers like birth certificates, social security information, and closing binders for the various residences my ex-husband and I had bought during our marriage.

As I skimmed through the closing statements, something I hadn't noticed before struck me. On most documents my ex-husband's signature came first with mine below. Jake was just "Jake" or like me, also "purchaser" or "borrower." On other documents, I received an additional designation, titles of my own—"wife" or "his wife." Even though I had contributed heavily to the family coffers that enabled us to purchase and furnish the homes, including the down payment for our brownstone.

When I was forced to reconstitute my life as a single adult, I discovered these odd hierarchies and titles had legal consequences. For example, when I tried to return our Jeep at the end of its lease, I wasn't allowed to, not without Jake's permission. I learned only then my name wasn't on the lease either, even though I'd been paying the monthly car bill. I had the same problem getting utility bills transferred to my name. In my struggle to refinance the house, the bank indicated I'd improve my chances with a letter from my ex-husband confirming his then payment of child support. I was tethered.

How did this happen? During much of the marriage, Jake and I kept most of our money separate. But one day, soon after I stopped practicing law altogether, he came home saying we should put our joint names on everything. I'd been so moved, "together" the only word I heard, that I quickly signed the requisite papers. And then shortly after my ex-husband left, I learned that without his permission I no longer had access to stock accounts I'd funded working long hours as a lawyer, sizeable sums once solely in my name. The checking account into which his paycheck was deposited, however, remained solely in his name.

Somehow, I hadn't intuited the rise and spread of feminism, with its critique of the effects on women of inequality in the law. I had been too busy birthing and raising babies and making a home, living in a supposedly financially secure dream-world. What did I know of middle-age or unemployment? Single motherhood or abandonment or what felt like second-class citizenship in the halls of justice? I can't deny the exhilaration that overcame me when I zoomed away from the Jeep dealership in a car in my name. Or the deep sense of accomplishment felt when I signed a mortgage on the top line, with no one else's name underneath

But was I truly equal or empowered even then? Or only a tad better protected than I had been? To be honest, having my family back would have made my life a whole lot simpler, although things in my marriage would have had to change.

"What happened to us?" I asked Pat after we ate lunch one day and headed upstairs for more shredding. "How did we end up single mothers, alone, and selling our homes?"

"We married assholes," she said. I ruminated endlessly over these sort of questions; Pat's opinion was quick and decisive. Even accepting her interpretation, however, led to the inevitable, unanswerable "why?"

The closing on Pat's Brooklyn house was approaching, but she was having no luck finding an apartment. Real estate in New York City was becoming increasingly cost-prohibitive for the middle class and, like me,

Pat hung onto her house as long as she could. She was also unemployed due to ageism and the raising of children, in her early sixties with no retirement plan. I wasn't far behind. Real estate brokers charged between 8 and 15 percent of the first year's rent for the privilege of entrée to an apartment in the City's crowded housing market too. Most landlords applied the forty times rule—dividing annual income by forty to arrive at the maximum rent they would approve a renter for. Because of housing competition, certain landlords used a fifty times rule of thumb.

With the negligible wages I earned as an attorney in 2013, I calculated I'd be approved for an apartment for me and Ella in the neighborhood of $400 to $500 per month, using the best-case scenario. I couldn't count rental income because after the sale I wouldn't have any. One legal recruiter I'd gone to the year before told me the kind of legal temp jobs I'd been doing were the best legal jobs, given the economy and my age, I could hope for. She nearly fell over laughing when I told her the amount of income Judge #7 said I could earn. Yes, for a few years I'd been highly compensated, but that had been more than a decade before and I'd worked long hours to earn it.

Pat tried to convince prospective landlords to take the proceeds from the sale of her house into account. They wouldn't. There were plenty of other takers—they didn't need Pat. And if they didn't need her, they wouldn't need me. Apartments sizeable enough to accommodate even a tenth of our belongings in a safe neighborhood would quickly dissipate the proceeds from our house sales too, funds we'd need to live on, maybe forever.

Some landlords would cut you a break if you found a financial guarantor for the rent. But who could I cajole? My ex? Another of my struggling single-mom or out-of-work friends? What about Pat?

She had periodic breakdowns and visions of homelessness. I told her I'd never let her go homeless. Did she sense the unspoken words between us that I knew I'd be moving too, and could not provide what I no longer had? The unspoken words filling me with resentment, followed by

NOT WORTH THE PAPER

loathing for any person, especially women, who suggested I stop whining like a victim? Resentment I nonetheless knew was a waste of my energy?

After Pat left for the day, I went upstairs to clean off the surface of my desk. I sang along to a CD of Merle Haggard's greatest hits as I shuffled through a pile of Post-its I couldn't decipher. I flipped through my two rolodexes, cards I hadn't used for years, people I hadn't seen in equally as long. Like the credit card statements and other papers, my rolodexes told stories of people I'd known and places our family had gone to. Mohonk Mountain House, the Red Lion Inn, Nelly Bly Amusement Park, Kreuz BarBQ in Texas.

Part-way through the CD, Merle started singing *Big City*. I joined in at the top of my lungs. Maybe I wanted Brooklyn—and my whole past— to set me loose too.

Earlier that month I had attended Ella's school production of Shakespeare's *As You Like It*. I'd hoped she hadn't seen me crying when the company's Jaques performed the play's most unforgettable soliloquy, "All the world's a stage." I listened carefully, more nervous by the minute as the young actor described each life stage that had already come and gone for me—infant, schoolchild, lover, and the soldier, eager, and impatient, striving for reputation. I tried to wedge my current image of myself permanently into the fifth stage—justice—confident and wise and enjoying the fruits of my hard-earned labor. Only I didn't quite fit there either: I was selling my house, needed a midlife plan of reinvention, and didn't feel all that wise having come to this juncture in the first place. Plus, I was acutely aware of my inevitable propulsion toward stage six—old age. And after that incapacity and death, "sans teeth, sans eyes, sans taste, sans everything."

Still, I had outlived my father, and deep down I sensed a growing foundation of hope confronting the paper that had weighed me down.

Did you know most people never look again at 80 percent of the papers they keep and file away? I examined every single piece of mine again, thumbing through thousands upon thousands of pages. I needed to put aside those to keep, but mostly I wanted to process it. It was torture, but cathartic.

I tossed rolodex cards for people who had died, and rubber-banded a small stash of contacts I would figure out what to do with later. While I packed up the last bit of important papers from the black filing cabinet for safekeeping, I came across the funeral bill for my ex-husband's aunt, an aunt who shared Ella's birthday and had died six months after Ella was born. She had moved into a nursing home near our co-op, and in her later years Jake and I took care of her.

Pine unstained casket, the funeral bill read. Pine trees. Paper. Casket. Dust to dust.

14

Meeting My Former Self

After polishing off my divorce files, I burrowed through the rest of the paper on the top floor. Maybe I'd discover evidence of that other life friends and family encouraged me to reclaim. Find the me I'd be if I hadn't gotten married and had children, me stripped of the reference points guiding me for decades: Beverly, distilled. After all, an online quiz I took said I'd live to be 115.

With Ella headed to college, I'd have the biggest dose of aloneness I'd had in over thirty years. But I'd done so much navel-gazing after my breakup the last person I cared about analyzing was me.

In addition to the black metal filing cabinet, I had two wooden filing cabinets in the war room, along with papers and other mementoes in several desk drawers, along the floor, and in a few boxes at the back of my bedroom closet. A third of one file drawer contained tear sheets of my published articles and executed contracts; I packed them up for safekeeping. Alphabetized manila folders labeled by subject matter filled another couple of drawers: dissections of magazines and newspapers, and notes related to pitching and demographics. Folders with how-tos on writing and finding an agent. Copies of articles in progress, background research, including interviews with experts. Ideas for businesses and screenplays. One completed book and partial drafts of three more, including a nonfiction book about tweens.

Years before I'd also tried my hand at writing a children's book. And become an overnight expert on the Pokémon and Digimon phenomena, interviewing dozens of kids about Pikachu and Hoothoot, and dozens of other characters for two nonfiction books a friend was writing. Such was the esoterica I happily immersed myself in to pay my writerly dues.

I slogged my way through the evidence of so much time, effort, and hard work that still didn't pay the telephone bill. Hard not to feel my writing career had been stunted—and maybe forever lost—by the demands of single motherhood and divorce. Hard not to hear the judge's voice pricking at my ear—*what are you doing with your days to be productive?* Hard to ignore the stacks of rejections, even though friends and fellow writers expressed amazement at some of the publications I'd broken into. Hard to ignore the inverse relationship between the probability of my dreams of writing for a living coming true as my age went up.

Still, after the early years of flailing about on the war room floor, I would stand back up and continue to pay my dues—attend book events, help other writers edit their work, sign up for classes, and practice my craft. I boosted my spirits with the requisite mantras: *Focus on your accomplishments. Trust the universe. It's always darkest before the dawn. Writing sucks. Be compassionate with yourself.* The picture-perfect bobblehead writer doll trying to maintain a cheerful demeanor while failure swirled around her.

Time had proven to me you can't always get what you want. Plus, I had lost faith in the scales of justice. And yet, if I gave up on my dreams instead of giving them say another year, or ten, or twenty, how would I ever know the outcome?

I couldn't imagine not writing, despite the unrelenting agony. I'd learned so much. I'd worked hard. And I'd published articles I was proud of, pieces that had drawn private emails from people who told me my words had helped them.

But what to do in the short term with my folders of ideas and partially formed projects? I had reached the point where I could edit my work without too much attachment, but shred even one paper baby? New ideas flooded my brain daily so paper multiplied.

Haunted by the thought I'd toss something I'd want later, I saved most of my drafts and haphazardly consolidated a bunch of ideas into a few folders. Pushing paper, it often felt like. But who said I had to be perfect? Still, I ended up with less than I started with, holding papers in my hands like a divining rod. *Stay? Go? Keep? Toss?* Assessing the pull.

Sometimes, as a last resort, I handed my troubles over to God, as in—I'm ashamed to admit—giving God an ultimatum. *If I'm supposed to be a writer,* I'd told him ten years earlier, after my husband left, *I'll know if I get three new things published in a row.* I had no idea what the hell I meant by "new." But that was the challenge, and for nine months God served me with a pile of rejections. In-between the rebuffs, however, I got published exactly three times. First by *Newsday,* then *Newsweek,* and then God's coup de grace as if he were wagging his finger at my impatience, *The New York Times.*

"And that was ten years ago," I said ten years later, cleaning off my desk and tossing a copy of *New Jersey Family Magazine* into a save box. It was April and the article had come out in January. It was the first time the word "new" had registered with me again, and I stopped in my tracks, recalling *The New York Times* had given me extensive editorial space the following month. *What came before those two pieces?* I found the answer later that day—the *New York Post,* with *The New York Times* third in a row again, God's double whammy to my juvenile doubt, whereupon I sat on the floor and blubbered like a baby.

Research about divorce filled another drawer, all alphabetized. Whenever I felt like throwing it in the garbage, invariably another shattered soul emailed to say thanks for giving them hope, unaware I regularly threatened to give up on mine. But I had written about the harm of divorce, the lack of due process, and the need for legislative reform, even co-founded a volunteer organization that received national attention and helped build awareness. Even if there were no paying jobs in the field, my life had had purpose.

I finished packing up the file drawers and set to work disassembling my office bulletin board. Horoscopes, Bible verses, song lyrics, quotes from Christina Rossetti, Thomas Merton, Ralph Waldo Emerson, William Zinsser, Rumi. Scrap paper with my doctor's "Resiliency" scribble. Ella's miniature red ink drawings of "Mom" and her school profile dubbing me "strong and brave." My notes to self—*remain flexible, do the opposite,* and everybody's favorite, *everything happens for a reason.*

"I'm sick of hearing my friends tell me everything happens for a reason," Sandra said one day while helping me straighten books on my bookshelves. I nodded. I was sick of hearing it too. Sometimes things happen for no good reason.

Coincidence is God's way of remaining anonymous. Albert Einstein. Another quote on my bulletin board. But God was not always so anonymous, although that seemed to be his preferred pattern. Perhaps Einstein was wrong. Perhaps paying better attention is what's required. And if so, what to wish for at this point?

Condemned to strength. One of my early editors had said that about me, so I added those words to my affirmations as well. Initially, the description seemed like a compliment; now I wasn't so sure. I envisioned a strong, brave, resilient woman walking up a steep mountain, never sitting down, never reaching the top, growing wearier by the minute, eventually sans teeth. *Condemned* sounded too much like a life sentence that did not end well.

Could I alter that? Keep the strength without the condemnation? Was my strength ingrained? If so, maybe other parts of me were too, parts I'd lost or covered over. Maybe I wanted to be someone altogether distinct than ever before. Was it possible? The "reclaim yourself" mantra friends chanted sounded alluring. But what if the other "me"s hadn't been creatures of free will, but rather an amalgam of confusion and contradictions, conditioned by experience? Maybe no one ever truly finds themselves. Maybe the whole of existence is one long endless futile search for self and then you die. Sans teeth. With that bleak, morbid view of life, why not just light a match to it all?

But maybe there was no self to search for either. According to Buddhist philosophy, the self is an imputation. No Beverly without the people who name her. No Beverly without the house, the kids, the possessions. Nothing to revert to except a figment. Search for Beverly and you'll find nothing more than millions of mini "me"s dependent on specific reference points, disappearing the moment perspective shifts. Nothing fixed except Buddha nature, the seed of compassion at the heart of every sentient being.

In one sense the concept felt liberating. In another sense, I envisaged swimming upstream against the current in a world filled with obligations and telephone bills. And one needs reference points for that. But which ones?

While Pat and I sat in the kitchen one day eating lunch, I sorted through my music. Hymnals I played from on my grandmother's piano after supper on Sundays. Show tunes the girls and I sang in the playroom after dinner. Sheet music from high school chorus days—*Let There Be Peace on Earth* and *Christ lag in Todesbanden*. A book of waltzes. A songbook for *Mary Poppins*, who I'd dressed up like for the county fair talent show in elementary school, carpetbag and all, singing "A Spoonful of Sugar." I blew a heaping pile of child support flying me and the children to London when the play opened on the West End. I'd ostensibly done it for my daughters, but maybe also for the girl in me that still needed honoring.

Doused in memories flashing at me all at once, I strained to absorb them, then make instantaneous decisions about which artifacts to let go.

On our way upstairs Pat and I stopped in Nicki's room so I could pack up the toddler clothes stored at the back of Nicki's closet.

"Look at this! And this!" Pat said, admiring the Renaissance outfits, velvet dresses, matching outfits, saris, and satin-striped Turkish pantaloons with vests and fezzes.

"You're the memory keeper!" Pat said as I told her stories behind each. "No one can ever take these memories from you. The girls will always have the memories you gave them." Those magical days I could not reclaim, the only ones I was certain I wanted to.

"You were always such an obedient child and I mean always," my mother told me often. "I used to bathe and dress you up and put you in the playpen, just so, every morning on the front porch for some sun." That's the strongest image I have of myself as a little girl, and I carried it around with me for so long, constantly comparing her with the flawed adult struggling to dot all her I's. And yet if I'd given up that girl, I might never have made it to New York City. Traveled extensively. Had advantages my mother hadn't.

But I also recall playing happily in my front yard making mud pies. Sprawled on the bookmobile floor and immersing myself in Nancy Drew and Ursula Le Guin. Was the girl afraid to get a spot on her dress the same one who liked to play in the mud and live in a dream world? Was I still both?

"I never had my teenage rebellion," I said to Anders after meditation class one night.

"Are you kidding?" he asked. "I've always thought of you as a rebel. You fought your divorce, you're studying Buddhism, and you left the law and are determined to be a writer." A real trifecta of crazy stuff. As he said it, I flashed back to the girl playing in the mud.

More traces surfaced while I waded through boxes of mementoes. Speeches I wrote as a teenager about democracy. Accounts of the Human Rights Day I helped organize in high school when integration was in its infancy. My fellow graduates voted me "Most Disagreeable" (would that be labeled bullying today?), a title I probably earned from raising my hand in class and my willingness to be the lone dissenter. I cried myself to sleep beneath the roof of my canopy bed instead of attending class night. A Sally Fields wannabe, only without the Oscar.

And yet as an adult I continued to make unconventional decisions, continually eliciting questions from friends, family, strangers, and acquaintances. Why do you want to be a lawyer? Why New York City? Why Buddhism? Why the Episcopal Church? Why do you still love your husband? Why give up your legal career and be a stay-at-home mom?

The only way to avoid answering questions—and being defensive—seemed to be compliance. To walk the conventional, or straight and narrow, or comply with someone else's expectations. Keep quiet when I disagreed, sublimate myself. Avoid full disclosure. I had done that at times as a wife, teenager, and career woman.

And it slowly ate away at me.

The more you're called upon to defend yourself for no good reason—or comply—you lose another piece of yourself. Yet the more you remain silent, you lose another piece too. Then struggle—and wonder—if you can ever get it back. So how to simply be yourself? Dodge the questions, yet not feel defensive and remain peaceful inside? What if I wanted to become a beach bum?

Entertainment agreements for clients I represented. Famous names on contracts. Offer letters from law firms I turned down. A folder of unpaid bills from a few clients. I found all these in boxes.

"What would have happened to us if we hadn't married our exes?" I said to Pat when I came across these papers, more a statement than a question. Reinvention had been the buzz word of the last decade or so for women, with opportunities for more than one career, three if you counted being a mother.

Before I married, I lived in a studio apartment on the Upper East Side of Manhattan. Jake's apartment in Brooklyn was slightly bigger so we moved there after our honeymoon, on the condition we find a place in Manhattan right away. This small-town Southern girl hadn't made it to the Big Apple to get stuck in one of the outer boroughs. But time passed and life became busy and then divorce, and, thirty years later, I still lived in Brooklyn, not much more than a mile from where we had started out. And then I hadn't wanted to leave, at least not until retirement.

Over the years Jake's frequent flyer miles often took us to Hawaii, the only other place in the world we could ever imagine ourselves. Brooklyn, however, was tops despite the images from our taxicab window on the drive back home from the airport via the Brooklyn Queens Expressway— dirt, filth, smoke, and metal—so far from the literal paradise we had just left. But our family waxed nostalgic when we saw the Manhattan skyline and the Hamilton Avenue exit.

"We're home!" we'd say and well up with tears. Could I get Brooklyn out of my blood? *Was* there life after Brooklyn?

"What are you going to do after you sell the house?" That constant annoying question. Maybe friends wanted to explore their own anxieties and uncertainties through me.

"Maybe I'll just sit on a porch somewhere in a rocker and drink lemonade," I told my mother. *Spiked lemonade.* The precise vision I got when I closed my eyes at night. It soothed me. Nanny, my great-grandmother, spent hours in her rocker on the front porch of my grandmother's house. Dressed in a crisp pink dress with her snow white carefully combed hair, cane resting at her side. I lazed about on the porch beside her, cutting paper and making cards. Fifty years later, I had visions of a porch again, and a rocker.

"Maybe I'll throw it all in storage and go away for a while too," I added when I talked to Mom. That was not a me anyone had encountered before.

"I think that's what you *should* do," Mom said.

I had thought I always wanted to be a lawyer but that wasn't true, and the evidence passed before me as I trudged through papers. Clippings from two newspaper columns I penned in high school for the local county paper. An article about an unstructured diet I wrote during my first year of practicing law and never sold. The program for a local community theater production Jake directed, for which I curated costumes for a cast of forty. Report cards for a semester's worth of classes taken at the Fashion Institute of Technology during my first couple of years practicing law. Creative endeavors every one of them. Missing that microchip to throw away my education, I suppose, one of the reasons why I continued on the straight and narrow for so long, even though lawyering hadn't felt creative enough for me.

As I dug through boxes, snippets of an ever more youthful me appeared. Letters from my father—messages from beyond the grave. Scripture verses and his notes to deacons suggesting they begin meetings with prayer and a loving and open heart. Samplers from my home economics classes in high school, perfectly preserved with an "A" pinned to one. Thirty years later I taught Ella how to embroider and make potholders. I called her up to my bedroom to show her my finds. And then ran to my closet to grab a jumper I'd stored at the back of it. A pink flowered jumper with crisscrossed straps on the back and ruffles at the hem, one of the many articles of clothing I sewed for myself as a teen.

"It's beautiful! Can I try it on?" Ella said, in a rush.

"You can have it, if it fits."

"Really?" she asked. And it did fit, and Ella wore it to school the next day with her tan wedge sandals and blonde hair flowing around her shoulders.

I shared prom and sorority photos with her, too, and programs from a prominent off-Broadway theater company where I had served as chairman of the board, resigning the year after giving birth to Nicki to immerse myself in motherhood.

"Wow! I didn't know you did that!" Ella said. She was shocked when I told her some of the well-known clients I had represented. Hadn't I ever told her or Nicki?

Today, women are warned stepping off the career ladder to hand out milk and cookies is risky business, especially given the reality of divorce and unemployment. But where's the choice in having no choice but to work outside the home while raising your children?

Thoughts swirled as I sat in the war room. *Go back to the past in order to go to the future.*

In a plastic bin from my closet I found my grandmother's green and purple fish order book I'd thrown in a box after selling her piano. In it she had scribbled random names and telephone numbers in no apparent order, along with fish orders: "10 roes, 2 rocks, Edna" and then the words "Billy Graham." Must save.

Next up a bunch of cards and love letters and drawings from former boyfriends, some of whose names and faces I remembered and others about whom I had no clue. One signed his letters with crazy made-up monikers and conjured up phony return addresses too, calculated to make me laugh. Reading them decades later still did.

No man in your lifetime is ever going to love you. Why couldn't I excise Jake's parting shot from my head? Here was the evidence it wasn't true. Men had loved me. Several of them, so why did I recall Jake's words and not theirs? I rubber-banded the letters, meaning to read the rest of them later, but thumbed through to search for one, a letter from a particular boy I'd dated in college.

"He was a *man*," my mother said when I told her about finding this letter. Technically it was true. He was twenty-one years old when I met and dated him in college, although in hindsight he seemed a boy. But he was a magnificent specimen of a boy that made him seem more like a man compared with his peers. He came to visit me one summer and, after returning home, wrote to say his weekend with me had been one of the best of his life. He was job hunting and said he wanted to find work close to college so he could visit me when I returned there in the fall—he had graduated ahead of me. He said he thought we might have a future together. I wracked my brain but couldn't recall what happened to us.

I logged onto the internet and searched for him. And there he was. Married for decades, photo of a big happy smiling family and beautiful wife. Still gorgeous in his fifties. And it crushed me. Try hard as I could to generate happiness, a tinge of jealousy lingered.

Suddenly I remembered the seventy-seven text messages I had kept on my phone from a guy I stopped dating two years earlier. Sweet messages, but from a safe distance, a texting distance. In-between our dates I hinted that I preferred talking on the phone. But he remained a texter, and we stopped dating. Why had I kept the texts? Why the gauge of someone else's worthiness of me and not my own? I looked at my telephone key pad and hit "delete all."

126

"You know what I see in your writing and everything you've been doing?" Pat said one day while shredding. "Sometimes you're jealous of your ex's money and love life. But maybe he's jealous of you. Maybe that's why he's still angry. You're the courageous one. You're the one who stood up for your convictions. You're the one pursuing your dreams." Was that possible? Stunned at her analysis I didn't know what to think. And yet I'd grown tired of wondering what he thought, and no longer cared.

In the middle of April, I drove to upstate New York for a meditation retreat and Tara empowerment. While there I made this note: *As leaves fall, I too will shed my former life. Springtime, I am cleaning out, a time of renewal. Spring to renew and fall to shed my former skin.*

In the Buddhist tradition, Tara is the holy mother, a symbol of wisdom and compassion, like our earthly mothers. Like the wind, she's swift, removing obstacles and granting protection from danger, suffering and fear, inspiring us with blessings. Who couldn't use inspiration and blessings?

I was more than a mother, but being a mother had been the most important part of my existence for so long. That skin I could never shed. As I grew older, my relationship with my daughters would change; it already had. I wanted to find joy in our changing relationship, in the worlds opening for us. Attempting to connect with Tara's qualities had always comforted me; now I wanted to connect with her mind of wisdom to find guidance. It's why I had also begun to pray the rosary several years before, even though the Virgin Mary was not part of my spiritual traditions. Mary, Tara, and me, all mothers.

I collected my girlhood diaries and various journals I had kept for several years and packed them away with mementoes. I had no time to read through them again but flipped through a few to see where they fell open. In one volume, covered with the face of a Buddha, the pages fell open to an entry made on July 18, 2010, during a five-day silent retreat at the Abbey of Gethsemani in Kentucky. It was there I had first prayed the rosary.

Who am I really? Who is Beverly? I had written those words after reading the famous prayer of Trappist Monk Thomas Merton again, the prayer in which he told God he had no idea where he was going and could not see ahead of him.

Peel back the layers. Declutter myself. My ex-husband's infidelity had so cut me to the quick I'd not only lost trust, but no longer felt I knew who I was.

"Be still. Simplify," my priest had said when I asked for his advice.

While at the Abbey, I had wandered through the library, my fingers landing randomly on spines of books, including *Becoming a Writer* by Dorothea Brande.

And then, after I opened the cover, this: "I hope this book persuades some who are hesitating on the verge of abandoning writing to make a different decision."

I had been struggling with that again in 2010, a year after the divorce judgment.

Later that day I spoke with Brother Rene at the front desk. He had introduced me to the rosary in the chapel outside the church the day before. I told him I had seen the name "Willett" etched on so many tombstones during my drives in Kentucky.

"Then you must be from Maryland," he said. Apparently in the 18th century Willetts from Maryland fled to Kentucky because of religious persecution for being Catholic. Baptist, then Buddhist, and Episcopalian. Was I destined to be Catholic too! I laughed.

"So what do you do?" Brother Rene asked.

"I'm a former lawyer," I said, a profession long gone, as if mother or writer wasn't enough.

"So you must be a writer now," Brother Rene said.

15

Exorcism

One day Pat and I came across more photos of my ex-husband. Several had duplicates.

"Should we shred one?" Pat asked. "Feed it to The Bitch?" We laughed.

The thought hadn't occurred to me. For more than a decade I pushed away thoughts of retribution even though fantasies of mayhem penetrated my dreams in the early days of our separation—using Jake's credit card to book a trip to Capri, tossing his clothes out the third-floor window and watching them float to the sidewalk below, envisioning him being run over by a bus. Impatience and frustration got the better of me, sometimes the pain explosive. Anger erupted in moments of exasperation and exhaustion even though the flames died down.

But I could not will myself to hate, although I felt certain my ex-husband thought spite or avarice fueled my attempt to save our family from the ravages of divorce, instead of love. Still, had I repressed some of my anger? Otherwise, why the dreams?

Another day of cleaning unearthed birth, death, and marriage certificates for Jake's parents. Finding them irritated me. Why hadn't Jake taken them or ever asked about their whereabouts? Why had I kept them nicely labeled among my personal files? No one would have been the wiser if I'd pitched them, so I couldn't. The ring of childhood taunts—*goody two shoes, goody two shoes*—nagged at me, cutting my solace at doing the right thing short.

Pat repeated her request.

I said, "Sure, let's shred one of those babies," even as I registered the false note in my assent. But what harm could shredding one photo do, given all I'd held back? Hundreds of photos containing Jake's mug still filled the family albums. Jake walked out, and to my knowledge, never looked back. Yet he also would not leave. Sometimes I sent stray photos back via the kids; on other occasions I put them aside. For years I methodically dated and captioned our photos and organized them in albums. After Jake left, the children regularly pulled them off shelves and begged me to join them in paging through. Twenty years of family stories waited in the hopper for them and their children, and the prospect of telling every single one hurt. So many memories I hadn't known what to do with. Would my children retain the good times or only the bad? And what kind of family legacy would they pass on to theirs?

But the past could not be helped Maybe shredding one photo would serve as a symbol to mark or galvanize my resolve to continue moving forward. Maybe I just needed to find out what would happen.

I walked to the shredder. But the photo was too wide. I tore it in half.

"Here's your half," I said, handing Pat the other portion. I fed mine first. Pat and I watched silently, each slice of paper disappearing beneath the shredder's serrated teeth. We giggled when her piece got stuck. And high-fived after she cleared the jam and refed it. And when all was done I felt no different than I had the moment before we accomplished our dastardly deed, nothing changed on the outside or the in. But I wasn't sorry either. It was a piece of anger I needed to expel. And a laugh for which I was long overdue.

The month before I had also found a silly card Jake gave me one Christmas. During our marriage, we had traded hundreds of cards for every occasion, most of them comedic. We always included our own annotations and had saved them all.

Right before our twentieth wedding anniversary I scoured the house collecting and arranging them in chronological order. This was to be my special anniversary gift to Jake, and I couldn't wait for him to open it.

He surprised me that evening, too, with dinner with friends at New York City's Oak Room, a supper club at the Algonquin Hotel. And a pair of emerald earrings I'd spotted in a shop window the winter before. Before our friends arrived, I handed Jake his presents: an expensive Fendi wallet, which he admired, rubbing his hands over the fine leather, then the special box. But when my husband opened it, he looked down, avoiding my eyes, distracted, embarrassed it seemed. "Uh-huh" and "thanks," he said, before quickly shoving the box under his seat.

The scene was nothing like I'd been imagining for weeks: Me leaning over my husband's shoulder as he opened his cards one by one, laughing with him over this one, our eyes misting over that one. My heart sank when I realized there would be no such scene. And when, for the first time in twenty years, he forgot to get me a card to add to our collection. There was no fight, no harsh words. But the evening ended with me falling asleep upstairs alone, crying softly in my pillow.

Three months later my husband had a girlfriend. Three months after that he left home.

"I left you, not the children," he'd said. A distinction without a difference. When we carved the girls out of our own flesh, we formed an entirely new molecule, all crazy glued together, called *family*. The whole of us became greater than the sum of our parts, our lives interwoven. The Supreme Court more or less said the same thing about marriage in its decision legalizing same-sex unions: "Its dynamic allows two people to find a life that could not be found alone, for a marriage becomes greater than just the two persons."

No way our bond, a tapestry of tears and joy, celebrations and heartaches, struggles and triumphs, could ever be broken. Yet in one swift motion my husband not only broke his vows to me, but dismembered our family, with the law's blessing.

Why had many friends, acquaintances, strangers thought moving on should be quick and easy? Get over it and get a boyfriend, like the family court judge suggested. I tried to excise Jake from the premises, and made headway, making a few alterations in the house. Painting over his name on my bedroom wall. I made some new friends, dated a little, worked hard to develop a writing career, and volunteered. I let go over time, in pieces. For decades my husband and I interlaced our lives. It took time to separate the strands.

But years later much remained the same. If it didn't belong to my ex-husband it was often something we had bought or assembled together, reflections of the life we envisioned and created as a team. Like our children, whose big brown eyes stared up at me from their seats at the kitchen table every morning after he left. Big brown eyes like Jake's big brown eyes.

On my silver wedding anniversary, two years before the divorce was final, I was at loose ends over how to spend the day. Finally I decided to brave the wooden doors of the Manhattan church where Jake and I got married, doors I had passed and thought about for several years.

I wasn't exactly sure why I headed there. Once inside, I looked around the empty church and stroked the red-velvet-covered pews; a few details of my wedding day came rushing back. The double aisles, one on either side, the rich wood. The rest was decidedly more majestic than I remembered—eight stained-glass windows, a cathedral ceiling, and a reredos adorned with intricate wood and gold filigree. The scale of my presence in the space where my husband and I pledged our faithfulness exactly twenty-five years before was humbling.

Surprised to find myself wanting to recollect more, I strode to the anteroom on the left-hand side of the church where I once waited nervously with my attendants on a hot Saturday afternoon. Our flower girl threw a fit in that exact spot, advising her mother she most assuredly was not walking down the aisle. I laughed, realizing the girl who stuck to her guns was grown up, probably an executive in charge of a vast number of underlings. And then I walked through the archway, as I'd once done, pretending to link arms with my dad, my head held high, tears flowing, while I marched down the aisle.

It's okay, I can do this, I said to myself, reaching the front pew. And that's when I realized flying off to Europe or partying with my girlfriends, ideas that had floated in my head about how to mark the day, would have been ill-advised. It was a time for being alone and making peace with my loss, for breathing in bright, white light and blowing the dark, smoky anger out.

As I ran my hands over the plush pews, my thoughts became clear, and I took out paper and pen and started writing my husband's girlfriend a note. "I imagine it will be as awkward for you to read as it is for me to write," I began. A month before, she'd been diagnosed with cancer. While I was still light years from forgiveness, what she and I had in common unexpectedly trumped the enormous gulf between us, at least in that moment: We were both mothers. Surprised, I found myself wishing her a complete recovery, though I hadn't always felt that way.

When I finished the note, it was time to go. I'd reenacted my entrance from the left; time for my exit towards the right. I turned my back to the altar, startled when the words "come on Jake" flew from my lips. Once I gathered my wits, I stopped dead mid-aisle, turned round again, and said out loud: "On second thought, I'm going to do this part on my own." And then I marched down the aisle and out the church, wondering who could possibly be channeling through me, feeling as light as the June air that greeted me outdoors.

Celebrating my twenty-fifth wedding anniversary in the way I had was a turning point toward accepting the dissolution of my marriage. But life became heavy again, with children to raise, bills to pay, and aging on the horizon. Each novel challenge could take so much out of me.

The more I unearthed my belongings, opened cabinets, pulled out drawers, sifted through papers, the more my ex-husband surfaced.

Like the day I found the silly Christmas card. Santa graced the cover and inside my ex-husband joked about husbands doing laundry. I wondered what I'd done with the box of cards I gave Jake on our twentieth anniversary—he'd taken the wallet with him, but not our cards. *I no longer wanted the orphan Santa card, but where to put it?* It dangled like a forlorn sock forever separated from its mate, a sock saved anyway for years, just in case. This time I tore the card up and threw it out.

And then I found the certificates for my ex-husband's parents. And shredded his photo. And on April 2, I suddenly knew where to find the box of cards, my reticence about entering the laundry room when Pat first came to help me clean out no longer a mystery.

I climbed the step stool in the laundry room and pulled the box of cards out from the back of the top shelf cabinet. I also pulled out my wedding album and several albums of honeymoon pictures. I had also pushed them to the back of the cabinet, far from view, forgetting where I'd put them.

Two large cardboard boxes filled with school portraits of the children and extra copies of family photos stood in a nearby corner. Photos of Jake before he knew me, photos of me and Jake before the children, more Father's Day cards buried at the bottom of the boxes, along with photos of the surprise fiftieth birthday bash I hosted for my husband and our tenth anniversary party. Pictures of our many trips to Hawaii before the kids and photographs of us with couple friends and colleagues who left me behind as Jake had. My husband looking boyish with a paintbrush in his hand, painting the edge of bookshelves I had designed in our co-op. An entire photo book devoted to Scruffy Red McFarlane, our first "child," a small stuffed animal dog wearing a Scottish tam that had come as a gift with one of my flannel nightgowns. We had posed Scruffy throughout the house—in the refrigerator, in bed, pretending to take a nip of beer— then added ridiculous dialogue bubbles like "Even Scruffsters have to go" alongside a photo of Scruffy on the toilet seat.

Pictures of my groom-to-be before our wedding with presumably pre-wedding jitters—I came across those next. He looked so handsome, so young, so full of promise. Before the lost dreams and broken promises. Before his *I love yous* turned into *I'm not sure I ever did.*

No man in your lifetime is ever going to love you. He'd left that message on my answering machine, shortly after he left. Piercing my heart a third time, as if betrayal and planting the seed of doubt whether he'd ever loved me wasn't sufficient for the cauldron.

So many things had once tugged on his heart. Why hadn't I?

Commentators to several of my articles about divorce called me a fool for trying to save my marriage and continuing to love a man who said he no longer loved me. But I could not will my heart to stone.

Besides, if love is easily defined, why have writers spent millenniums trying to explain it? I never believed my ex-husband's broken vows gave me license to ignore mine. My vows were my vows, my conscience my conscience. It hurt when people called me a fool, at first, but now I'm okay with it. Keeping your promise is not a burden, it's a joy. It made me feel more like myself.

Right before I made the decision to fight the divorce, before I irrevocably traveled that road of trying to save my marriage, I called my mother for advice. For twenty years I'd kept my marital problems hidden from most everyone, including her. But my divorce had provided the opening to draw us closer, and her words resonated with me.

Mom said her views weren't important.

"You just need to ask yourself one question," she said. "No matter what happens, what choice you make, will you be able to live with yourself? The next day and the day after that and for the rest of your life."

At that moment, I knew that ignoring my inner voice and ending my marriage was not a choice I'd willingly make, not without going the distance.

I'm not sure I ever loved you. No man in your lifetime will ever love you. Both statements were false.

My marriage had ended, yes. But my ex-husband and I had both loved each other. That I was sure of, certain our marriage had not been a mistake either or else the children would have been a mistake. And the truth and the proof? It was in that cupboard, in those photos, in those cards in the laundry room, in the wedding preparation folder which I took back out of the filing cabinet. And in my heart. I no longer needed my ex-husband's validation or anyone else's. I didn't care what my critics had to say. I knew the truth about us. I'd always known it. The truth about the past. The truth I wanted to bequeath to my daughters. That they were loved and they had been conceived in love by parents who loved each other and that this was something they could depend on and always be absolutely sure of.

I grabbed a black plastic bin and inside placed the folder, the wedding album and portraits, and the honeymoon albums. The photographs of the newlyweds in love. Pictures of them watching the sunset in Hawaii where they planned to retire. And the cards—Mom and Dad's box of love letters. Proof Mom and Dad had loved each other. Proof my children had been conceived in love. Proof Nicki and Ella were not mistakes. Proof that perhaps we had been that family on the prairie once, even if only for a moment, even if we had forever lost our way.

As I lowered the souvenirs from my marriage into the bin, I glanced at a photo of me and my former husband taken on a catamaran, the Pacific Ocean our background. I heard the thought "the best days of my life are over" in my head. Once, I had believed that wholeheartedly. Throwing something away often reminded me that I too had been thrown in the garbage by the man I loved. For years I could not get beyond that thought. Now, I no longer believed all my best days were gone. And I knew that the past had held memorable ones too.

I wrote a note to my daughters, folded it, and placed it on top, and then I closed the box and taped it shut, adding a wall between my past and my future. One day when my daughters opened their time capsule I hoped they would know the truth as indisputably as I did. For me, though, I vowed it would be the last time in this lifetime I would ever look at those cards and pictures again.

I could not go back and rewrite the history of my marriage or make things turn out in a way they hadn't. But I could take back the power of those memories to cripple me.

After taping the box, I folded my hands in prayer and bowed. I lit a nearby candle and sprayed perfume throughout the war room. I walked from corner to corner, clapping to cleanse the air. My tears dwindled to a trickle.

16

Bangladesh

Ella occupied the typical teenager's room—close your eyes and shut the door. With the house being sold the room not only required hauling out, it had to appear more spacious, like nobody inhabited it, let alone a teenager.

"It's my room," Ella said every time I raised the possibility of my entering it to clean. "I'll do it myself."

"But you said that yesterday," I'd say. "Let me help you. It's going to take more than a few hours after school." It was already April, and once summer arrived, purchasers would dwindle as school ended and families sped out of town on vacation.

"Please, Mom. I'll do it, okay?"

"Okay, but you have to start tomorrow," I'd say. Tomorrow came and Ella and I would have the same conversation. But Ella was juggling a full plate and continued to shuttle between two residences. No mystery why tomorrow never arrived.

When we moved into the house, Nicki was seven and Ella two. Ella slept upstairs in a toddler bed in the space that later became my office.

Once my dread of her tumbling down one of our many staircases eased off, we built up the wall enclosing the precarious open staircase leading from Ella's room to the kitchen, added a door, and Ella moved downstairs into her own room.

We bought her a yellow metal Art Deco bedroom set with twin beds, a dresser, and a vanity with a matching stool and two round Art Deco mirrors. Our handyman painted Ella's walls yellow with Bazooka bubblegum trim. I hung multicolored 1960s plastic beaded curtains in the windows. Atop the half-wall surrounding Ella's staircase, a local carpenter constructed a whimsical, open, cage-like series of interconnecting rectangles with ledges of varied sizes where Ella displayed her special trinkets—a Chinese doll, a pink felt unicorn, a miniature wind-up merry-go-round, and more.

Nicki favored an old-fashioned look so we painted Nicki's walls light pink and bought her a queen-sized pine canopy bed with carved flowered posts. I found a small chandelier in a neighborhood flea market and hung it in the middle of the room.

By high school Nicki decided her pink room was too childish, about the time Ella began calling her bedroom set my "baby" furniture. Time for sprucing up.

Nicki chose forest green for her walls, and Ella an eye-popping royal blue. In the pocketed moldings beneath Nicki's shutters, she and I had once held up a blue plastic stencil with flower cutouts and used slender paint brushes to fill in, painting the flowers pink and the petals green. When the handyman painted Nicki's room green, Nicki wanted to leave our collaboration intact. I found the stencil fifteen years later, curled up and still bearing the residue of pink paint Nicki and I had brushed on while sitting on her bedroom floor when she was only seven. The same age Ella had been when her father walked out. Sometimes I forget how my daughters looked at other ages. Seven I remember.

The handyman had also repainted my bedroom. And Ella had begged me for the iron and brass queen-sized bed my ex-husband and I had slept in, along with our burled walnut furniture. An unconscious way of linking herself more inextricably with her father and me?

Before I knew it, Nicki grew up and was gone, and Ella was on the verge of college.

"Can you move across the hall to Nicki's room?" I asked Ella one day when she came home from school. "It's the only way we can get into your room to clean. And it's too hard with your trying to sleep and do homework there."

"Okay," Ella agreed.

"You can still go in and get what you want," I added, teeming with guilt. "But let's put some of your spring clothes in Nicki's closet and drawers so it's easier for you."

"Okay," Ella said.

I hesitated before delivering my next line. Ella surely knew, but I had to make certain: "You know after you leave you probably won't ever be back here."

"I know," Ella said.

"I'm not trying to make you sad," I added, making sure it registered.

"I know," Ella said. "It's okay." Was it? Was any of this okay? And would she tell me otherwise? Ella had suffered so many losses in her short life—Nicki too—and mostly kept her thoughts inside. Strong and brave even at seven, and way too young to have to be.

It was only in hindsight I realized the summer before Nicki moved out would be her last at home, that the smell of pies she baked all summer would be no more. The realization hit me hard. How had Ella felt when she realized? Was I wrong to prepare her now as if preparation was possible? Would foreknowledge have sapped the joy of watching Nicki roll dough? Would my ex-husband's betrayal have devastated me any less if I'd been cautioned?

The cleaning tasks before us included these: Ella's closet, along with two shelves on the top and lots of stuff stored on the bottom; the insides and surfaces of a dresser; a chest of drawers and vanity, including inside the vanity stool; a five-foot-high stainless steel shelf system laden with games, toys, books, CDs, records, a record player, and puzzles; a painted cabinet with two shelves inside, which held Ella's flute, sheet music, flute stand, helmets, sports gear, Game Boys, and other miscellaneous items; wall hangings (posters, a bulletin board, and a kimono); Ella's staircase trinkets; books propped up against the window; dress-up clothes and costumes stored in zippered plastic bags under the bed; and cardboard boxes containing schoolwork that were upstairs.

Ella finally agreed I could help her, although she presided over the decision-making. After all, how can one person decide the value placed by another?

"I want none of it," Ella said as we began. I understood. The same thought had initially coursed through me. A hollowness, a feeling of nothingness. A potentially enlightening thought too, but one that could also trigger depression. Better to pretend not caring than acknowledge having to face it.

Sealing up the remains of my marriage had been restorative. Sorting through my other possessions was at times liberating too, but also overwhelming. My heart welled with sympathy when I imagined the time my daughters might spend one day even pouring through the things I was saving. An endless ring around the rosy.

The month before we began digging through her room, I threw Ella a surprise eighteenth birthday dinner at our home attended by a dozen or so of her friends from high school, Nicki and her boyfriend, Helen, and Dirk. Ella's friends laughed and snapped photos, and then quietly stood in the living room, giggling silently in the dark while they waited for Ella to appear, running into the vestibule and yelling "surprise" as Ella's key turned the front door lock. Then rushing to the dining room table and gobbling down every last crumb of Helen's Italian cooking like they'd never eaten.

"We love your house! It's so cool," Ella's friends said, appraising our decorations. I'd spent decades making a home, and a certain offbeat comfort and elegance had settled in. Scratched and weathered from wear, the whimsy still shone. Masks on the walls, folk art wooden dining room chairs painted like fruit—a pineapple, green apple, strawberry, and watermelon. A Buddha here, a chandelier there, a Chinese wall hanging nearby. A mirrored table that lit up, and a red and black lacquer Art Deco tea cart with matching wall unit. An entire wall ran the length of the loft-like parlor and was painted Granny Smith apple green, my favorite color. I thought of that wall as a painting.

"You've got such great stuff, Bev," Sandra said, surveying the same scene a few days later.

I said, "I don't know whether to keep the masks."

"That's a good question," Sandra said in her British accent. Sandra was from the U.K. We sat on the couch and stared up at the masks.

"They'll look good for the open house so I'm leaving them up for now. But I don't want wherever I live one day to look like I merely reassembled everything from my old life." Although, couldn't keeping even one serve as a placeholder for the entire lot? Would getting rid of at least a portion lessen the memories and therefore dull the pain? And yet, would scrapping the collection scrub them and their painful associations from my mind? Or simply cure the attachment to the masks themselves without erasing the psychic meaning I'd bestowed on them and so much else? Is a memory forgotten necessarily a memory erased? And why did I torture myself with these questions?

Of course, possessions can as easily conjure up joy, as some clutter experts have pointed out. In truth, though, pleasure is probably a better word because joy in possessions and people is nearly always bound up with attachment. The only way to lasting joy is through achieving inner peace.

I bought the fruit chairs with Jake, but still wanted them simply because they were fun. Maybe that was enough. So hold onto so-called joy and drop the memory and the attachment? Could I do that with the masks? And when the joy, or rather pleasure, was gone from the chairs, let them go too?

"Sometimes when I look at them I imagine my future grandchildren visiting me one day saying *Grandma, what are those?*" I said. "And I hear

142

myself telling them the stories about how their grandfather and I collected each one, and the trips we took. But I don't want to tell those stories again. And I don't want to be sad anymore. Our family—that family—it's gone." Sandra listened.

My sciatica returned with knife-like stabs in my buttocks and pain that shot down my legs. I popped Advil, took warm baths while sipping a glass of chardonnay, and told myself it was in my head. I returned to meditation classes and one night heard a teaching on the emptiness of the self, in particular the loser self I sometimes identified with. The one who lost her husband, lost her career, lost her youth, and now was losing her house.

"Sometimes we love our loser self," Anders said. "It's often comfortable to identify with." Because who and what are we, if we don't have the loser self and the loser story? How to acknowledge myself as a victim without becoming one "me" I didn't need? Stuck in a valley of loss, it could be a slippery slope to loserdom.

Anders had called me a rebel and said he'd always thought of me as one.

"A *radical* rebel if you ask me," Sandra said. "Just look at what you're doing, Bev."

Perhaps getting rid of the house would be the ultimate detox, reversing the cycle of loss by losing even more.

But I urged Ella to keep more than she purged. And the more I urged the more Ella kept. Perhaps she hadn't wanted to disappoint me. Had wanted to be brave and strong, and not overburden me with more boxes to keep. Lighten my burden while taking it on herself. If so, I wanted to take it back.

While Ella was at school, I threw out what was clearly garbage—multiple cans of Red Bull from under her bed, food wrappers, crumpled paper, empty bottles of Poland Spring water. I gathered up loose items strewn about her room—coins, hair ties, erasers, pens. I arranged other items into matching piles, breaking the tasks down into more manageable ones for Ella to sort through—clothes, books, makeup. While organizing, I came across photographs I'd never seen before, and couldn't help looking. Ella at her dad's place with the dog I'd never seen, sitting on a couch I knew nothing about, in an apartment I'd never entered, smiling a smile I'd never witnessed while laughing a laugh I had never heard. Millions of moments with my children lost—no, stolen.

Another day I found a batch of outdated calendars and thought I'd count the number of days I'd lost with my children due to divorce over the prior decade. But I couldn't bring myself to start. The final count would be too great a number to absorb. This was a tally best left unknown, in a past I couldn't change.

It was the same with the photos of Ella in her father's apartment. I put them down and got back to cleaning.

Twice yearly the girls and I weeded out their outgrown clothes, once before school started in the fall and a second time before spring. Ella and I now sorted through her drawers and clothes for the final time.

We cleared ledges and shelves and the tops of her vanity and dressers. I matched the blue paint on Ella's walls, and walked around the room touching up a nail hole here and a paint chip there.

"Can we keep *Where in the World Is Carmen Sandiego*?" Ella asked while we sorted through her games. "I want to play it one more time." Into the save pile.

Once Ella got into the rhythm she seemed to enjoy herself, especially the hours it took to comb through the contents of her vanity, which contained trinkets from toddler days. When I looked in at her from the doorway putting what resembled junk into the "save" pile, my heart sang. When she placed items in the discard pile, my heart sang then too. One day she came up to the top floor where I was cleaning.

"Can I have my passport?" Ella asked.

"What for?" I appreciated her pursuit of independence, but with the mess, prudence required my keeping track of our important papers.

"I want to be honest with you," Ella said, like music to my ears considering her father's betrayal. "I want to buy cigarettes."

Don't air your dirty laundry in public was drilled into me growing up. So much so that I didn't know my own mother had smoked for forty-three years until I was thirty.

"I've got a secret," Mom said, breaking down one night as we sat at her kitchen table. My father had died, and I'd stayed on after the funeral to help her organize papers. Dad was a chain smoker, and Mom hid her smoke behind his all those years, smoking only at night after I went to bed and while I was in school. I had never seen her light up.

"I knew smoking was wrong," Mom said, "and I didn't want you to do it." But she was distraught over Daddy's death and desperate for a smoke.

Once the shock of my mother's admission sank in, I got mad, although I never let on. Maybe if I'd known her flaws, I wouldn't have been so hard on myself to be perfect.

Quinnie had another take: "How sweet of your mom to want to save you from becoming a smoker." It was the first time I'd seen it that way.

After my mother spilled her secret, I shared one of my own. "I drink," I said. Drinking was against our religion growing up. But I had a bottle of wine in the car and minutes later, we sat at the kitchen table breaking bread, Mom with a cigarette dangling from her lips, puffing and exhaling through her nostrils, me sipping wine from a crystal dessert goblet. Me, despite my annoyance, feeling closer to my mother than perhaps I ever had.

Ella's declaration caught me off guard too.

"I'm trying to cut down," she said before I could form words. "But will you please tell me where my passport is, because I'm not allowed to legally buy with my student ID only." I didn't ask her how she'd purchased cigarettes before.

"Smoking isn't good for you," I said.

"I know," Ella said. "And I'm going to quit. But I can't right now. And I want to be honest with you and tell you things." More music.

I love her so much, I said to myself after Ella walked away, passport in hand.

I carried the boxes of Ella's schoolwork to the dining room table, and Ella left them until nearly last. Half a dozen boxes with folders of work separated by year, including Ella's second grade folder, which I'd pored over many times. Filled with poems about sharks and sea monkeys and rock stars and family tales involving Mom, Dad, and Sister about baking bread without yeast and lobster ice cream.

Another box contained a hot pink three-ring binder filled with loose-leaf paper. I began making it when Nicki was a toddler, then added to it later for Ella. The girls loved playing school and I used the notebook to teach them to read and spell. They loved it so much they usually begged for more. Ella was excited when she came across it again. In it I had pasted pictures of items cut out from magazines, and then I made corresponding index cards with printed words to go along with the pictures. I jumbled up the index cards, and the children sounded out the words to find the ones that matched the pictures. The early pages were the easier ones, with items beginning with different letters. As the book progressed, I devoted an entire page to words beginning with the same letter. Years later this same woman would be so overcome with grief after her husband left that she'd help her children with homework, play the piano while they sang after dinner, then contemplate suicide after her children went to sleep.

One day while sorting through her preschool folders, Ella found a story she had written about an imaginary place. "Villameltland!" she yelled, running off with her cell phone, saying, "I've got to call and tell Dad!" Did my children's love for him help keep my own love alive all those years?

After she finished going through her schoolwork, I repacked Ella's "saves" and took a private look at her rejects before throwing them out, integrating a few back into the save pile.

"Please forgive me," I said to Ella one day after she came home from school, her room nearly hauled out. "I just can't keep the house any longer."

It was silly to blame myself, but I still felt guilty.

"It's okay if you're sad," I'd said to her while we were cleaning out her room. "It's natural. I'm sad too." We were both about to be unmoored.

"It's okay," she said, returning the words to me. "I'll have a home wherever you are." And then I started to cry and Ella said, "Whether it's in Tennessee or Bangladesh." And then I started to laugh.

17

The Wall of Mom

Pat finally found another buyer and an apartment for herself, a $2,500 per month rental less than a quarter the size of her previous living quarters, an hour and a half away into deep Brooklyn. She had a hard time finding that, landlords not wanting to rent to her given her unemployment. Still, she'd turned the corner, at least in her mind, determined to make a new life for herself and start a business at sixty-one. Somehow we'll make it, we assured each other.

"What are you going to do?" Pat asked.

"No clue," I said. "I want to keep writing but have to sell the house first." Maybe I'd get swept off my feet by a well-heeled widower or mysterious elves would finish my manuscript while I slept. And then Oprah would call.

"Where are you moving to?" people continued to ask.

"I haven't a clue," I replied to their shocked faces. Some tried to draw me out, but I resisted. It seemed they were more nervous than I was. It wasn't like me to feel nonchalant, growing more comfortable with uncertainty the further I descended into it. But it was still early, the house not yet on the market. None of it real yet.

"You want to move back into your room?" I asked Ella after we finished cleaning out.

"That's okay," she said. "I'm fine sleeping in Nicki's room." I suppose that was alright with me too; it might help with the transition. But I worried whether divorce had primed her for a lifetime of involuntary resignation to loss, forced numbness to hide disappointment. And when it came to men, possibly worse. But if she was truly okay, why did it bother me? Why was I partly sad she no longer yearned for her room when longing could bring about suffering? Ella had lived longer without an intact family than she had with one; conceivably she no longer recalled what an intact family felt like. To me that was sad too. I struggled to arrive at a comfortable place in the middle with my thoughts, balanced halfway between expecting the worse and hoping for the best, mindful of not tricking myself into a false sense of security either, a place I had certainly inhabited during my marriage.

When I woke up on Mother's Day, Ella frantically called up to me as I began walking down the stairs.

"Don't come down!"

"Why not?" I teased. I already knew why not. Ella was busy whipping up a breakfast surprise in the kitchen. She and Nicki had done so every Mother's Day.

"I'll call you down in an hour," Ella said.

"We don't have much time," I said. Church started at eleven and we'd scheduled a stoop sale for one. Besides, what could take an hour?

"Thirty minutes," Ella said. "Go relax. I'll bring you coffee." I propped my pillows behind my back and settled back in bed with my thoughts. Nicki wouldn't be coming later—it was her boyfriend's birthday—and next year Ella would be in college on Mother's Day. When would I have another day like this one?

Sometimes I think it's the holidays that kept me going all those years as a single mother. Every other Thanksgiving the girls were gone, but

Christmas quickly followed and the girls spent every Christmas and Easter with me (my ex didn't celebrate either). The same applied to Mother's Day of course. And somehow Valentine's Day had always landed on my visitation schedule too.

How would I celebrate my future holidays once the house was sold, with Ella gone to college and me who knows where? A rush of panic had hit me on Easter, but then I knew Mother's Day was ahead. With the arrival of Mother's Day, however, I was about to cross a line and march toward more uncertainty.

On Easter, I had hidden plastic eggs around the living room and dining room and in the foyer. From the time the children could walk, our indoor Easter egg hunt had been a yearly tradition. Though seventeen, Ella still expected chocolate on Easter morning for breakfast along with the Easter egg hunt, especially since the loot inside the eggs had graduated from pennies and penny candy to dollar bills and a fistful of quarters.

There were only so many spots to hide eggs, but I came up with a few obscure locations every year. The girls delighted in going straight for the familiars—inside a shoe in the foyer, behind a chair pillow, in the toilet paper holder in the bathroom. We played "hot and cold" when they struggled to find the last one or two.

Navigating through the first several cycles of holidays without Jake had been challenging. When my husband and I were first married, time was measured by our years together. Then the children became our yardsticks, each passing milestone giving structure and stability to our lives. When my husband left, however, time began anew and with it a resifting of significances. His leaving became the new benchmark, with milestones measured from when he left, computed by loss instead of gain, and marked by the passage of time gotten through. And so when Ella's eighth and Nicki's thirteenth Christmas rolled around that second year, for example, instead of these markers, it signified our second Christmas alone.

Gradually these reference points faded. And then Nicki left for college and I no longer saw her on Valentine's Day or our birthdays,

Easter or Mother's Day. College loomed for Ella, and with our last year in the house, a new reference point began to emerge, somehow attached to the house. And so instead of our eleventh Christmas without Dad, in December we celebrated the last Christmas in our home, followed by the last Valentine's Day, birthdays, Easter, and finally my last Mother's Day. Once I moved, would I experience new points of reference? And what would they be tied to? And would it be loss or gain? Or might my reference points disappear altogether?

Of all the holidays, I knew I'd miss Valentine's Day with them the most. Each year, after the girls fell asleep on February 13, I would leave presents for them at the breakfast table then tiptoe into their rooms to decorate—hearts on their bedroom doors, valentines to stare back at them from the bathroom mirrors when they brushed their teeth in the morning. *Cute Stuff. Be Mine. Forever. Luv Ya.*

"How much do you love me?" my daughters began to ask even more after their dad left, or so it seemed. I wasn't sure whether it was a humorous impulse, a continuation of the game we'd played when they were young, or whether they really did need to know.

That first Valentine's Day as a single mom, I went to wake the children, but their beds were empty. Downstairs, they had set the table with placemats, bowls, spoons, napkins, cups, and two kinds of cereal. And in the center of the table sat a vase with a red rose. The girls stood at the edge of the kitchen table smiling.

After Nicki moved out, Valentine's Day landed on a weekend.

"Who am I with on Valentine's Day?" Ella asked.

"You're with me," I told her, having already looked at the calendar months before.

"Oh good," she said. "Valentine's Day is my favorite. I love it when you decorate."

While I waited for Ella to call me down to breakfast on Mother's Day, I stared up at her handiwork from Valentine's Day the year before, which I'd saved for over a year, unable to bear taking it down. While I slept, Ella had cut out paper hearts and strategically placed them in a path leading from my bedroom all the way down to the kitchen, a heart landing on each place my eyes would alight after waking. A Hansel-and-Gretel trail that followed the footsteps I took every morning. I saw the first heart while reaching for my watch on the nightstand on Valentine's Day morning, the second as I sat up in bed and looked at the mirror on the wall opposite my bed. Ella had taped heart number three to the light switch in my bedroom. Then dozens and dozens more hearts followed, the next on the bathroom door, then down the side of the wall leading from the third floor to the second-floor landing, with a heart on the mirror that greeted me at the bottom. Hearts continued along the hall of the second-floor hallway, then picked up again on the left-hand wall of the staircase leading from the second floor to the first. Ella had taped a heart to the center of the pier mirror too, in case I stopped in the foyer before heading into the kitchen. The last heart appeared at my last stop—stuck on the coffee pot in the middle of the kitchen counter. Ella's trail of love.

Had Ella ever watched me walk all the way down to the kitchen from my bedroom in the morning? Probably when she was little, although I was often the first one to rise. To place her hearts, though, she'd had to intuit my movements and picture the precise path I followed. To truly know me.

I'd kept those hearts up for over a year, even the one on the cof-feemaker, seeing them every single day first thing after I woke up. As I waited for breakfast on Mother's Day, I began to unpeel them from the walls upstairs, stopping to stare when I reached the Wall of Mom, another testimonial of love, which I'd also waited until the last moment to disassemble.

I thought of Mary Kennedy, Bobby Kennedy, Jr.'s wife, who had committed suicide the year before, a few days after Mother's Day. Her husband had filed for divorce and obtained temporary custody of their children. Prayer, meditation, my resiliency—they'd all played a part in my recovery. But the courage and love from my own children had played the biggest role. If I'd lost them, I can't say for sure what I might have done. Their father's love for me had changed, but theirs hadn't.

"Ready!" Ella called up the staircase. I smelled her cooking on the way down and realized I'd passed down my family legacy of cooking to my daughters, along with so much else. Because as potent as the smell of Ella's cooking was, I could still place myself in my grandmother's kitchen, watching my great-grandmother curl up dough around her apple dumplings. And with both Nicki and Ella, somehow I knew the legacy would continue.

During her last two years in high school, Ella also insisted on preparing dinner on a number of cold winter nights.

"It relaxes me," she said when I told her not to bother. But I relented, because she'd also done it to relax me. The prior winter I'd been working at a particularly demanding job, temping through the weekend, sometimes sitting twelve hours a day behind a computer screen, when for a second night in a row, Ella announced she was cooking dinner and had the menu already planned. Neither of my girls could afford expensive gifts. Nor could they fix the problems that had affected our family. But they could remind me of what was most important, what I sometimes forgot. And they could feed my tired, hungry body and in so doing, feed my soul.

I walked down the stairs that last Mother's Day morning in my house and there propped up against the front door was a three foot by two foot Mother's Day card which read, "Mom You Are the Best, Happy Mother's Day." In the kitchen, Ella stood beside the breakfast she had prepared. Her first-ever eggs benedict with homemade hollandaise sauce, her inaugural homemade crepe topped with sliced strawberries and powdered sugar, and a side of crispy bacon. A slab of butter and a dollop of raspberry jam sat in tiny glass bowls alongside a glass of orange juice. Ella had placed a red and white placemat underneath the green plate. In the left-hand corner was a red vase sprouting a pink zinnia.

I snapped a picture, wanting to retain the memory forever.

After church, Ella and I spent the afternoon until dusk sitting on the stoop, presiding over yet another stoop sale where we mostly gave things away or sold them for a buck or two.

"Are you sure?" people asked, holding their treasures.

"I'm sure," I said, watching them walk away, the Hansel and Gretel procession continuing to spread throughout my Brooklyn neighborhood.

18

Cartage

In mid-May I put a temporary halt on hauling out upstairs and headed to the cellar.

"You can leave the junk downstairs," my real estate agent said when I queried her about cleaning the cellar before the house went on the market. "Cleaning it now won't add to the value of your house, so most owners leave it until they sell. Maybe get rid of the old mattresses and tidy up a bit."

That meant I'd have to find muscle to help me. But why sink so much effort into pushing junk around? Who knew how much time I'd have to finish cleaning out, pack up, and move once the house sold. It was a seller's market, and my neighborhood was hot for real estate. Odds were a sale would happen quickly. Plus, Ella started college in August. I couldn't stand the sight of rubbish anymore either and was on a roll. The behemoth that was the basement junk had to go. I was determined to tackle the task quickly.

My agent knew a man with a cartage business and sent Carl by for an estimate.

"I can haul out in a day," Carl said, and so we did. Carl, a slight, tattooed, fiftyish white man, and I and half a dozen black and Hispanic men worked and laughed together, comrades for one long exhausting day, all of us covered in sweat and grime.

They arrived on a Thursday, the only day Carl's truck could grab a guaranteed parking space in front of my house after the street sweeper drove through. After they parked, two of Carl's men followed me to the roof. The railing wiggled from neglect. The deck planks were weathered, some rotting, many warped.

It was a crisp late spring day, and, except for an occasional fire engine whistle or church bell, the roof was the only place for me in Brooklyn where silence reigned, where worries could shuffle into insignificance. There were no other roof decks in sight, so no people either, only the tops of other houses and buildings, church spires, and steeples. In 1997 when we moved in, the roof provided an unobstructed view of the Manhattan skyline. A few trees had grown above my sight line over the years, obscuring part of my view of lower Manhattan where the Twin Towers had once stood. My vista also included a portion of the East River which separated Manhattan from Brooklyn and over which the Brooklyn Bridge stretched to connect them.

I'd stood on the roof on September 11, 2001, my mind and body in a state of red alert, where it remained for years. I had gotten the kids off to school and was in the midst of cleaning up the kitchen when I heard a loud bang, right before my friend Rachel called.

"Are you watching the news?!" she asked, out of breath.

"Just go upstairs," she said when I asked why.

"I'll call you back," I said, rushing up to the roof where I saw the North Tower on fire. Within seconds the vision was too much to take in. From the distance, it was impossible to observe the particulars. But there was no mistaking them: People were dying. Letting them do so in private seemed the only offering I could make, so I turned my face away.

Minutes later, I stood at the kitchen door and watched grey snow showers land on the deck, then cover the garden below and sink into the soil. The sky remained dark for hours, ashes falling from the sky, the smell of death permeating the air.

The following year Jake left and the year after that we had the August blackout in New York City, the day before the real estate appraiser appointed by the court had come to appraise the house. I'd gotten the house, like the appraiser predicted, but now I was leaving it.

Upstairs on the roof, the ailing picnic table wobbled, unsteady, warped and rife with splinters. Previous owners had left it, already ramshackle when we bought the house, since there was no way to lower it down the spiral staircase without disassembling it first. I watched Carl's men hack it to pieces, then tear apart the wooden barrel that had split, scoop out the dirt and weeds, and load everything into heavy duty garbage bags which they dragged behind them, sweeping the deck, floors, and stairs, working their way down and out to the truck. The sight thrilled me.

"What took so long?" Carl asked his men. He was paying them by the hour, having bid the cartage job for a fixed price, and was already behind schedule. My real estate agent wanted to hire a stager. But the stager seemed to rubberstamp most of my ideas, so I asked her to pay Carl instead. After all, the agency would gross 5 percent from the sale of my home off the top. And I had to pay Arman to paint and make repairs.

I put on plastic gloves and a facemask and followed the men to the bowels of my house, an unfinished cellar with cement floors and concrete walls. The exposed ceiling was a maze of joists, wires, and pipes upon which 120 years of repairs had been grafted. A layer of dirt, grease, and oil drippings coated the floors. We bought the house "as is," basement debris and all. And then we moved in and mingled our overflow with that of previous owners.

"You might have something valuable down there," my mother, an aficionado of the *Antiques Roadshow*, said. But I was preoccupied with more than I had time for. What I didn't know couldn't hurt me I supposed. Would I even be standing in the cellar if I hadn't reached for the cell phone inside my husband's pocket? And yet.

A series of doors and framed openings divided the cellar into six discreet spaces, the first, an alcove at the bottom of the staircase. It contained mostly old cans, paint paraphernalia, and a rickety ladder. A door then opened into the main room, where most of the junk resided, including an old washing machine and sink, both operational, and the apparatus that controlled the sprinkler system which looped throughout the house.

A doorless room at the front of the cellar held the fuel tank, a couple of wooden tables left by previous owners, miscellaneous boxes, and a fair amount of dust and debris. A corresponding recess jutted out at the back of the main room, and to its immediate left, a closet with old magazines.

"What do you want to do with these?" Carl asked, gesturing to a pair of shiny skis I'd never seen. Carl also owned a secondhand shop in Brooklyn where he sold items collected during his house cleanouts. My former tenants were skiers; I told Carl I'd call the former tenants and let him know.

Before we moved on, I stepped into the back room, realizing I'd never investigated the space, passing it by each time on my way to drain the boiler. Inside I found several cartons of dishes and wine glasses I vaguely recalled buying for the surprise fiftieth birthday bash I threw for Jake a decade and a half before. In addition to what appeared to be two worktables, there were a slew of drawers and cubbyholes. Up close I could tell it had once been a carpenter's workshop. Old tools. Metal rulers. Who worked down there and when and what had they made? Hard to believe this airless atelier had once been someone's refuge.

The last rooms in the cellar—the boiler room and a small room off to the right—were situated at the back of the house, separated from the rest of the cellar by a metal door. The light bulb had gone out in the room long ago, but I had no reason to enter the small room. I could still make out bedroom furniture belonging to my ex-husband's parents, which we'd used when we first got married, then dragged from one residence to the next. Jake didn't want it after he left, so I somehow got stuck with it.

"Save this room"—the small back room—"until last," I told Carl after we completed our tour of the basement, knowing the grand prize was stationed there—the crib both my children had slept in. The Lover Crib, as it was called by the product maker. *Beautiful Things for Beautiful Babies*, the company motto. A white crib, rectangular but with soft, rounded corners and slats. A dream of a crib that provided the perfect backdrop to the outstretched arms of my beautiful children. Mom splurged beyond her budget when she bought the crib, matching dresser, and changing table. Jake and I installed pink carpet in the nursery, and I draped a white sheet over our brown rocker and cinched it with pink satin ribbons. We added a six-foot-high puffy palm tree and a purple-covered futon, embellished with turquoise pillows and a hand-embroidered quilt from Hawaii. We wallpapered with scenes of the skateboarding bears, Fritz, Willie, and Goober, performing their antics against a backdrop of palm trees. At the back window, I hung white curtains on which I had embroidered green and pink palm trees along the border.

The girls knew I was passing the crib on to them, and I dreamed of one day reaching for the outstretched hands of my grandchildren. The crib was tucked securely in the back of the basement, where movers had deposited it sixteen years before, out of the way of foot traffic. It would be a taxing day, but seeing it again was something I looked forward to.

There were three ways in and out of the cellar, the most convenient on foot through the ground floor and down the staircase. But this route was also the slowest and most inefficient. Construction of the mud room cut off primary access to the playroom and necessitated creation of a sharp right angle off the hallway to the cellar door, resulting in a tight squeeze for getting all but the smallest of items in and out. Exterior vaults opened in the ground in back and front of the house, the latter of which became the primary path for Carl's men to carry the contents of my cellar to street level, walking straight up a metal ladder bolted to the side of the front shaft.

After Carl's men paraded each of the items in the cellar before me for inspection, they gave Carl dibs on what I chose to ditch, then placed Carl's selections for his side business on the sidewalk for loading into the truck last. During the day Carl choose a couple of lamps, posters, and the bedroom set.

The more the men loaded into the truck the more room it seemed to make. It reminded me of the 1950s fad of phone booth stuffing. And the 8 mm home movie I saw as a young girl of my grandmother and grandfather attempting to cram as many people as possible into their car, my grandmother, probably twenty-five or thirty at the time, giggling as she piled in last. Then laughing again, and hopping out first when the film was played in reverse. Somehow Carl's truck had evoked an association with the home movie of my childhood.

I took periodic oxygen breaks during the day; Carl used his breaks to catch a smoke. Late morning, after one of our breaks, I skittered back inside and down the stairs before realizing Carl wasn't behind me. Through the hatch, I heard him talking with a woman outside. I only caught snippets but sensed the urgency in Carl's voice. When the conversation dragged on, I walked back upstairs to investigate.

"I have to talk to you about this later," Carl said to the woman, but the woman, a neighbor on my block, kept insisting. A woman who, not once in the eleven years since my ex-husband had left, through snowstorms and knee surgeries, when she'd seen me hobble up the stoop on crutches, had ever asked how I was faring or offered a helping hand. Yet Teddy, my neighbor to the right, an elderly man with persistent serious health problems, could not be talked out of constantly helping me. This woman also had a possible project for Carl, who she'd snagged in front of my house. Even though Carl was anxious about being behind schedule, she pressed him for quotes, refusing to accept his polite "later." Meanwhile, Carl's profits dwindled by the minute.

"Carl can't talk now," I said, inserting myself into the conversation.

"But I was just asking him because I have to…" she said, before I cut her off, the I's and "just" setting me off.

"Go away," I said. She looked at me, stunned, clueless, responding with another "but" and "just" and implied "me," before I lost it.

"Get the hell off my property!" I screamed, backing her up onto the sidewalk. "Go away," I yelled until she finally did.

I had maintained my neighborly decorum for sixteen years, before I blew. But what a relief to have her gone.

"Thank you so much," another neighbor said to me later that week. By then shame competed with relief, and I hoped no one else on the block had heard me, that only this neighbor had. In truth, I'd screamed the F word, not the H one.

It wasn't like me to curse like a sailor, as my mother would say. In the moment my words poured out, I'd felt empowered. And for the split second I calculated my decision I'd thought adding the F word would clinch my liberation. But that was my carefully scripted illusion, and I regretted it. Not the speaking up for Carl and myself and my neighbor part. My neighbor said he'd kept his own frustration inside for years, and she'd needed the wake-up call. True wisdom wouldn't have required me to resort to angry words. But I was still learning. So I poured forgiveness my way.

"Wow, look at these," Carl said after I followed him back down to the basement, remarking on the elaborate poster boards that accompanied Ella's science projects, one with colorful photographs of soil samples Ella collected from the parks and gardens in Manhattan and Brooklyn I drove her to.

What are you doing with your days to be productive? I often heard the court's words when I came across evidence of how I spent time with my children. I heard them again when Carl remarked on the poster boards. An associative memory of the most egregious kind, compromising the most precious of my memories. From red alert to red rage that I tamped down with guilt or meditation or fear. Was there a way to strip out the joy, nurture and protect it, along with the memory, and forever neutralize it from the pain? A scientifically-based mechanism for overriding the judge's words? Triggering an associative memory of a different kind, a positive one that could be layered on and programmed in a way to be automatically invoked?

"Do you have kids?" I asked Carl.

161

"Yeah, I got four kids," Carl said. "Three from my first marriage and then my eight-year-old daughter with my wife. She goes to school around the corner. She likes to read. I saw some books on your stoop. You throwing those away?"

"I put them there for people to take. Help yourself."

"Beautiful. She'll love them. Thank you," he said.

"Lunch time," Carl called, and instantaneously the men put down what was in their hands and headed upstairs, where Carl took sandwich orders.

"No thanks," I said when Carl asked for mine. "I've got something inside." Carl sat inside the truck to eat while I ate on the stoop with the men.

Afterwards I ushered Carl inside to see my grey and black lacquer Art Deco coffee table. It occupied too much space for staging, but I'd had no luck selling it even at a fire sale price.

"Would you like to have it for your shop?" I asked Carl. "You'd be doing me a favor taking it away." Carl quickly agreed.

Four mattresses; two lamps; clothes; sixty or more cans of paint, shellac, and other chemicals; particle boards and other wood; a wooden door; a trunk with a broken latch; framed posters; a TV stand; two suitcases; a scratched Art Deco ashtray stand, minus the ashtray; books, papers; two rugs; rusted pipes; a fireplace grate, and screen. The men carried these items into the truck. Carl took an electric saw to a rusted dryer and stove left by previous owners, slicing them down to size and heft small enough for his workers to carry them up and through the shaft. The worn-out water heater passed through the hatch intact. I watched the men struggle with it, pushing and pulling until, in due course, they glided it out. I worried about the strain on their bodies. And wondered if they had other work options.

Midafternoon Carl's guys came across half dozen or so banker's boxes that had been buried beneath the mattresses and other junk.

"What do you want to do with these?" one of Carl's guys asked.

"I've got to go through them," I said after peeking inside one of them. I'm embarrassed to say I've forgotten the men's names, including the more than middle-aged tall black man who remained with the truck all day, sweeping the sidewalk and helping lift items through the hatch and then into the truck. He refused to let me pick up boxes and brought each one to me in turn while I sat on the stoop. I understood only a word here and there, and when I smiled or shook my head or said "thank you," hoped he could not detect my ignorance. He had a speech impediment; I couldn't tell whether he was also learning disabled. Was this a steady job for him or did Carl grab day laborers whenever the occasion arose?

I found textbooks from law school and the blue books I took tests in. Client's files, many confidential, some privileged. Papers I had an ethical duty to protect as a lawyer though more than a decade—and in some cases two—had passed, although I was free to finally throw them out. Some from a period when unbeknownst to me I'd been training the lawyer who would replace me at one job.

A's on the blue books. Complicated contracts I had drafted, beautifully crafted briefs. A couple of treatises I had assisted a partner in a prestigious law firm with, researching while I worked my way through law school. Smart, and yet so incredibly naïve in my marriage and then again when it came to office politics. I wasn't brought up or trained to mistrust, and so Dante's ninth circle of hell, betrayal, simply did not compute.

On the stoop, I tore paper in a frenzy. Hair flying, paper flying, wearing threadbare black leggings, a camouflage tank top, and a mask. Half a dozen men milled around me amid junk on the sidewalk. I amused myself contemplating what kind of crazy woman the passing vehicles in my chichi neighborhood must have imagined me to be. Who cared? I was having fun.

"Why don't you let me take this stuff and shred it for you when I dump the garbage?" Carl asked.

I said, "It's okay, I need to do this." I had promised confidentiality to my clients and felt grateful for the opportunity and the wherewithal to maintain my commitments. I'd earned my battle scars. And I liked tearing paper. It definitely severed something. Completion stage. Purification. Erasure.

Inside, the basement was almost empty. The men stacked a few boxes I still had to sort through—mementos, baby clothes, Christmas ornaments, my old T-shirt collection—to one side.

On the other, they set the few items I was keeping—a fireplace set, my childhood rocking horse, a pair of antique wooden doors from Bali, the dishes and wine glasses, and the sewing machine I stitched my clothes on in high school.

As usual, the cleanout unearthed more of Jake's things—a Louisville Slugger bat and a framed picture of his brother as a boy. He'd obviously forgotten about them, and I could have thrown them out. But, again, I couldn't do that, not without getting angry. And by now, what was the point?

My former tenants didn't want the skis so I gave them to Carl.

The men swept the cellar cleaner than I had ever seen it.

And then came the denouement of the day—the men brought out the crib. I turned to face it and burst into tears. It was corroded and covered in the telltale brown residue leftover from a leaking pipe. The white coating had peeled, eaten away by brown gunk which had leached into the wood, underneath the protective base. One of Carl's men patted me lightly on the shoulder.

"It's okay, ma'am," he said. But, of course, it wasn't.

"I'm sure somebody can fix it." But, of course, no one could.

"It's gonna be okay, ma'am." No, it would never be okay, even though I'd have to find a way to make it more or less so.

I could not pretend I didn't care, that the crib was merely a thing, that I was so much luckier than most folks who suffered far worse in their lives than I had. I'd felt so strong and powerful throughout the day, but the crib crushed me and I felt so extremely fragile and in need of protection.

Because it had been my fault. My fault for not wrapping the crib up better after we moved in. My fault for becoming preoccupied with manning a four-story house, raising children, working, dealing with Jake losing his job shortly after we bought the house. Knee surgeries, betrayals, single motherhood, nearly seven years of divorce litigation. And so much more. I hadn't wrapped the crib securely. I hadn't been perfect. There was no one for me to forgive but me.

I ran upstairs and screamed at no one, "Stop taking things away. I'm not Job!" How ridiculous I feel admitting it now. But the crib was gone and I wanted it back. I wanted to lift my grandchildren from it while I told them about Fritz, Willie, and Goober. Not show them masks and coffee tables and Waterford crystal vases.

I walked back downstairs and told Carl's men to throw the crib away. I couldn't watch them load it into the truck, so I turned my back, waiting inside until they were done. When they were finished, I went outside and thanked them before closing my door for the night.

It was dark before Carl's truck drove away. But I could still make out the men, huddled beside it while Carl counted out their cash.

19

Open House

My house went on the market shortly before summer.
"I want to schedule a broker's preview for June 6," my real estate broker Mona said. Had I heard correctly? A broker's preview would give other real estate agents with potential buyers the first opportunity to tour my home, which was fine. It was the date that threw me. I graduated from high school on June 6. Thirteen years later, on the same day, my father died. Eighteen years after that my husband's divorce trial began on the same day. Now the date for my house to go on the market. Each June 6 had been a watershed, and none scheduled by me. If I had any concerns about selling my house before, my doubts vanished, at least for the moment. June 6 was my D-Day.

After my marriage broke up, I started paying attention to signs, particularly so-called coincidences that came in threes. I had questioned my own intuition, especially in those early days when I'd been so fragile.

So when I saw Nicki's birthday on a license plate while driving, and then again on the door to my hotel room where I'd arrived for a retreat, I thought, *I'm supposed to be here.* The ancient rule of threes repeated itself when I got those three "new" articles published in a row and exactly ten years later when on the verge of giving up I discovered I'd had another three "new" articles in a row. In-between I received a powerful affirmation when I stumbled into Barnes & Noble, where I had unraveled after trial one day, following my natural inclination to reach for a book when I needed comfort. As I hurried to the section on religion and spirituality, the name Kierkegaard (who I had never read) hammered in my head, which was weird. My eyes landed immediately on *Fear and Trembling*, right before I heard the words, g*et another book*. My eyes drifted over to Anne Lamott's *Traveling Mercies*. I began Lamott's book that night and a few days later reached the part where she described her lurch of faith after reading *Fear and Trembling,* at which point I sobbed. Certain that I'd been led precisely to that spot in the bookstore for help.

"I'm so worried about you losing your home," my best friend from law school said, when she came to New York for another round of experimental treatment for breast cancer. I tried turning the conversation back to her while Laura fretted about me.

"Maybe rent it and put your things in storage once Ella goes to school," Laura said. "And stay with friends to give you time to plot your next move. I hate for you to give up your principal asset. If you wait, your house will fetch an even higher price."

"It's okay," I told Laura. "I've made peace with it. I've accomplished the main thing I wanted, giving the kids a chance to grow up in their home before going to college."

Laura had a house and family of her own. She knew what those things meant to me. But new signs pointed elsewhere. And then Pat called to say the closing on her house had been set for June 6. I had prayed for signs so how could I ignore them when they came?

My to-do list kept growing, with trips back and forth to the hardware store. Arman and I were a team again. "What would I do without you?" I asked.

Arman laughed. He might be moving too. The wealthy woman he took care of properties for had sued to evict him and his family from their rundown basement apartment so she could refurbish it and charge a higher rent. The neighborhood was becoming so popular that landlords were getting greedy.

"You know, Bev, my family and I used to eat around her table at holidays. She treats us like family and now she wants to kick us out," he said. "I thought she was friend, but she wasn't really friend. But what you going to do, huh?"

"I'm so sorry," I said, stuck for words. "I'm your friend, Arman." How could anyone treat this kind man so? I felt the tears coming.

"I know, Bev. Don't cry. I am fine. I finally retire. I have saved money for house. You'll be fine too. I have heart, you have heart like me," Arman said, touching his chest with his fist. And then he laughed again. And whistled while he spackled.

After Arman finished painting the kitchen, he painted the entryway and top floor. The chair railing and floor molding that lined the foyer and ran alongside the staircases hadn't been painted since we moved in. Neither had the spindles. There were nicks everywhere, so I bought paint samples, trying to match the light yellow cream. While Arman made broad strokes, I applied touch-ups, understanding as I glided my brush over the molding why painting seemed to soothe Arman so.

Arman fixed kitchen cabinets and door hinges and installed a new shelf to replace the warped one above the kitchen sink. He glued down peeling wallpaper and regrouted the kitchen and bathroom tiles. He unclogged the drain in the basement sink and installed a new pipe. He screwed in switch plate covers and removed the nail and puttied the front door where I had hung the yearly Christmas wreath. He unbolted portable air-conditioners, so I could clean the outsides of windows, holding the windows open while I washed.

"So why you sell this house?" Arman asked yet again. "You have beautiful house." Was Arman's question an omen for me to reconsider or a chance to reaffirm? It wasn't always easy deciphering signs.

"It's too much to take care of. And I can't afford to keep it running."

Every little thing ate up so much time and energy. Like the episode with the glass door panel in the bathroom I had intentionally smashed the summer before, which Arman now replaced. Our cat Thunder had been sick, so I left her in the bathroom while I temped. The doorknob on the inside of the bathroom door had been missing for years so I closed the door carefully when I stepped inside, and not all the way.

But in a hurry to get to work one Friday morning, I accidentally slammed the door shut behind me and heard the doorknob on the outside fall to the floor. The door wouldn't budge. My cell phone was three floors below. Ella had already left for school and would be at her father's all weekend, not home until after school on Monday. I screamed for her anyway while Thunder clawed at the door. There was a skylight high in the air, directly over the tub, but it probably hadn't been opened in decades and was tiny, not even wide enough for a child to slither through.

Finally, I resorted to the only thing I could, besides being stuck in the bathroom with Thunder for four days without food. I set Thunder in the bathtub, wrapped a hand towel around my right fist, ducked my head, and thrust my hand through the glass panel. Glass shattered everywhere. I reached my hand through the jagged fragments and somehow pried open the door. Thunder shot out of the tub, through the door, and down the stairs.

The scene sounds comical now. Back then I hadn't seen any humor in the episode, however. I spit fire sweeping up the glass shards, then crawled on my hands and knees in my work clothes amid the dust bunnies under Nicki's bed, trying to catch Thunder before trudging off to Manhattan to temp.

Outside, Arman screwed in new floodlights. He secured the railing on the roof deck, then took his hammer to protruding nails and loose planks. Inside he replaced light bulbs I couldn't reach. Davit, his son, came by to straighten out the Nixalite bird spikes in the crevice above the front door, a typical place for birds to nest in Brooklyn brownstones.

"What shall I do with this?" Davit asked, after ringing the doorbell, in his hands a nest. I gasped when I saw the baby egg. Davit had already lined up the spikes, so he climbed the ladder and placed the nest on a low hanging branch in the tree in front of my house. Later that day we watched a bird fly back and forth to the crevice, swooping and caulking. Davit and I waved wildly at the bird, as if it could read our minds, until the bird flew away. A few days later the nest was gone. I was so torn up, I convinced myself the mom bird and soon-to-be baby bird had surely been reunited.

The gardener planted flowers. An architect that Mona had sent sketched floor plans, then a photographer shot photos for the real estate company's website and house brochure. In retrospect I felt guilty not retaining another mom I knew from Ella's school. She had shown me apartments over the years, knew about my divorce, and was sympathetic. She said she'd personally roll up her sleeves and help me. But she'd given me a contract to sign, so for her it was a business arrangement too. I wasn't eager for another crutch, someone who knew my past, who I was more likely to break down in front of. I'd been successful as a landlord, but my businesswoman muscles had atrophied. Mona knew I was divorced, but she was a stranger I thought I could maintain my distance from.

I was also moving into a new phase where I wouldn't be raising children full-time. I wanted to create a new slate. A life-without-Jake slate. A life-without-Jake's-things slate. A life-without-talking-about-Jake slate.

Before Mona came by, Moving Man helped me move rugs and furniture around.

"And the bench in the hallway should go in the cellar," he said. "It's a nice bench, but you've got to empty out the foyer," he continued, walking upstairs to find a place in Nicki's room—now Ella's—to stash the entryway table. Moving Man helped me do what Walt had suggested ten years earlier when I'd not even been ready for the couch to switch places with the chairs.

I hadn't been able to sell the red velvet sectional and needed to ditch it—there was too much furniture in the parlor. The week before the open house I saw an appeal for free furniture on Facebook from a dad going through an unwanted divorce. So Moving Man delivered the couch and matching ottoman to yet another part of Brooklyn.

I staged the house, observing through fresh eyes, searching for eyesores at eye level. My goal was to create a minimalist tableau of serenity and order, upon which prospective purchasers could impute their own imagination. I was selling more than a house. I was also selling an illusion and luring buyers into it.

Flat surfaces cleared, except for a few carefully choreographed items—candlesticks here, a basket there, a few classic glass pieces. Countertops and sinks clutter-free—making them appear more expansive—along with desks and dressers, tossing loose items in drawers or beautiful containers.

Cardboard boxes and plastic bins stacked neatly in the laundry room and closets. CDs and videotapes either on the stoop for takers or tucked out of sight. Shoes that normally lined the foyer where we removed them after coming in were now in boxes or shoe cubbies. Electrical cords for computers, printers, the microwave, toaster, telephone, television, VCR, CD player, DVR player, were hidden, as if unnecessary. Cords for necessary lighting concealed along floor molding and taped down. Hallway runners gone.

I organized the contents of drawers, cabinets, and dressers, folding every top and pajama bottom, neatly stacking dishes and glasses and cookware. Removing superfluous hangers from closets, grouping clothes neatly by length, eliminating dry cleaning plastic. Paring down clothes to make closets appear underutilized, rather than overstuffed, with plenty of room for growth.

Sandra helped me align the spines of books and tidy office supplies. We dumped out the contents of the linen closet, purged, and then refolded linens to within an inch of their life. We stored sheets and one pillow case inside the second pillowcase, a trick I saw pictured in a women's magazine.

In-between showings Ella and I swept our bathroom necessities in and out of containers I stowed away before prospective buyers arrived.

I've struggled with my predilection for perfectionism all my life. The realities of single motherhood forced me to lower my bar. Now everything had to be perfect again. Somehow this felt deceptive, not only selling an illusion, but removing the evidence of life I had tried so hard to hang onto. Perhaps that's why I refused to take the children's portraits off the walls. And proudly displayed their high school graduation photos on my bookcase upstairs, still wanting my house to resemble a home.

Otherwise I was obsessed with precision. I had no job, no retirement paycheck, no partner, no alimony, and in a few months—although I didn't know it yet—no more child support. My entire future was riding on the sale of my house.

Mona knew the photos of my girls were staying, but otherwise nodded her approval of my staging. But she suggested I strip curtains off the picture window. And how I loved sitting in the parlor until the house was gone, staring out at the Brooklyn plane tree that had been hidden from inside view, watching how the summer sun fell on the oak floor in my living room. The shadow part of the décor.

"Where can people leave their strollers?" Mona asked after photographing the garden.

"What do you mean?" I said. I assumed parents would leave babies and rambunctious toddlers at home. My house was a minefield of antiques and breakables. Prospective purchasers could easily afford sitters for an hour; some certainly had nannies.

"You need to put it all away, especially breakables," Mona said. "And up high."

"Can't they leave strollers inside the gate?" I asked, no rain forecasted for the open house.

Mona gave an emphatic *no*. "They spend so much money on their strollers, they don't dare leave them outside where they could get stolen or dirty. And they won't want to fold them up either. You need a place for several at a time." I pictured a mob of drooling babies and grabby-handed toddlers eating Tofu Pops. The neighborhood had transformed around me. But it was more than my aging and my own children growing up. I

172

was well educated, but still carried my small-town Southern girl part of me inside. A new, wealthier generation seemed to be taking over my once Italian working-class town, a contingent with whom I had less common ground.

"I guess they can leave strollers downstairs in the ground floor hallway, although it will be hard for my tenants to get in and out," I said to Mona.

"It's better if your tenants leave," Mona said. "And please ask them to clean up their apartment."

I already knew Ella and I had to exit the premises. I'd been floored by that news. But it was standard operating procedure in the industry, at least in New York City. It was inconvenient, of course. I asked why I had to leave and was told it was to protect me from prospective buyers asking questions. Maybe that was a nice way of saying I had to give up control.

"Will people look in my drawers?" Ella asked.

"They shouldn't," I said.

"Will people look in our drawers?" I asked Mona.

"They shouldn't," Mona said. But I knew betrayal all too intimately and put little stock in shouldn'ts. Easier to have Arman install a lock on one of the upper cabinets in the laundry room and stow away bills, jewelry, and important papers. Nothing I could do about the rest. Strangers examining where I ate, slept, brushed my teeth, showered, and dressed. Maybe opening drawers when Mona and her helpers weren't looking. I replaced the locks after Jake left, but he laughed at me one day in court, reminding me the children had keys so he could come in anytime he wanted. Not that he did or would have. Not that I trusted him not to. Not that I ever knew. Tomorrow and tomorrow, fretting and fretting over some grand fantasy of privacy. Because isn't that what I had done? Time to choose prudence over fear and let the rest go?

After Mona took photos, I gave the house a master cleanse. I hired a cleaning lady, Maria, and her sister, and the three of us wore our knuckles out for ten hours straight. After they left, I kept going, and two days later Maria's sister returned for another round with me. Scrubbing wallpaper, baseboards, doors, floors, windows, and shutters. Polishing doors and banisters. Cutting through layers of cooking grease on the top of kitchen cabinets. Bathroom tiles scoured until they sparkled. Brass cleaner rubbed onto doorknobs and kick plates. Refrigerator, stove, toilets, and bathtubs sponged down until my knuckles bled. Dusting every surface that could be Pledged.

The vacuum cleaner clogged up the first day. I uncurled a wire hanger and Maria and I spent a couple of hours snaking the hoses and nooks and crannies, pulling out hunks of gunk.

I dusted every ceiling and wall with a Swiffer mop. And swabbed every air-conditioning vent with a Q-tip. Better than cleaning closets!

Mona brought flowers, plants, and food. The broker preview went well, she said, some mild interest. There would be a showing the following day, and a public open house on Sunday. I had two days off to rest and clean all over again.

Mona emailed on Saturday to report my house key must have slipped through a hole in her dress pocket. She asked to stop by to make a copy of another key.

I saw red, the old fears from the early days after Jake left, when I'd been afraid of nearly everything and everyone, rising through my gorge. But I also saw clearly my pattern over many years of constructing an illusion of security to protect against the loss of what hadn't existed in the first place.

"The key wasn't in any way labeled by me, so there is no chance anybody could know what home it is for," Mona said when I questioned her. But what if it had fallen out in front of my house? In the final analysis, a locked door could not protect me against the inevitable. And yet it would be foolish to cavalierly leave a door open. So I asked Mona to pay for a locksmith. After all, I was now a businesswoman.

The following morning Ella helped me clean again. We stowed pens and papers and schoolbooks away. Hid dirty clothes in the washing machine. Folded clothes from the dryer and put them away. Unplugged electrical appliances and hid cords again. Made beds, put shams on pillows, and adjusted throw pillows on beds just so. Finally, I opened shutters, shoved books and reading glasses in the nightstand, and locked valuables in the cabinet.

Ella came upstairs while I was smoothing the comforter on my bed.

"Floors are clean and beautiful," she said, smiling. She had already mopped the floors downstairs and made her bed, all on her own. Executing these tasks with love and grace that seemed to come naturally, and effortlessly, to her. Grace I had to work harder at.

I continued with my tasks, dusted the furniture, applied Pledge to the banister and wood polish to the front door. Windex to the windows and glass doors. I wiped down window sills. Ella sprayed plants in the garden, while I watered them on the deck and front stoop.

Next up, the kitchen countertop and top of the stove. Washing the coffeepot and putting the teapot away. Clearing smudges from the microwave and refrigerator door handle. Loading and unloading the dishwasher.

After Ella and I showered, I cleaned the bathroom—swishing the toilet, wiping down the tiles, lifting hairs from the tub and toothpaste from the sink. I placed a fresh mat in the tub and new towels on the bars. New rolls of toilet paper on the holders. Kleenex boxes in their holders. All multiplied times three bathrooms. Then I got dressed and stowed away my and Ella's bathroom necessities and emptied garbage cans times three—bathroom, office, and kitchen.

Scoured the house for anything else out of place.

Turned on lights, adjusted dimmers.

No dirt, no dust, no crumbs, no smudges, no smells, except for the chocolate chip cookies baking in the oven to make the house smell like Betty Crocker.

With time to spare, I sat under the green umbrella on the kitchen deck, drank coffee, and watched the squirrels skitter alongside the deck railing then over to my neighbor Teddy's fire escape. "Shoo," I said, when a squirrel retraced its step and headed back towards me. When Ella was three, a squirrel had fallen from the fourth story ledge and onto my head while Ella sat on my lap. I had been reading to her, waiting until it was time to walk her to her first day of preschool. I was decidedly shaken and had migraines for weeks. But later on my husband and I and the kids had laughed about it when telling the story to friends and family members. Before Jake left and sued me for divorce, alleging my panic about the squirrel incident had somehow caused him stress and strain. Treasured family memories turned from good to bad with the flick of a lawyer's pen.

I could be happy here, I thought. *I am happy here now,* a decided revelation. And then, *I need to move.* Need to, for the physical distance to feed the mental. I felt like crying, but there was no time for that so I held back.

"We'll get through it, baby," Ella texted me while on her way to the subway, off to spend the afternoon with friends until after the open house.

And then Nicki called, excited to tell me about a place in Manhattan that served high tea. The girls and I had loved tea parties. While cleaning out I had found an invitation Nicki made for me when she was eight inviting me to join her for tea and cookies one night at "8:30 p.m.," and then to play Scrabble. I placed that invitation into my own save pile.

I cannot imagine a life beyond these two sweet girls, I thought, walking to the bagel shop to wait out the open house for the sale of my home, which was at last on the market.

20

Home

There were no immediate offers on the house. Real estate agents I interviewed had recommended the house be ready by April when buyers would be more plentiful, before the summer lull. I'd injured myself, though, and had been temping. In retrospect I should have quit temping earlier and put all my efforts into hauling out. Too bad retrospection manifests only in the present.

Still, I'd devoted considerable time to the project. I needed to process the letting go, just as I'd needed time to heal from divorce. Stuff flew in front of me. With no instantaneous buyer, I became antsy.

Homecoming. Welcome home. Home for the holidays. Ella would be with her father at Thanksgiving, but I worried about failing her at Christmas. What home would she have to come back to then? My mother started holiday shopping in the summer so there I was, like mother like daughter, in June, thinking ahead to December.

Home of the brave. How to continue being brave and hit a home run selling my house. Find my way home to a new home base.

Selling my house, selling my home. Home furnishings vs. house furnishings. Starter home, starter house. I'd used the terms interchangeably. The brain chatter overwhelmed me as the words vied for equal position, scrambled and jumbled up. When my house disappeared would my home vanish with it? Distinctions without a difference? Hearing Bing Crosby sing "I'll Be Home for Christmas" in my head, I collapsed in a puddle.

Join the witness protection program. I'd fantasized about that after my ex left. Where was the safety net for distraught mothers and children?

I'd once thought of running away from home; then my house became the place I was scared to leave.

Confined to New York City, I'd panicked during those first few months of 2003, at times panic turning to paranoia, convinced my phone was tapped and my husband listening in on me.

One day I'd seen a phone repair truck parked across the street and walked over to "Mariano," the name printed on the guy's shirt. I asked him what he thought about my phone. Mariano probably thought I was crazy. But he said the clicking noise I heard was probably the sound of my cordless phone switching to another frequency when I moved around.

"But I've never heard this sound before," I told Mariano.

"It's probably nothing," he said when I pressed. "But you never know," he said. "And if your husband's clever"—and he certainly was—"you probably never will. Even cell phones can be bugged."

I thanked Mariano and walked calmly back across the street, toting up Mariano's probablies in my head. Once inside I proceeded to tear the house apart, searching for hidden wires, pulling out desks and filing cabinets, getting down on my hands and knees and examining baseboards. I had no idea what I was searching for but found nothing that appeared suspicious. But when I called my mother, she heard clicking too. And the phone clicked even when I stood still. A cloud of fear hung over me in my own house. The house Jake and I built. Storm the house. Haunted house.

Stay away from your husband, my therapist warned over and over. *Don't talk to him on the phone. Limit the emails.* Married twenty years with two kids. How was I supposed to do that?

That first Memorial Day weekend I herded the kids into the car and drove nine hours in a torrent to visit my mom in Maryland. Home away from home. Hometown. Going home.

"I wish we could live here," Ella said after we arrived. With holiday traffic, the usual five and half hour drive also took nine hours in reverse. Eighteen hours on the road to put temporary space between me and Jake and the family breakup awaiting us back home. It was sunny, too, and Mom had a giant yard for her city grandchildren to pick windflowers in. And Grandmother spoiled them.

The night after we returned to Brooklyn, my husband sat one seat away from me at an awards banquet at Nicki's school. Nicki squeezed in-between us. We chitchatted with other families and pretended to be something we were not. A house divided. House of cards. House on fire. Light the frigging house on fire. With all my might, I reined in my tears and snapped Nicki's picture when she accepted her award. Home of the brave. Sick and tired of being brave.

In time, once my nightmares had subsided my Brooklyn brownstone became a safe haven, and I burrowed myself inside again. No place like home. Safe house. A place I clawed my way back to and fought to maintain. Eating me out of house and home. Bring home the bacon. Temping night and day.

As a girl, my childhood house in Maryland served as the family vortex, a giant nest I crawled back into whenever I returned from college. My mother used to leave little presents in the middle of my bed to welcome me back and in turn, I left small gifts on Nicki's bed when she returned from college. The bed Ella now slept in. The one she would vacate in less than three months. And where would she go at Christmas? It was June.

No place to call home. Ella had always had a place to call home. Nicki, too. Homing pigeon. Hearth and home. Home fries.

My father's home fries were legendary. Medium thick slivers of potato with loads of pepper and sliced onions, fried in Crisco oil until a thin burnt crust formed around the edges. My father, a sweetheart of a 1950s man, was at home in the kitchen and helping out around the house long before feminism said he had to. A gentle man I adored, who died on me long before life got so unbearably hard and I needed him most. A man so unlike the man I'd married.

Gimme shelter. Living a sheltered life. I had lived a blissfully sheltered life while growing up. Sheltered from the storm.

When Nicki was a young child, we sometimes got caught in rain without an umbrella on our way home from school or running errands. We'd often take cover under the canopy of an enormous weeping willow tree a few blocks from our house.

"Let's go to our umbrella tree," either one of us might say if it began to rain, even if it meant walking out of our way to reach our tree. And there she and I would stand beneath it, enveloped in our soft bubble, the tendrils draping so thickly over us rain could not break through while it poured down around us.

Psychologist Abraham Maslow placed shelter at the base of his hierarchy of needs, along with food, air, and bodily functions. His five-tier pyramid graduated from there to safety and security, then love and belonging, followed by attainments that promoted self-esteem, with self-actualization at the apex. Nicki and I sheltered underneath the branches of our umbrella tree.

Why had Ella placed *Hansel and Gretel* in her pile of books to save? Hansel and Gretel, who left trails of pebbles then bread crumbs to find their way back, but to what? The evil stepmother and spineless father who abandoned his son and daughter? Or to home?

Was I confusing home with family, and yet, didn't they somehow go together? Was home—like family—an ever-evolving designation, illusory? Not having a fixed reference point for myself and the children in the future made me uneasy. Did I need to leave a trail for myself to find my way back home after I left? And where would it lead? And what would it look like? And was I overthinking?

I had left my childhood homes—or houses. My ex and I had moved a few times before settling on the house we planned on living in until retirement. Housewarming. Full house. Dream house. And then Jake usurped my illusion of security. Perhaps I should have thanked him for illuminating my delusion. A delusion I'd reconstructed and clung to. Had I regained my balance sufficiently now to crawl back out, this time on my own?

"Start with the Psalms," my parish priest said when I asked him where to turn for help. I'd read straight through them, but chose Psalm 23 for my mantra, reciting it on my walks down to court and in my toilet stall inside the courthouse whenever I took a bathroom break. Soothing green pastures metamorphosing to vistas of pure lands whenever I reopened the courtroom doors. Home of the brave. *Strong and brave,* Ella's words for me.

The summer my house went on the market I sent Ella a text while she was at her dad's.

"What are you up to?" I asked offhandedly.

"I'm on my way home," she said, referring to her father's apartment. She'd never referred to her dad's latest residence as "home," at least not to me. Nor had Nicki.

"How can you have two homes?" I texted back, crushed. I don't remember Ella's reply, so caught up I was in a fresh well of sadness.

Once my children became teens, they commuted to school on their own and enjoyed a later curfew on the weekends. The phrase they texted most often was "I'm coming home." There were no more comforting words.

And suddenly, there I was, mad at Ella over a word. A word I could not define yet clutched so tightly, caught up in a misapprehension. And yet "[t]he ache for home lives in all of us," said Maya Angelou. It is a word "stronger than magician ever spoke," Charles Dickens wrote in *Martin Chuzzlewit.*

Stay-at-home. The comforts of home. Home ownership. Where would Ella go at Christmas? Where would I? Bing singing in my head again. It was June.

In the spring of 2007, Nicki and Ella and I toured colleges, then took a side trip to Savannah for a few days to decompress. I returned several times over the following years, with Ella and on my own, including after my divorce became final when I took a day trip to Gullah country. Gullahs, descendants of slaves from the West Coast of Africa, settled in communities along the coastal regions and islands of Georgia and South Carolina and once worshipped in praise houses usually built on plantations during slavery. A reverend opened one for me on St. Helena Island in South Carolina, a wooden hut where slaves and descendants of slaves once sang and clapped hands. I sat on one of the wooden benches lining the interior perimeter and stared at the whitewashed walls and bare floors. The walls were bare too, except for cotton curtains on the small windows and a large wooden cross nailed to the front wall behind a crude wooden pulpit covered in plastic. Someone had painted the words "Praise House" on the inside of the simple latched door. House of worship. House of God.

Spiritual literature is filled with departures. New Testament Apostles and disciples, monks, spiritual seekers of all faiths left their homes. Heavenly ascensions. Swift spiritual progress. Departures without separations. The original declutterers. Could I leave my house but not my home?

Shortly before the open house I threw my journals into a plastic bin. In late June, I reopened it and thumbed through them, drawn to an entry written during the Fourth of July holiday in 2008. I'd joined about ten other strangers from assorted faiths from around the country at a retreat center in Kentucky affiliated with Thomas Merton's Abbey of Gethsemani. I wrote:

"I feel more at home in the South. Life stretches out and lengthens. Strangers who become friends. Lives out there like mine on an unknown spiritual journey. I have felt my own whole person here. Doing what I believe in the sphere of my own life which is mine to determine. Maintaining a mind of flexibility that life is change. I am not here to do. I am here to be, to move with the currents of beingness, as it should always be."

I returned to Kentucky the following year, the day after spending July Fourth with Arman and his sons buying lumber at Lowe's. On my way from the airport, I noticed a sprawling cemetery off to the side of the road and pulled over, stunned at how many tombstones bore the name "Willett" while I strolled the grounds.

When I arrived at the retreat house, a place had already been set for me in the dining room. Dinner for one served on a Blue Willow china plate, my grandmother's pattern. The same plates I'd eaten off of as a child. As the director of the retreat center appeared in the kitchen doorway, the word "home" burst from my lips.

"You used to own this house, didn't you?" he asked.

I shook my head, perplexed. "No."

"Willetts are big in this part of the state," he said. "For some reason I thought you used to own this house." I'd only been to Kentucky once, the previous Fourth. But I was drawn back the following year, and the July after that when Brother Rene, a monk at the Abbey where I was headed, told me about the Catholic Willetts from Maryland who fled to Kentucky because of religious persecution. My Old Kentucky Home. Were some of my ancestors buried in that cemetery?

I called my daughters after I settled into my room. Delight registered in their voices when they picked up the phone and heard mine so I must have sounded happy because Nicki said so.

"You sound so relaxed, Mom. Happy," she said.

21

Independence Day

// "Why don't you come down," my sorority sister Jolene texted me the week before Fourth of July, inviting me to her beach house. We'd gone to college together in the 1970s, when I'd gone from a hometown of probably no more than five hundred residents to a university with an undergraduate population of more than thirty thousand. Jolene and I became sorority sisters, and then life-long friends.

"Ella's with me on the Fourth," I texted back. "I'll talk to her and let you know." In my head I was already packing.

"My daughter and her friends will be here," Jolene said, upping the ante. Jolene's daughter was off to college in the fall too.

"I want to stay in New York with my friends," Ella said when I told her about the trip. "But you should go. I'll stay with Dad." I enticed and cajoled, but Ella was firm and so was I. And so I did what I hadn't done in the previous decade of being a single mother. I said the hell with it, texted Jolene, and said, "I'm coming" and hopped aboard Amtrak alone.

After I got off the train, I stood on the platform squinting, scanning the parking lot for Jolene's blue soccer mom van. It wasn't there so

184

I figured she must be running late. My eye caught a woman standing beside a royal blue Mustang, smiling and waving frantically at someone. She was too far away to make out, but I started walking in her direction, headed toward another parking lot to search for Jolene. As I got closer, I heard Jolene's familiar girlish giggle and realized she was the waver. It took a moment for the scene to add up because it didn't.

"Where's the van?" I asked. She told me it had been in an accident and was beyond repair.

"So I just decided this time to get what I wanted!" Jolene said. We hugged and slid into the car.

"It suits you," I said.

"Hell yes!" Jolene said, taking a sip of Dr. Pepper and then expertly maneuvering her way out of the parking lot and onto the highway. She and I had been driving since we were sixteen, both skilled behind the wheel. Neither of my daughters drove yet—they were city girls. My first car had been a Mustang too—a used 1967 silver blue metallic car my parents bought me after I got my license. In my rural middle-class town, having your own car to drive to high school and work was the local teenage status symbol, not expensive clothes or gadgets. And sitting in a bucket seat, low to the ground, the symbol of youth and possibility.

Jolene switched the radio dial to an oldies station.

"Do you remember our trip to California?" she asked. "And the guy you met from one of the networks who took us on the set of Hollywood Nights? I sat next to Olivia Newton-John while she practiced! And wasn't Elton John playing the piano?" He was. I'd forgotten.

We must have been twenty-one or twenty-two at the time. And then we went to Disneyland and to Chasen's, the original Hollywood celebrity restaurant. I'd saved up money from my summer job to buy a Gucci purse on Rodeo Drive. We thought we were something.

Except for Jolene, decades passed after college before I saw most of my sorority sisters. In recent years, a few had surfaced on Facebook. Then about three dozen of us had converged in Delaware for a reunion to celebrate a sister who had nearly lost her life in a car accident. We wore our sorority pink and chanted college songs until hoarse, picking up our friendships where we'd left off in college. We promised each other to be more in touch, and we had been. Another reunion was coming up in October, although I wasn't sure if I'd be able to go, not knowing what would be happening with the house.

The past couple of years Jolene and I had fantasized about taking another trip together. But with working and raising kids there was no way either of us could see our way clear. Not now either with me selling my house and Jolene out of a job. But riding in Jolene's car with the windows down, reminiscing and singing oldies, the idea had potential.

The morning after we arrived at the beach I planted myself outside on the deck which overlooked a canal that fed into the Chesapeake Bay. I slathered myself with lotion and cocked my head back and faced the sun. It was July 4, 2013. Immediately my mind jumped back a decade to July 4, 2003. The children had been at sleepaway camp, Ella's first year going, the year I hadn't wanted to send her because she was so young. But I had acquiesced when my ex-husband tempted me with a chance at a second honeymoon that was never to be. I had glued myself to the computer screen that day until well after midnight, writing and rewriting the same five hundred words of a story about the day Nicki and I jumped into a fountain in midtown Manhattan. The editor I phoned said my idea sounded promising. A month later he rejected the piece, telling me to shorten it and try again. I battled with myself for hours, and then I sat down in my chair again and wrote and rewrote and whittled it down to three hundred words. Determined to be a writer. I hit the send button, and forty-one minutes later the guy replied: "We'll take it."

The same year my mother suggested I make July Fourth my personal independence day. I'd told her I wasn't ready for liberation. And then came a rain of litigation.

I heard Jolene bustling about and went back inside. On my way to the kitchen I looked around at the photos and furnishings in Jolene's family room and wondered how much of the room remained as her mother had left it. So many attachments to my own possessions had kept me in the past, but hadn't some also propelled me forward? Given me the foundation I needed to slowly move on?

Inside, Jolene and I and her children and their friends traded college stories while we sat at a table in the living room eating donuts and bagels. After breakfast was over, Jolene joined me on the deck.

"Do you know what today is?" Jolene asked, leaning over to whisper in my ear.

"No," I said, sitting up.

"It's my wedding anniversary," she said, whispering again. "But I just filed for divorce." That's why her husband wasn't there. I stood up and hugged my dear friend. She and I had done our best to hold our families together.

"We deserve better than our past," I said.

"Hell, yes," Jolene said, smiling.

"Here's to independence," I said, raising my coffee mug. She was ready. So was I.

22

Hurry Up and Wait

By the time I returned home from Jolene's, my house had been on the market for a month with no bites. Four weeks may not seem long, and it certainly wasn't in other parts of the country. But Brooklyn was super-hot. For a year I'd been hearing stories of bidding wars after a single open house.

All that forward momentum and then wondering what to do next. I thought by then I'd be packing up, searching for a place to live, and ridding myself of items kept only for staging.

One woman expressed interest but declined to extend an offer. Mona said she was content to wait for the "perfect" house, so I guess she's still waiting. Other buyers remarked on the necessity of gutting the marble bathroom and kitchen. Admittedly, I was jealous. If I had the money perhaps I'd have been renovating too, though not the sort of renovations becoming neighborhood mainstream. Like the $200,000 gut kitchen renovation immediately bulldozed by a subsequent owner to make way for a $300,000 one. My friend Charlie from church recounted that tale. He had also been the one to clue me in about the "leftovers," the term some neighborhood newcomers applied to the older Italians.

As instructed, I had removed so many of my personal touches—though not the portraits of my children—to create a landscape upon which purchasers could impute their own imaginations. So where was it? Why couldn't they see past the flaws to the beauty of how the sunlight slanted in through the back door? Or the ideal second floor set-up for siblings? The move-in ready condition of the ground floor for nannies, tenants, or out-of-town guests? I'd spun gold from my imagination, where was theirs?

Idling about in a no man's land of uncertainty, and cranky, that was me in July. A couple of days declaring my independence at the beach followed by the reemergence of my loser self, who began filling my head with negative mantras.

Maintaining the vigilance required to show the house on short notice made it challenging for me to relax. No dishes lingering in the kitchen sink or clothes unhung, encouraging piles to grow. Shoes off immediately after entering the house—fine, because I had done that anyway—but then pronto up the stairs to stash them out of sight. It became easier to wear out the same pair of shoes, and just slip them on and off as I entered and exited.

When I write I spread out papers—on the kitchen counter, floor, nightstand, desk, sometimes on the dining room table. It took too much time and effort, however, to lay papers out only to gather them up again. Not that I was having much luck forming even one respectable sentence.

The house was also somewhat sterile for my taste. Too much like a hotel or museum. Or mausoleum. Dressing up the corpse to reanimate it. Flowers and plants on every floor as if I were hosting a wedding. Or funeral.

But I did love the simplicity. All that purging and decluttering triggered a permanent high I still enjoy. I loved living with less.

With less chaos, I instantly detected when something was out of place. And with it, a tug to instantly return items to their place. Maybe that's because the house was for sale. I'm not normally an everything in its place all the time kind of girl and don't think I ever will be. Live with any condition long enough and even perfection will start to wear on you.

Whenever Mona scheduled a showing, Ella and I deployed a slightly modified drill of the one enacted the first time around, sans fresh baked cookies. I was amazed at how quickly the black Brooklyn dust settled on surfaces in-between viewings. One day I spent three hours tidying up—and wasn't done—only to have the potential buyers call last-minute and permanently cancel. With the house going nowhere fast, it was harder to push myself to get there.

Ella was a tad grouchy too, but never failed to be a marvelous, generous helper. Her increasing maturity over the summer reassured me of her ability to succeed at college.

After a short burst of activity, the phone stopped for four days in a row when no one called for an appointment. Four days when I dared to allow myself to crawl back under the covers and tangle up in my sheets for a few extra minutes. Before my anxiety bounced me back to worrying.

The lease with my tenants was expiring in September too, and they wanted to renew. I kept them dangling, although in the loop. Mona said I needed to keep my options open. Mona said houses delivered vacant brought more cash. I thought ready-made, impeccable tenants would be a benefit for buyers requiring help with the mortgage. But Mona said the purchasers for my property probably wouldn't need help. Indeed, Wall Street was just across the river. In the meantime, I needed the rent money to pay my own mortgage, and yet I owed my tenants the courtesy of sufficient time to move if they had to. So I fluctuated between being courteous and diplomatic on the one hand, and protecting my own interests on the other, while hoping my periodic reminders to "pick up your dirty underwear" before another set of buyers trudged through wouldn't push my tenants too far.

One day I was walking home from the pharmacy, dipping my hand in and out of a bag of potato chips, when I saw my next-door neighbor

Donna, Teddy's wife. She was sitting outside in a chair next to her stoop wearing a scarf to cover her baldness from chemotherapy.

I smiled at Donna, swallowed one last potato chip, and was about to open my mouth to speak when Donna said, "Come over here, Beverly," and motioned for me to come closer. I bent down and she kissed my cheek.

"Thank you for taking care of that girl," Donna said. "Teddy told me what you did." By that time Teddy had come outside.

"How are you, Honey Bunny?" he said. "We're going to miss you."

"Don't cry," he added, just as I started to.

Teddy and Donna had been having trouble with one of their tenants, a well-educated professional. She was a complainer before she'd even signed the lease; Teddy and Donna had nonetheless been accommodating. For safety reasons, however, they asked her not to party on the roof over the extension to their kitchen, which she could access from her back window, although they allowed her to plant herbs and flowers. But she partied with a throng of friends anyway and kept me up half the night a couple of days before my first open house. Teddy and Donna were too afraid to say anything—she'd called them "Mafioso" though they were no more Mafioso than I was.

The day of her party I had paid a gardener to spruce things up and plant flowers. The following morning, a huge splatter of potting soil trailed down the side of Teddy's house and then onto the white tiles in my garden below. The woman feigned ignorance when I knocked on her door, but bags of potting soil sat on her roof and the mess hadn't been there before her party started. She shrugged after I pressed and said she'd sweep it up "later."

"Do you have a broom and dustpan? And a garbage bag?" she asked when she arrived at my door, after dark, holding a peace offering of drooping carnations.

After that she began locking her bike to my wrought iron gate, blocking a portion of the opening serving as the way in and out of the ground

191

floor. I never caught her in the act, but Teddy said he'd talked to her. That's when he told me about her calling him and Donna names.

"I appreciate it, but leave it alone," Teddy said when I offered to intervene. "Donna and I aren't going to renew her lease." But they had eight months more to wait. And then she locked her bike to my gate again near the end of July, when I felt my least friendly. I began yelling in the street for her to get her bike the hell off my property. (This time I used the H word.)

"What's the big deal?" she asked, opening the second-floor door and staring down at me. "I only left it there for a few minutes."

"Move your bike now!" I screamed. "I'm an attorney and you're trespassing and the next time you do I'm calling the cops!" She walked down the stoop in a huff. I hovered nearby while she unlocked her bike.

Teddy silently looked on. I was embarrassed for yelling. *It's fine not to be perfect*, I told myself. *It's okay to feel the pain coming from your anger while you try to absorb the loss.* Maybe next time I could separate the anger from the yelling, though sometimes there are people with whom you need to lay it on the line to protect yourself and others. Like Teddy and Donna, so-called "leftovers," sweetest people on the planet.

Back inside my house, I combed my closets for what I could dispose of without a full scale opening up of boxes. And then I grabbed a few more books to place on the stoop. Ella handed me a few more items of clothing she was never going to wear. I had to feel like I was moving forward, even if I was blowing the doubts away as they floated back up.

"Your house is going to sell," Pat said. "You know that."

"Come over for lunch and I'll help you," my friend Janet said when I told her things weren't going according to plan. Janet had been studying a technique called focusing which helps individuals turn their attention inward to assess bodily sensations. To unearth the feelings that precede or might be unavailable in words and thereby create awareness about situations and discover solutions.

"So I gather the house isn't selling," Janet said in her precise British phrasing. "And that you're not feeling able to move forward and, with the unknowns, you're feeling sort of stuck?" She hit on my thoughts exactly.

"So where in your body are you feeling this stuckness?" she asked, telling me to close my eyes.

"I feel it in my throat. And in my chest," I said, after scanning my body.

"Okay, so just sit with it," she instructed. "And ask it what it wants."

"It feels like this giant boulder I have to push," I said after sitting for awhile. "It's so large I can't get my hands around it either. It won't budge. And I'm trying to get to the future, but it wants me to stay here in the present. The boulder's telling me I've done all I can to move it, and I can't do anymore."

"Anything else?" she asked. I concentrated.

"Well, it says I'll need someone else to come along and help me move it. But for now just to wait and sit and lean against it. And take the weight off my legs and let it support me."

How easily I had forgotten what I learned years before when I studied the teachings of the renowned 8th century Indian Buddhist pandit Shantideva, and discovered one of his most famous sayings about worry: If there's something you can do about a problem, why worry? And if there's nothing you can do, why worry?

The boulder provided the reminder. Because if I couldn't move the boulder by myself I just had to prop myself against it and wait. Waiting gave me time for reflection on what I had first taken pleasure in with my newly streamlined house. Feeling the clean wood beneath my feet while I walked around the house barefoot. The routine of making and unmaking my bed and putting a deliberate break between sleep and wake. The calm brought on by observing the unobstructed visual lines that emerged after the decluttering. I focused on enjoying the solace from these rituals once again.

When my tenants asked about the likelihood of their being able to stay on I breezily said, "I don't know."

When friends and churchgoers asked again about where I was going to go I said, "I have no idea."

"It's hard sometimes," I told Quinnie. I had met her through a mutual friend at a Christmas party in 1999. Her eyes were red, and she was sick with a bad cold. But she trudged out in the snow anyway to bring her son to a party she had no business attending. In those days, we Brooklyn moms had all done that. Perhaps so glad we'd gotten under the wire of our biological clocks we'd have gone anywhere and done anything for our children. And so we did.

I had started meditation classes that fall and invited Quinnie to join me one evening. She came right away, and we'd go arm in arm to classes for more than a decade.

Quinnie and I both grew up in the South, were both raised in the Baptist Church, were both left by husbands having affairs. We raised children at the same time, embarked on artistic careers while juggling homes and families, and even had hot flashes together.

Just do the best you can, Beverly. I have faith in you, girlfriend, was her consistent advice and encouragement.

A few years after we met, she moved to Manhattan, and then her husband's work took them a thousand miles away. As I was about to leave my nest, however, Quinnie was moving back. One afternoon we strolled arm in arm through the Museum of Modern Art.

"You know you can do anything you set your mind to, Beverly. You've already accomplished so much and one day you are going to have a room of your own to write in." I pulled Quinnie closer.

We wandered through the exhibits and were drawn to Adrian Piper's glass jars filled with her hair, fingernails, and skin entitled "What Will Become of Me," turning to each other and acknowledging what was becoming of us. Next we saw Douglas Gordon's installation entitled "Play Dead; Real Time," projections of films he'd taken of a circus elephant inside an empty gallery room while an off-stage voice issued rote commands in monotone for the elephant to sit, lie down, and get up. The films were mesmerizing in their stark elicitation of despair. Before heading off to lunch, Quinnie and I stopped to laugh at Jeff Koons' stacked vacuum cleaners.

The following week I scheduled a meeting with Mona and her colleague Rick at their agency. Other houses were selling and mine wasn't. But Mona's track record for sales the previous year was sound. Was this another test of trust for me?

"I think we should pull the house off the market in August," Mona said. It was still a seller's market, though not as many people were coming through as in the spring. She handed me charts of comparables, purchasing trends, and inventory.

"So why isn't my house selling?"

"There's no way to predict these things with certainty. People might think the price is too high, if they want to put money into renovating. I think you'll start to get offers if you lower the price," Rick interjected. But I didn't want to lower the price with hefty taxes, closing costs, and a jumbo mortgage to pay off.

"I don't want you lowering the cost now unless you agree to lower it again another step in September," Mona said. Steps are price intervals buyers deem meaningful when the price of property is lowered.

"We're going to feature your house in our company brochure inserted in the Sunday paper," Rick said, pulling out a sample. Who knew how long the seller's market would hold. I hadn't been prepared for the 2008 market crash or divorce. Meanwhile, what to do about the tenants, and a job, and the mortgage? Walls began closing in around me.

Rick said if I kept the listing active until September without lowering the price buyers would perceive the listing stale and start to wonder if something was wrong with my house.

"But nothing's wrong," I said. "My house is better than others that sold for more."

"Buyers can be funny," he said. "And that was in the spring."

In the end I had a decision to make. Lower the price or start over again in September after Ella went to college. So I cut the price. I let go. Unexpected things had happened in the past when I let go, so I entered a new realm of uncertainty.

After Jake had left, I worried myself into sickness about so many things, about not being able to cope as a single mother, and having no option but to work long hours as a lawyer and leave what time I had left to raise my girls to a babysitter. And losing our house. But none of that came to pass. I often struggled to keep going. I fought like hell to defend my rights and keep my sanity. But there were also times of plenty and showers of blessings that rained down on me and the children. They would do so again.

I told Mona to schedule showings whenever she wanted during the last week in July because I would be away.

With the worry and responsibility in someone else's hands for the moment, Ella and I hopped in the car and drove to Maryland so she could say goodbye to her grandmother before college. While I was away, Mona called to say she'd received an offer on my house.

23

Empty Nest

Near the end of summer Jake and I took Ella to college. During the flight, Ella curled up in the airline seat next to her dad and napped. My ex worked on his iPad while I sat in the aisle seat, two rows ahead. Ella and I had barely slept the night before. We had our final Girls' Night Out, packed, and then arose at 4:30 a.m.

The week before Ella had been out saying her goodbyes to friends one night. I was home, packing and cleaning, when I heard the text message prompt on my cell phone.

"I truly love you and I'm going to miss you," Ella had texted. I abandoned my chores and cried. Ella's precise insertion of the word "truly" ensured I understood the certainty and depth of her message.

My ex hadn't gone to college with me and Nicki, but insisted on accompanying Ella. Certainly, that was his prerogative and at one time there was nothing I'd have wished for more. Now though it would be awkward, at least for me. Jake and I had rarely been able to co-parent. He'd gone to parenting therapy with me for a few weeks, once, but as soon as I thought we were making headway, he called it off.

The month before Ella started college Jake had also cut my child support (payable in New York until Ella was at least twenty-one). He claimed he was entitled to a credit, since Ella was going to college. But a clerk I called in the family court told me he had to get the court's approval first. Never mind Ella hadn't gone to college yet. Never mind that while the judgment said he could take a credit for Nicki's room and board, the judgment did not specify what would happen with Ella. Never mind alimony had ended years before, and the same clerk told me that often meant child support would not be reduced but increased. Never mind I had earned about $20,000 in legal income the year before, instead of the $200,000 the court imputed to me as an obtainable salary. Never mind child support was payable in addition to college expenses. Never mind so many other things.

The palpability of my anger over Jake's latest missive momentarily blinded me. But maybe it was about time. The thought of setting foot in a courthouse again caused stabbing aches in my chest. My doctor had warned me about them for years. What would have been the point of going to court again, when I believed the justice system wouldn't protect me? Along with what else I was giving up—or losing—I had to relinquish the idea of achieving justice too.

And now I was supposed to spend several days in proximity with Jake taking Ella to college?

If my ex-husband had any qualms about my accompanying him and Ella, he said nothing. Maybe he thought reducing child support would make me cancel my plane ticket.

"I'm not sure I can go," I told Ella.

"You have to," she said. "I want you and Dad both there." Of course she did and of course she was right. And of course there she was, a normal child, trying to cope with divorce when the adults in her life should have spent more time trying to cope with their marriage. I could not disappoint her, not with something like this. If I didn't see her off, I would regret it. My anxiety stemmed from the frustration of trying to get inside her father's head—something I'd been trying to do for over a decade without success—and letting him get inside mine. Allowing the past to muck up the present and compromise the future.

So I turned my mind to wood, a technique I had toyed with in meditation. It was hard to sustain, but I'd only be gone a couple of days. I did not want to repress my anxiety, but rather will my anxious thoughts not to arise, to engage in non-thought about my ex while attempting to be totally and fully aware and present and experiencing the occasion of taking Ella to college. And when I felt about to latch onto negative, angry thoughts, I would flick the switch and blow out the match.

The night before we left, I told Ella to take one final look around and point out anything else she wanted me to save for her besides what we had already packed up. Before Ella had said she didn't want anything except the mementoes we had boxed up, but now she began to identify a few items she'd like to have for her first apartment, a 1930s lithograph, the tea cart, a couple of masks, including the fierce looking one with bulging eyes and real animal whiskers my ex-husband and I had bought in Yelapa, Mexico.

The next morning she and I took a cab to the airport. We met her father in the lobby, and then the three of us proceeded to airport screening together, boarded the plane in unison, deplaned as a group, and stood in tandem at the luggage carousel. We shared a rental car to the same hotel—Ella and her dad sat in the front seat while I occupied the back. And then we drove to Bed Bath & Beyond, where I slipped into the familiar role of list maker and orchestrator. Although there were a few tense moments negotiating over which plastic storage bins would fit in Ella's dorm room, after several hours of shopping we got through the ordeal, our humor relatively intact.

Ella and I had also shared a few inevitable tense moments packing the week before. After all, we were about to live a thousand miles apart and forever leave our family home.

"Where's that nice grey hoodie I bought you for Christmas?" I asked one day while we were sorting through her clothes. It was a familiar refrain, and my patience blew. This time Ella yelled back.

"It's hard living in two houses," she said. It had taken her more than a decade to say words she'd probably been holding in for years. But I was glad she had finally said them.

Ten years before, when Ella was seven, she told me she wanted to get baptized in the Episcopal Church, where a person can be baptized as an infant, youth, or adult. My ex and I had agreed the children could make their own religious decisions, but our parish priest wanted to talk with Ella first to make sure she understood the terms of the sacrament. When I picked her up after her meeting with the priest, he pulled me aside to say that Ella's mind had been on other things—things she didn't want to happen. Things like the divorce and Daddy leaving. Things she kept to herself for years.

The day after was Thanksgiving. Ella was still in her pajamas, and Nicki had a playmate over. I grabbed my coffee and went upstairs to Ella's room.

"What's going on, Mommy?" Ella asked, as I propped her up in bed, her golden hair fanned across the tattered, pink velvet pillow that said "Princess."

"Wait and see," I said, winking, going into the bathroom and bringing back towels, lotion, and a bowl of soapy water. Ella played along and swooped a thin, frayed remnant of blue nylon she pretended was silk over her shoulders like a cape.

"Close your eyes," I said, proceeding to bathe Ella's feet with warm water, wipe them dry with a soft towel, and file her toenails. The girls loved these rituals. Hand rubs, foot rubs, a quick back massage before going off to sleep. One time after I had a facial Nicki wanted to know what it felt like. "Close your eyes," I said, using my fingertips to make soft circles around her eyes, down her cheeks and then above and below her lips, trying to replicate the motions on Nicki's face that the facialist had made on mine.

I filed Ella's toenails and massaged each leg, foot, and toe, marveling at each tiny flaxen hair and hard-earned bruise from Saturday morning soccer. Once I'd been able to protect her from every sort of bump and scratch. *If only I could put her back inside,* I thought that day, gently lower her head and curl her petite fingers and toes and place them carefully back inside my womb. No worries or wondering about things that had happened, or were about to. And eventually did.

Ella hadn't wanted to leave her first home. She arrived nearly two weeks past my due date, only after labor had been induced. Any thoughts I had about control had been mostly illusory. From the moment the hospital nurse took her and Nicki from my arms to the first time they smiled and reached for someone besides me, they had already begun fleeing the nest. Ella had fallen down on the soccer field, and I'd been powerless to prevent it. Unable to spare her from her father's departure, even though I had tried to shield her. Soon I would be dropping her off at college, just as I had Nicki, and she would be on her own.

Fighting over Ella's lost hoodie was a feeble attempt to camouflage our helplessness.

"Let's go to the beach," I announced while we were packing. "We need to get away." I searched the internet and found a motel at the Jersey Shore for two nights.

After dinner there our first night, we grabbed beach chairs and planted ourselves in the sand. The air was crisp and a billion stars and a waning moon filled the clear sky. Ella shoved her hands in her pockets and kicked the sand.

"I'm cold," she said.

"Look up and see how big and beautiful the world is and what a speck we are," I said. "Let's stop fighting. I love you more than anything, baby girl."

"More than Nicki?" she said, her mischievous grin lighting up her face. It was a familiar tease among me and Ella and Nicki.

It had been a grueling year, but we'd slogged through it. High school, graduation, and college applications while I temped, managed tenants, and hauled out nearly every possession, Ella not knowing what she'd find missing next when she came home from school.

But our love was intact. I'd kept my deepest fear, that my children would grow to hate me, hidden. My ex had spewed his words in anger, but he'd nonetheless planted the seed of doubt that sprouted inside me whenever tension arose between me and my daughters.

Before Ella and I had binge-watched *Hoarders*, we'd watched back-to-back crime dramas, my favorite produced by Jerry Bruckheimer, hers, Mark Gordon.

"Jerry Bruckheimer," she said one night as the producer credits rolled, playfully mocking my taste in television. She said it in this high-pitched nasally voice that instantly made me crack up. At the end of her favorite show, I retorted with "Mark Gordon." Somehow our call and response took on a life of its own, becoming one way we said "I love you" and offered reassurance to each other of just how much.

"Jerry Bruckheimer," I said to my daughter out there among the stars at the Jersey Shore, a few nights before she'd go to college and leave our home forever.

"Mark Gordon," she immediately shot back.

"I'm cold too," I replied, putting my arm around her shoulder and leading us back inside. Lose the bonds between me and my daughters? Nope, that would never be.

~ ~ ~

AFTER JAKE, ELLA, AND I RETURNED to our hotel room from Bed Bath & Beyond, we showered and changed and drove to a fancy restaurant for dinner. My ex was hosting a wealthy client he was anxious to court, along with the client's wife and their son, who was starting college with Ella. Jake had invited me to join them. I didn't ask why but wondered if he wanted to present a corresponding portrait of a happy family. Still, I wasn't going to spend the evening apart from Ella, so what did it cost me to play along? My girlfriends were agog at my participation in the *Brady Bunch*.

"Just think of it as my cameo in a Woody Allen-like movie," I'd said. The other couple talked about their life, trips they'd gone on. I had no clue whether they knew Jake and I were divorced, but at one point the wife leaned over and whispered in my ear that she knew. Had she sensed something behind my words, wanted to spare me the effort of further pretense, or had my ex filled them in? No matter, I carried on being upbeat, the evening surprisingly tension-free.

The following day was move-in day, and the three of us acted in concert. Jake drove and I stage-managed and we all helped carry and unpack boxes. We met Ella's roommate and her parents, and there were handshakes and introductions all around. Jake clowned with his hat and the other parents laughed and Ella's roommate's mom asked, "Can we get a photo of you and your lovely wife?"

The last time my ex-husband and I had been on the other end of a camera had been at Ella's high school graduation in June. Before then, at Nicki's college graduation the year before. I suppose I would have to smile for wedding photos one day too.

"That's okay," Jake said to the mom, nonchalantly declining another photo op. Ella was silent. My body froze. I waited to see what Jake would do.

The other mom begged and Jake acquiesced. I stood still and sensed him coming up behind me and lean into the camera's frame. I smiled broadly and imagined my ex did the same because the real Mr. and Mrs. leaned close enough to touch shoulders and tittered on about how lovely the photo of us had turned out. Neither Jake nor I asked to see it.

Ella slept in her dorm room that night, and the next day her father and I met her for brunch, then drove her back to college. We hadn't had that much togetherness in over a decade. After we settled Ella in, she walked us back to the car, gave us hugs, and said goodbye. I slid into the front seat with Jake.

"Is she going to be okay?" I asked, my voice breaking as we drove away from campus.

"She's going to be fine," he said. "You're the one who's going to have a hard time. But you gotta let her go."

"I know," I said.

"I miss her already," he added.

"Me too," I said. And that was the sum total of our shared moment as parents. Mom told me she and Dad had teared up after dropping me at college, and often talked about the long car ride she and Dad shared home, sitting close to one another. I longed for someone as well, but it was no longer my ex I wanted. And, for just an instant, I was sad it wasn't Jake, because in that tiny moment I had seen a glimmer of the man I thought I'd once known, the one who shook with tears when Ella came out of me with her mop of red hair. But then it disappeared and so did he, and I let the moment go.

My ex-husband parked the car and once inside the hotel, he went his way and I went mine. Five years earlier, after taking Nicki to college, I drove back to the hotel too. Nicki had wanted to go to the dining hall and begin her college experience, so I ate dinner alone. Feeling vulnerable out in the open, I sat in a corner table in the hotel restaurant, shielding myself from view of couples who had dropped their children off together. Every time the waiter spied me crying he refilled my wine glass.

"Don't worry," he said. "It's on the house. I figure you just took your kid to college." And so it was with Ella, almost. I went to my hotel room, ordered room service, and ate dinner alone. But I prayed a prayer of thanksgiving for Ella's sake that both her parents had seen her off.

Before I flew home the following morning, Ella messaged me to ask if she could meet me to say another goodbye. Forty-five minutes passed; Ella was still waiting for her bus to my hotel. I was in danger of missing my plane.

"Wait there," I told Ella, hailing a cab and heading in the opposite direction from the airport, toward campus. Ella tumbled into the taxi and we drove around the college's circular drive before it was time for Ella to hop out and leave. I handed her a bag filled with microwave popcorn and ramen.

"I love you so much, Muffy," I said.

"I love you more, Mama Bear," she said.

I waved until Ella's figure disappeared. And then I flew home, the nest I'd built verging on empty.

The house was unusually quiet, and I waited until I showered to have a good hard cry, to mix my tears with the shower spray and have them washed away. "There is sacredness in tears," Washington Irving said. "They are not the mark of weakness, but of power. They speak more eloquently than ten thousand tongues. They are the messengers of overwhelming grief, of deep contrition, and of unspeakable love."

My role as wife had ended years before, and the role I had taken on as mom *cum* daily nurturer had come to a close as well. I chose those roles lovingly and willingly, and it satisfied me to see them through. The universe would eventually open up time for me and wipe out the last bit of residual sadness I still clung to from the lost potential of my past, right?

I ate dinner in silence. To save money, I scrambled to find evermore creative ways to reduce my expenses and had turned off the cable shortly before Ella left town. So there was no TV to cling to.

See this as a good thing had become my mantra to myself whenever the latest adversity struck. Remove all crutches and excuses not to feel to the fullest and then let go. Some days I managed more or less; some days I failed miserably.

A month before getting rid of cable TV I had also released my home telephone number. Even with the proliferation of cell phones for every member of the family, every family I knew with kids still had a landline. The other moms I queried weren't sure why they kept one, even when the kids got their own cell phone and were practically adults. In an emergency, a landline had seemed more secure, more reliable. The school and medical papers I filled out each year for my kids asked for a home telephone number, so I'm certain a part of me would have felt negligent leaving the space blank. My cell phone reached me; the home telephone number called home. But where was that? Would home exist without it?

I had recovered from my back injury and had been searching for temp work to tide me over until the house sold. Finally, a two-week job with normal hours had surfaced. During a bathroom break, I called Time Warner customer service from the hallway.

"Are you sure you want to let your home telephone number go?" the representative asked. It was Jake's before we met, and then it became ours, and then the family number, which I'd kept even after Jake left. I had had the number for over thirty years, and I knew it as well as I knew my social security number.

"You can never get this phone number back after you let it go," the man said during the second of silence I took to make certain I was fully present when I uttered my response.

"Let it go," I said.

"Let it go," I said again.

24

In Contract

now had three offers on the house. The first, submitted by a wealthy Wall Street couple, requested a price reduction, and ultimately fell through. Personal appeals accompanied the second and third, both from couples with young children. Their names meant nothing to me, their letters, everything.

I found it odd hiding behind the shield of real estate agents and lawyers, although perhaps I needed the buffer between my business hat and my emotional one. But the conveyance of my house from one family to the next was more than a business transaction to me. My house formed a part of the intricate fabric of the neighborhood. Its continued legacy depended on my passing it on to those who would not only maintain it but also appreciate its historical context.

The second set of purchasers included a note at the bottom of their offer form. They asked for a price reduction too; they couldn't afford the house without one. Their three elementary school children were already enrolled in a neighborhood school and they'd been house-hunting and finally found the "perfect" house—mine.

"We love its character and charm," they said. The ground floor rental was a bonus, not a detraction.

Couple number three, with two young children, also found the rental income and ready-made tenants a benefit and met my lowered asking price. A separate full-page letter containing the handwritten signatures of both husband and wife supplemented their offer. They mentioned they had both been raised in old houses and said my home's "old bones" spoke to them. Even the third-floor bathroom, sorely in need of renovation, stood out, nearly identical to the one in the wife's childhood home. A vision that to her evoked fond memories, instead of the potential for a wrecking ball.

"Our children are currently crammed in a two-bedroom apartment and would so love to have more space to dream, play, and build in," the couple said, noting the convenient second floor set-up. For them the house also raised possibilities for backyard kickball games and seed planting. The inside, sufficient space for childhood sleepovers, fort building, and visiting grandparents. All those things that go into making a house a home. Even the roof called out to them, as it had once called to me.

"The view provides a taste of the sunset, and a glorious panorama of Brooklyn's church spires and the skyscrapers of lower Manhattan, helping to remind us where we are, and of all the life and city that is around us," they wrote.

No mention of the many flaws in my house. Instead, memories of their own childhoods, and the family life they imagined having within my walls. They wanted to make it their dream house just like I had once yearned to make it mine.

They understood the importance of preservation, to treat the house with the reverence required not only to sustain it, but move it into the next century, noting the green improvements they hoped to make. My worst fear had been that a purchaser with no vision or appreciation for history—or devotion to family—would gut the house, then redesign it to resemble the high-priced, soulless, cookie-cutter townhomes being erected two blocks away. My house had traveled with dignity from the

19th to the 20th century. I stretched it the best I could into the 21st. Now new owners would carry on with its care.

By the time I reached the end of the letter, I knew my house had found its proper owners. I accepted their offer.

It was odd not being able to share my excitement with them. Even my tenants got to meet the new owners before I did, with lease discussions proceeding smoothly.

For half a minute, I thought of renting the ground floor myself. I didn't know where I was going to live, and time was evaporating. College for Emma had seemed so far off when I'd renovated it. Even with the purging remaining to be done, I would need to ship some belongings to storage. But I could move the rest downstairs. The one-bedroom would be tight living quarters when Ella came home, although perhaps cozy. But Ella would be away at college most of the time until spring. Without the pressure of moving, I could catch my breath before the next transition. Take time off to write. Maybe travel and visit friends, take a road trip. These fantasies floated in my head, including an assessment of the perfect spot for the Christmas tree downstairs.

"I don't think it's such a good idea," my lawyer said when I pitched the idea. "It could throw a wrench into the contract negotiations, although the purchasers seem pretty easygoing. And what if they decide to renovate? Do you want to live with renovations going on around you? And how are you going to feel living there?" I was silent.

I had thought that with so much on my plate, moving downstairs would be easier on me physically. But maybe I was still trying to hold on to my old life.

After my divorce, I cringed at the thought of entering another courthouse or ever hiring another lawyer. Yet here I was not only retaining one for the real estate closing but listening to her counsel. It seemed even real estate transactions were more complicated in New York than elsewhere. I interviewed three lawyers, but when I met Ziporah, a compact powerhouse of a woman, slightly younger than me, I knew she was the one, and my reticence disappeared.

"I box," Ziporah said when I remarked on the amazing ripples in her arms. After our initial conversation, I sensed her real power came from within. She'd survived her husband's untimely death and was working and raising children on her own.

And then there was the matter of another coincidental trifecta. Our daughters had attended middle school together, a member of her family had once worked with my ex, and a female priest who had trained at my church had retained Ziporah to handle her house closing. Over eight million people reside in New York City. But these intersections happened often, so in many ways I found New York to be a small town.

How fortunate to have Ziporah in my corner of the ring—only there was no cause for duking it out. Contract negotiations proceeded smoothly and swiftly. Before signing on the dotted line, I forsook my fantasy of continuing to live under the same roof.

In the moment I stood in Ziporah's office signing the contract of sale, I realized leaving wasn't the far-off proposition it had once been, a prospect so unreal the likelihood had been hard to imagine. I would definitely be vacating my house forever and venturing out into the universe alone, with a blank slate, for the first time in over thirty years. Up until then I had been working toward the goals of preparing the house for sale and then finding a buyer. From that point forward, my reference point was about to drastically shift. The goal I would follow—the goal that would direct my path—would be the one to leave.

So many things remained to be accomplished. So many things could go wrong before my property transferred hands. Pat's first deal had fallen through, and she and I had experienced many similar ordeals, so I couldn't help but wonder if my deal would track hers. But I never had serious doubts that my deal wouldn't happen. Not after reading that letter from the buyers.

Worry had started to drop away, and I wasn't all that concerned when the termite inspector showed up. Even though, in addition to squirrels and bird mites, I'd had termite troubles in my previous co-op. Neighbors told me not to worry about the current inspection—recent inspections on the block had sailed through. And sure enough the inspector declared my house termite-free. Whatever critter karma I'd experienced for decades apparently had burned itself off.

The general inspection proceeded like clockwork too. The inspector noted obvious repairs and upgrades, but nothing major, and otherwise pronounced my house suitable for sale.

"It's a solid house," Mona said she overheard him say. A sturdy solid house built for occupancy by strong—brave—people. Hearing his words I felt proud to have been a part of its history.

The bank appraisal, the owners' creditworthiness, the survey, all ensued without a hitch. So many appraisals occurred in the house while I lived there. Appraisals to refinance while my ex-husband and I were together, appraisals during the divorce litigation, an appraisal for my own mortgage, and another for my failed attempt at refinancing. The bad appraisal karma no longer presaged doom and gloom either, and the buyer's bank gave my house and the buyers its seal of approval.

While this was happening, I'd been trying to reach Laura, my best friend from law school, who was battling breast cancer. I'd seen her the previous winter when she'd come to New York for treatment. We had talked in July, after she recovered from a collapsed lung. Since then, she hadn't picked up her cell phone when I called or returned any of my emails, although she'd told me in July she was feeling better. When I phoned her house, there was no answer either.

After I returned from taking Ella to college, Laura's name kept pressing on my consciousness more and more. I sat in church one Sunday morning unable to concentrate as Laura's name pounded in my head. A few days later she died. Her family finally answered their home phone; they had been unable to reach me on mine because I had disconnected it the month before.

As soon as I heard Laura was gone, I remembered she'd given me those French onion soup crocks, when I was in my twenties. Somehow I knew that in opening my cabinets I would now notice their absence and thus remember Laura all the more.

I have never known anyone quite so fearless and committed to justice. Laura juggled a marriage, a house, and three children, and flew around the world reacquiring assets and money that had been laundered due to international crime. One night during law school we were walking back to Laura's car after dinner when Laura, who was under five feet tall, took off down the sidewalk, running at top speed. It took me a moment to grasp she had dashed off, but I caught a glimpse of a tall male Laura seemed to be in pursuit of. It was late, and not a safe area of Washington, D.C., to be in after dark. I had yet to have the first of my six knee operations, although my knees were already weak from a major car wreck when I was eighteen. I felt that if I lost sight of Laura I might next see her lying on the sidewalk. I hobbled after her as fast as I could, sobbing when Laura's shadow turned the left-hand corner at the end of the block and disappeared. As I neared the middle of the block, I saw her shadow walking back toward me, swinging the purse the snatcher had taken. The closer Laura got to catching up with the guy the more he realized he was not going to win and dropped her purse in the street. Righting wrongs was instinctive to her and in equal measure, kindness. Laura is the only person I can think of that I can't recall uttering an unkind word about anyone. Of all people she was gone. It was sad, tragic, and unfair, and had happened for no good, damned reason.

"Write your book," Laura said the last time we spoke in person. "And I'll throw your book party in D.C.," she said, refusing to succumb to despair. As she spoke, I thought of all the times I had wallowed in it.

And then her words, "I'm just so worried about you losing your home." Now Laura was no longer around to worry about me. But she no longer needed to.

By the time I returned to Brooklyn after attending Laura's wake, I had less than six weeks to purge, pack up, and find a place to live. Somehow I knew I would.

25

Countdown

With less than two months to go, the real task of hauling out began. The fate I assigned to my possessions—sell, toss, donate, or keep— was more sure-handed this go-round as intuition guided me from one item to the next, answers sifting of their own accord. Similar to the way priorities instantly reordered themselves after my children were born.

I'd go to sleep at night and visualize the tasks to tackle, then walk myself through them in rapid succession the next day. I began again in the kitchen. *She won't be back, ever,* I thought, tossing out an opened box of Ella's cookies, uneasy as I felt a tad complicit in somehow erasing her. *Stop the silliness,* I reminded myself.

It was the first time I had lived alone since those initial few months on my own in New York City before getting married. I'd been by myself during retreats, and when the kids were with their father. But this was different, the aloneness never so thick.

The house was now a mess again, and piles grew before they receded. I zigzagged around, scattering bits of progress all over as I hauled out. Astounded I still had so much. The middle drawer of my desk held hundreds of loose paper clips in various shapes, sizes, and colors. Where had they come from? Why so many more than I could ever use?

The world is too much with us, Wordsworth's words continued coming to me. The churning round and round, depleting the scarce time left while complaining about never having enough. The false sense of security and abundance we construct with stuff, propelled by fear.

I filled a stationery box with enough paper clips and rubber bands and discarded the rest. Literally harnessing time for the future and admiring the efforts of my labor as the results coalesced. Boxes—taped, labeled and ready for moving—accumulated. I numbered each one with a felt tip marker and made a note of their contents for my master list so I'd know where to find things later on.

Momentum pulled me along as I held objects in my hands, or stared at them, sometimes for no more than a few seconds, while I assessed their fate. A human Geiger counter playing the childhood game Hot and Cold. Do I need this? Is it interchangeable with that? Is it more costly to move and store than replace? Is it replaceable and do I care? Will it keep me stuck in the past or escort me peacefully into the future?

From time to time a slight uneasiness registered. I was avoiding a few things—the engagement ring my ex-husband gave me that had once been his mother's, my wedding gown, our mask collection. The answers about what to do with them had not come. I had the ring appraised, and it was only worth a few hundred dollars, but I couldn't release it. I brought the ring to brunch one day with Nicki. I don't know why I hadn't thought of it before. Nicki said yes right away, eager when I asked if she'd like to have the ring belonging to the deceased grandmother she had never met.

Moving estimates were high, so I continued packing on my own, calling on friends for assistance. Every few days I made another run to U-Haul for more supplies. I downsized at least three-quarters of my stuff or about 27,000 pounds, according to estimates from movers. Much more if you counted heavy-duty items in the cartage! All of it gone.

"So what's your new address?" the movers asked.

"I don't have one," I said.

"So where are we moving your stuff to?"

"I don't know," I said, sensing restrained, though polite, agitation. "Just give me an estimate within the City. And maybe one to Maryland?"—I'd grown up there. "And another to Delaware"—a sorority sister said maybe I should consider the beach. "And another to Savannah"—I'd been there on vacation several times. I wanted to have options floating around in my head.

"And another just to put it into storage and a price for storage too," I added.

"Storage for how long?"

"I have no idea," I said. The one thing I did know is wherever I ended up it would not involve shoveling snow.

I listed furniture for sale on Craigslist and a few other websites. Most people bargained me down, but that was okay. I met people from all walks of life. A lawyer who had once been an actor, an artist, a couple expecting their first child, a woman with her own television talk show. A textile designer from Arkansas now living in Yonkers because she couldn't afford New York City said she was going to reupholster my bar stools. June, an Asian man who I had assumed by email was a woman, bought the foyer table for use as a nightstand. I could barely lift it, but he picked it up and carried it from the second floor to the first and then out the door and down the stoop to his car waiting below in one fluid motion. About a dozen people wanted the Djembe drum and kept emailing to find out its availability. Strangers walked in and out of my house. We conversed about their lives and mine while standing on my stoop or in the foyer.

"Where are you moving to?" people asked.

"I'm not sure," I said.

"Wow, that's so exciting!" they said.

In the throes of shrinking my possessions, the world kept opening up.

One day the owner of a neighborhood vintage shop stopped by to look at some items.

"And what about this library card catalogue?" I asked, steering him into the kitchen. Pat told me she'd sold hers to pay for groceries. The closest I'd come to selling mine was to a woman online who bargained me down and then kept stalling. *Can you take more photos?* (I'd already sent three.) *My van fell through so can you deliver it to Long Island?* I finally told her it was no longer for sale, remembering what I had learned about drawing lines.

"I love it," David said when I offered it to him. "But I don't have room in the store now."

"How about fifty bucks?" I asked.

"Done," he said. At that point I was practically—and in fact literally—giving stuff away. The lift I got at the end whenever I said yes to someone who wasn't taking advantage of me was so satisfying.

My friend and longtime writing partner, Ethel, spent several days helping me fill dish packs with stemware and china. I'd forgotten about the Christmas ornaments in the cellar so I brought them up and she helped me wrap and sort through those too, marveling at my decorations. "Fascinating" and "just beautiful," she'd say while holding them up, especially the angel we placed on the treetop.

"Now I know what WASP Christmas is like," she said, laughing. Ethel was Jewish and had never celebrated Christmas. But she loved my baubles.

"Look at all these pretty linens I folded," Sandra said, when she lifted the sheets and towels down from the linen closet and into boxes, linens it seemed she'd just organized.

"And I remember putting these books *on* the shelves!" Sandra added, as we took books off and loaded them into boxes. We got punch-drunk, laughing at the foolishness of the undoing of what it seemed we'd just finished.

"My friends asked me what I was doing this weekend," Dirk said one Saturday afternoon when he came by. We were standing in my bedroom where we spent the next three and a half hours bubble-wrapping a long, odd-shaped mirror, then constructing a cardboard box around it because I couldn't find one big enough.

"I told my friends I was Beverly's bitch for the weekend."

I cracked up. I'd encouraged Dirk to write. His stories of the random people he met and observed in New York kept me in stitches. When we finished with the mirror, we packed up more artwork downstairs, then scouted about the house, yanking nails and molly bolts out of walls, some buried so deep Dirk had a hard time pulling them out.

Holding it back would cost me later so I allowed myself to cry. Sometimes the tears simply erupted, like the day I was walking up the second-floor staircase and thought, *What's going to become of me?* Whenever I told myself, *not now,* however, and pushed the tears back down, sure enough I'd soon be doubled over with abdominal pain.

"You're trying to digest so much emotionally. That's why your stomach hurts," my doctor said. A top to bottom detox, pulling up deep dark roots.

The month before I closed on the house my ex stopped paying court-ordered child support altogether.

"How can he get away with it?" friends asked. He wouldn't answer me when I demanded an explanation. He said he'd heard I was leaving New York. From whom? That was news to me. I'd made no long-term plans and hadn't even closed on the house or moved. Our parenting agreement had restricted me from taking the children out of New York City without the court's permission, tethering the children to New York. I had obeyed the agreement. But Nicki was already living on her own; Ella was going to college. The agreement specified no such restrictions on me.

And my options? Start depleting my house proceeds back in family court, where I didn't feel protected, with family courts becoming notorious nationwide for their many injustices? I would not allow myself to get distraught again after I'd done so much hard work healing and distancing myself from the poisons of my past.

Years before I had told Anders about a recurring dream I'd been having after the divorce started. "It's a dream where I'm struggling to grab onto Jake's hand. And no matter how hard I strain I can't latch on," I told Anders. "When I finally do, Jake whirls me around and around until I'm dizzy. And then let's go."

"Stop reaching for Jake's hand," Anders said.

217

I'd refused to take it several times over the ensuing years, but at times the old habits pulled me back. But not now.

To the finish I uncovered more of my ex's things. By then it no longer surprised me. In the cellar, behind the Christmas tree ornaments, I found a slideshow my ex-husband's groomsmen had made for his bachelor party. He'd thrown me in the garbage but wanted the slideshow from his bachelor party that was a prelude to our wedding? Go figure! I no longer cared to figure.

My church friend Charlie said he bet my ex was the one who couldn't accept the split. Hard for me to believe under any stretch of my imagination. But Jake had surprised me before. Many times, about many things. I'd made great progress healing though because the need to know why no longer tormented or interested me.

Still I felt peculiar splitting up our collections. The wedding gifts, the Art Deco furniture, the masks. Jake had disassembled the family and now I was disassembling our home, our nest. Except for the family photograph albums, deconstructing all evidence of our union and family, this time the orchestrator of it myself.

"I'm horrified by divorce," Charlie said, holding up his paper napkin at dinner one night, tearing it in two. "It's a cutting, only you can't really tear marriage asunder particularly when you have children. So there's this constant agitation over what can't be done." Charlie's explanation captured the oddness I'd felt, performing a seemingly unnatural and impossible act. And yet I had no doubt disassembly was required, essential even to my future.

Charlie said there was power in the assemblage too. I saw that. The shapes, lines, colors, intersections, ordering, and compositions of items, imbued with deep meanings and associations imputed upon the entire assemblage, thus giving it power too. This entire collection now dismantled, stripped of the last trace of power, and dispersed by me, the memory keeper, as Pat had called me.

Ella wanted a few of the masks; I kept two for myself, one the least valuable monetarily, a paper-mache folk art mask Nicki had made in middle school. Ethel had admired the collection so I asked her to choose one. I left the leather mask from Venice on the stoop one evening and donated the rest to the annual church auction.

Dirk helped me load the car with things for the upcoming church rummage sale. Other parishioners carried furniture and other items down the street to the fellowship hall to await the auction—the grand dining room table and four chairs, my Art Deco cherry leather couch with black lacquer arms and two matching chairs, an Art Deco torchiere, a flawless Steuben bowl, a limited edition lithograph my ex and I had gotten as a wedding present, a gilt-framed still life my ex-husband had an artist paint for me one Christmas. I'd always wanted my own Cezanne.

Right before my church friends carried off the chrome Art Deco sling chair from my bedroom I plopped down in it one last time. It was so comfortable I wondered why I hadn't relaxed in it for years. I was about to say I'd decided to keep it when Mandy from church walked in with Jack and said, "And look at the beautiful lines of this chair Beverly is donating!" I smiled, got up, and let them slide it out from under me.

Hard to believe that more than a decade before I'd been so scared of my husband walking off with our things I instantly followed my attorney's instructions to take inventory before the children and I went away for the weekend. Parting with things I'd held onto so tightly now felt so freeing, my longing evaporating as I let them go.

Each night I placed more and more goodies on the stoop. Vases, jewelry, throw pillows, Christmas ornaments, crystal pitchers, cameras. Each morning I hurried downstairs to look out the front door, even before making coffee. All the things I'd laid out the night before would be gone, and I'd smile on my way to the kitchen.

"Surely, you're not leaving that magnificent chandelier in the foyer for the new owners, are you? And those matching Art Deco designer fixtures in the parlor?" And on and on, friends aghast when I said yes I was, including leaving the lavender crystal chandelier with tear-shaped dewdrops that was the crown jewel of our home and had once graced a stately home in Louisiana. But the more I let go of, the lighter I felt.

These things had no inherent value, only the financial value placed on them by the world and the emotional value I'd once infused them with, thereby allowing them to weigh me down or lift me up. But even the lifts were short-lived. When you reach the point where it doesn't matter whether you keep something or let it go, that's the place of perfect balance, of inner peace. And then it doesn't matter what you do.

As floor space opened up around me, I began to imagine the space for a new future, my reference points continuing to drop one by one.

26

Reclamation

The closing date shifted back and forth. Meanwhile, I packed. It was October.

As I continued to wade through my belongings, it was as if I had left Hansel and Gretel-like crumbs for myself, trailing from girlhood on up. The accomplished woman side by side with the small-town girl.

In one box, I found my sorority paddle and a certificate from Outstanding Teenagers of America. Programs from the Kennedy Center. A Hawaiian newspaper account of Hurricane Iwa that Jake and I had survived. A 1973 Texas license plate—where had that come from! A bumper sticker from "South of the Border" where we'd stopped during a family road trip to Florida when I was a child. Results of the office football pool I'd won. And my eleventh grade report card, all As except for one B and five black marks for being tardy. Even today I brush up against the clock.

All along I had this sense that at the conclusion of my weeding out, when I'd peeled away the layers, a grand epiphany of sorts would occur. And there I'd stand, surrounded by a warm glow, a blueprint in hand for whatever came next.

In *The Silent Life,* Thomas Merton wrote that "if man is constantly exiled from his own home, locked out of his own spiritual solitude, he ceases to be a true person…He becomes a kind of automaton…no longer moved from within, but only from outside himself."

This disconnection from myself is what I had sensed in my early forties, while married. Adrift while stressors kept popping up. Panic attacks in the middle of a relaxing meal with friends or while out shopping. Arguments with my husband. Biting back tears as I traveled for work, hailed airport cabs, and counted the hours until I could return home to be with my children. Was this a midlife crisis? I didn't know; I'd never had one before.

But one day it culminated in the thought: *I am living a reactive life.* The bolt was so strong I can still witness myself in the spot where it occurred after I returned home from the bagel shop, coming in the front door and setting my parcels down on the bench in the foyer where I removed my shoes.

After that, the more I drew within, the more settled inside I began to feel. By then I was at home full-time with the children. I had started writing, taking meditation classes, and had returned to church. At the same time the distance seemed to grow between me and my husband, a wedge that grew the closer I drew to what felt life-affirming for me. I didn't pinpoint the gap widening then, but after my husband left I'd wondered, given the proximity between the return to my spiritual life and the end of my marriage. As I returned to myself, I definitely felt more distant from him.

And yet, shortly before I discovered Jake was having an affair, I'd felt the most lighthearted I had in years. It was a hectic fall, but we seemed to be managing better than ever, flourishing even. I'd gotten through my fourth knee surgery and had surprised myself the night I came home from the hospital and walked up two flights of stairs to bed. Within a few days, I relied on meditation alone to tolerate the pain. My husband had a new job, the best one ever, and said he felt he was finally getting the recognition he deserved. The kids were off to a fine beginning at school, and then my husband suggested Ella go to camp and we have a second honeymoon. Was this optimistic woman the real me?

And then my life blew to smithereens. My husband left, and I spent the ensuing decade clawing my way out of the wreckage.

Silence proved essential at times, though I initially cursed it: Divorce stole my children for weekends and holidays at Dad's. I'd violated no laws, but the most precious thing to me had been stolen away, time with my children. Silence was the last thing I wanted to hear, being silenced the last thing I wanted to endure. And yet in solitude I could hear myself think. Again and again, I plummeted to the bottom of the well, anchoring myself at the depth of my soul, searching for my voice.

"[People] need enough silence and solitude in their lives to enable the deep inner voice of their own true self to be heard at least occasionally," Thomas Merton said.

When I started the process of selling my house, I'd been counting down the months. Now I was down to days, with less than two weeks before the closing. Nevertheless I hopped in the car and headed off to my sorority reunion at a sister's house several hundred miles away. I'd hemmed and hawed about attending, weighing pros and cons, until I surrendered.

Two years before we'd had our first reunion in thirty years, with sisters flying in from all over the country, dozens of us, many of whom hadn't seen each other since college. But it was effortless to be together again. This bond I'd forged as a teenager lasting far longer than the one I'd fashioned with my own husband. It should have been the other way around. I felt more myself in a roomful of women I hadn't seen in decades. So what had my teenage self known that the grown-up me had repressed?

Mothers, lawyers, one judge, women who ran their own businesses, stay-at-home moms, far-flung geographically. Was our ease at being together after so long an indication we hadn't changed at our core? And that our young selves were closer to that center?

Maybe if we'd continued living in the same place after college, then mixed and mingled as couples and families, the atmosphere would have been different. Perhaps we'd be wearing one of our adult facades. Perhaps our reunion provided the safety that allowed us to separate from our other lives and be our true selves.

The weekend before the reunion one sister posted our pledge formal photo online. She said nothing had ever divided us, and she trusted each of us with her life. I cried when I read her message. That word, trust, it was huge. It hit me hard. I'd struggled with it for so long and maybe always would. Sure, I'd had breakups with friends and boyfriends. A slew of disappointments. A few backstabbers here and there at work. But nothing had ever rocked my faith in humanity the way my husband's desertion had.

"Come on up here and sing, Willett," one of my sorority sisters said, handing me the mic to the karaoke machine. I sang my heart out, like the youngster in me had on stage at the county fair talent show. And the girl singing hymns at her grandmother's piano. The mother driving her children home from the first Thanksgiving without Dad, singing those words on the CD with her children about when you're down and in trouble. And the woman holding the liner notes from the song *House* while looking out the bedroom window at the tree in front of the stoop to the house she was about to leave. The same full-grown self, too, who sat on the basement floor of her friend Maggie's house that first New Year's, belting her way to the final note of Gloria Gaynor's "I Will Survive." And somehow she had. I had.

After I returned home from the reunion, I scooped up the two boxes I'd slung in the trunk of my car after a visit to my mom's in Maryland and brought them inside. They'd been in my mom's attic for decades, then sat in my car for another three years. Before I opened them, Quinnie dropped by to help me sort through my clothes.

"So where do you want to start, hon?" she asked, plopping down on my bed. I'd dropped off many bags of clothing at the Salvation Army, but still had clothes ranging from size 6 to 14 with no clue where I'd end up. Hippy chick or professional? Wearing leggings and tunics bought in the junior department, a jumpsuit, or a caftan? And yet the eclectic looks I'd cultivated suited me.

"I feel like I still have too much," I told Quinnie.

"It's okay, hon," she said. "Have fun with it, as long as you know you could just as easily get rid of it." And by now I could: What remained no longer felt sticky.

I pulled out pajamas, socks, and underwear and laid them on my bed. Then scarves, tops, and hats and gloves.

"I like these," Quinnie said, holding up a pair of off-white hipster briefs with lace I'd bought a size ago. We discussed the merits of granny panties vs. thigh highs, bikinis, and thongs. Two middle-aged postmenopausal bosom buddies examining a decade's worth of bras and panties, gabbing about intimacy and the ways our bodies had failed us and would.

Quinnie folded each of my selections, like they were gold. I'd never folded underwear in my life—throw it in the washer, toss it in the dryer, then fling it in the drawer was my method.

"You gonna get rid of this, hon?" Quinnie asked, trying on a black fur-rimmed hat I'd placed in the donation pile and tying it under her chin. She resembled a schoolgirl—one I wish I'd known—and I snapped her picture.

"No snow shoveling for me!" I said, giggling with Quinnie.

"If you're sure you're gonna get rid of this, maybe I'll take it. It'll keep me warm this winter," she said. I was content knowing it would.

"I had this dream the other night," I said. "My ex wanted to date me again. And I was listening to him and wasn't saying no. Only I wasn't excited either. And then I woke up at five thirty and shouted, 'But I don't want to date you anymore!'"

"That is huge, honey," Quinnie said. "I'm so proud of you."

"I'm so tired," I said. "I keep waking up early."

"Well how in heaven's name can you sleep like this, hon?" Quinnie asked, pointing to the suitcases, boxes, and clothes strewn about my bedroom. "You need to keep a peaceful mind, girl, so let me help you move this stuff to the other room."

Her ministrations reminded me of another occasion, more than a decade before, when she'd prepared another place for me to rest, soon after I'd learned about Jake's affair. I was about to leave for a Friday night meditation, or at least that's where I told my husband I was going. He was watching Ella while I first drove Nicki to a party at school. But I never made it to class. I couldn't bear talking with anyone. If it hadn't been for Quinnie, I'd probably have turned up the heat and sat in the car for two hours while I waited for Nicki, rather than going home. Quinnie's Brooklyn home hadn't sold yet, but she'd already moved to Manhattan, so her house was empty. One night, a few weeks before, Quinnie had pressed a key to it into my palm and told me to keep it in case I ever needed a safe place to go. I hadn't known what to think. But somehow Quinnie knew a night like that would come.

When I opened the door to her house a wave of peace I hadn't felt in months permeated the night air. I closed the door behind me, pressed the light switch on the right-hand wall where I knew to find it, and walked down the hallway to the back room. There, in the dark, Quinnie had prepared a place for me to rest.

The bed in the back room faced a shrine, a table covered with a simple cloth upon which Quinnie had placed a Buddha statue, one candle, a pack of matches, and a note: "Enjoy the bed! Light candle. Exhale your anger, fears, and doubts out. XO, Quinnie." I lit the candle, prayed, ate the sandwich I had stuffed in my purse, and wrapped myself in the thick white down comforter. If only I could stay in Quinnie's house forever and disappear, I thought, not wanting to be found. Except for Quinnie, no one would have known where to find me.

Two hours later, though, like the responsible girl I was, I wiped my tears, walked to my car, and drove to pick up Nicki.

The day after I had the dream about my ex, he stopped paying child support. I told Quinnie. I showed her some messages I'd gotten from him.

"They are meant to stab the heart. Don't read them anymore," she said. "They are not helpful to you and your future life." I grabbed Quinnie's hand. She and I had often held hands; it felt so natural.

"You are in great shape in the house, Bev. You have done so much and you can do the final push. Yes, it's hard, but you are so strong," she said. I smiled. "Don't follow the mind that rears its head to tell you negativity. I believe in you and your potential. I see Mother Tara, and she moves swiftly. You go see yourself now, moving to where you need to go."

I knew what she said was true, but I also allowed my failings to pull me down. It couldn't have been easy for my daughters living with a mother going through divorce, then menopause. Scared while trying to be brave. The stress boiling over sometimes, and torturing myself with guilt even though I'd imagined myself their protector in my heart. But I too deserved a chance to start over.

I plowed through the rest of my keepsakes from the trunk boxes, unearthing silly slang books from middle school, my Sunday School attendance pin, an "I Love You 4-Ever" card from my high school sweetheart. A couple of photos of me and Laura from the law school newspaper, Laura with her blond ponytail. A copy of *The Washington Post*, July 21, 1969, with the headline "The Eagle Has Landed." A program from the Country Music Hall of Fame. A "Women for Nixon Agnew" button I had no memory of whatsoever, except that my father had been a Nixon fan before Watergate, and that I had been a fan of my father.

I found one of my college recommendations from the County Treasurer I had worked for several summers. "It did me good to stand there and watch the public enjoying the splendid courteous treatment this fine girl extended to them," he wrote. A "fine girl" he said a second time, from a "fine happy home." When I reached that phrase I lost it. More than anything I had aspired to pass on that inheritance to my own two fine girls. Those three contiguous words a primary reason I'd fought my divorce. This, above all, was perhaps the hardest attachment to give up. I wondered if it were possible to become dehydrated from crying so much.

In the spring I'd come across clippings from sports columns I'd written for the county newspaper while in high school. Now I was deluged with them, including clips from the neighborhood column I'd also written about the comings and goings in my town, parties, births and deaths, marriages, birthdays. By today's standards, it was a trivial feature, but it demonstrated the sense of community connectedness I came of age with and the ideals that shaped my life.

Seems I'd been writing all my life too, first in a more journalistic vein, then transitioning into law. In-between I'd written an independent study paper in college, a mini-dissertation of sorts which I unearthed while cleaning out the cellar. There I also found brief upon legal brief, which I'd shredded. And those well-regarded treatises.

A couple of weeks after I returned to Brooklyn after dropping Ella off at college, I learned that one of my favorite writers—a woman I personally admired too—was reading from her latest book in the City one evening. There was no way I could imagine dragging myself into Manhattan on a hot subway car, even though I'd been wanting to meet the author for years.

Beverly, you have a car. Get in it, turn on the air-conditioner, and drive. Somehow I found myself following that voice, driving into Manhattan, finding a free parking spot on a busy street, half a block from the venue. After the reading, I waited to get my book signed. When I reached the front of the line, the woman looked at me and said: "You're Beverly, aren't you?" We were Facebook friends, but famous writers have thousands of friends.

I was floored. Moments before I'd been preparing myself to sound literary-like and intelligent, but now I had a mouthful of mush and stumbled my way to "yes," reminding her how she'd remarked on an article I'd once published.

"I know," she said. "And you've got a house in Brooklyn and a daughter who just went to college." By then it was a miracle I could form speech.

"I'm trying to let go, as I know you've had to in life," I said, fumbling. And yet maybe we're at our most authentic and vulnerable when we haven't prepared the words.

"Wonderful," she said.

I felt the line swelling behind me and did not want to take more than my share of time. So I wished her well and said thanks.

"I'll be following you," she said, as I turned to go. I ran to the car, got in, flicked on the air-conditioning, and slumped over the steering wheel and cried. The lingering undercurrent of despondency and exhaustion I'd been struggling against the closer I came to the house closing had burst.

Weeks later, as I neared the bottom of the second box from the trunk, another treasure emerged—my first writing rejection. I thought I'd found it during the cellar clean-out when I came across the dieting piece I'd written in my twenties. But my passion for writing had evidenced itself long before that.

I had no memory of this earlier occasion, but there it was in my hands, an envelope addressed to me with a letter inside returning a fiction story I'd written at thirteen. The letter from *Ingenue*, a magazine for teenage girls, read, "It is not right for us at this time."

Rejections typically hit me hard. But when I found that one, I was overjoyed.

And to think I hadn't known who I was when the evidence wasn't far away, encircling me, inside, waiting in my trunk even. I'd given others the power to make me doubt myself, succumbed to hiding myself at times. Worried so much about what others thought that I'd neglected to embrace what I thought of myself.

Strong, brave, hardworking. Fiercely loyal. Mother, memory keeper. Writer. Woman who had been loved and deserved to be. I was pleased with my bio.

In the end, I had my epiphany. I'd been searching for what had not been lost. I was who I had always been. What a relief at last to know it.

My teacher Anders had been right. I was a rebel. It is, after all, a divine act of rebellion to simply be yourself.

27

Homeless

People continued peppering me with the same question: *Where are you moving to?* Early on I fantasized about not moving anywhere. It started as a joke between me and my mother the first time she asked, my house not yet on the market, when I'd told her maybe I'd sit on a porch somewhere and drink lemonade.

We'd laughed because it was exactly the sort of thing Beverly wouldn't normally do. Yet somehow the idea took root in my mind.

So where are you moving to? I asked myself. What would it be like to have no fixed roots, no permanent address to designate on an intake form, no reference points?

At one time the prospect would have petrified me. Now the possibility had the opposite effect.

I toted up the reasons to exit New York. It wasn't hard. The cold, snow, expense. The traffic, sidewalk stroller slog, and parking nightmare. The cramped space I'd inevitably be living in, without sun. My ex lived in New York.

One morning, while I sat on the subway during rush hour, on the way to a temp job, the man standing in front of me leaned back to let other passengers off and stuck his butt firmly in my face. I pressed my body against my seat as hard and far back as possible. But the distance wasn't enough so I gently poked the man in his back.

"Don't worry," he said, not bothering to turn around, aware of his doings. "I took a shower today." He finally moved, and I opened my mouth to breathe while closing my eyes to concentrate and avoid getting nauseous.

It was epiphany time again.

Sure, I'd miss friends if I left New York. And Nicki. Members of my parish and sangha at the Buddhist center. Certain people I'd miss a lot. But support from friends had contributed to the strength enabling me to leave.

How wonderful, I imagined my teacher Anders saying when I told him of my decision. "How wonderful," he said when I did.

"I'm worried for you," Mom said. "I want to know my kids are okay before I leave this world." Mom was in her eighties, and I could imagine feeling the same way about my own children one day.

"I'm concerned about you being a vagabond," she added. I chuckled. In the strictest sense of the word, we're all vagabonds. It didn't sound half bad. Some of the greatest leaders in history were vagabonds. Perhaps down-and-out is what Mom meant. But that wasn't happening, far from it; selling the house would give me back some of the financial security I'd lost, providing a tidy nest egg for starting over. Nor am I a wilderness gal. I don't like tents or bugs. I prefer hot and cold running water and a warm bed with soft sheets. Still, I'm strong and brave in my own way.

In fact, that's what most people said: "Wow, you're so brave." Ella wrote that very word at seven to describe me, although it had taken me a long time to start embracing it. And yet I didn't feel this surge of overpowering bravery stepping out into uncertainty either. Letting go felt natural. No longer constrained by debilitating fear, I felt the least afraid I had since, I couldn't remember when. After all, what was there to be fearful of? And if I could be brave, well, anyone could be brave.

Months before Mom had concurred with my idea of sitting on a porch somewhere. Maybe because it had been mere whimsy on my part. An off-the-cuff remark about a situation wholly imaginary then.

Now, the future was real. And though my confidence had amplified over the summer, I'd only started dipping my toes into uncertainty. What would it be like to plunge in all the way? Leaving town might bring me even closer to myself.

Home, family, and marriage had operated as reference points for so long and each had fallen away or was about to. *Come visit!* out-of-town friends and Facebook friends I'd never met urged when they learned I was selling my house. As my reference points shrank, the world expanded. I'd been pulling up deep-seated roots and dealing with dreams that had been plucked from me, why immediately put a stake in the ground? Why not pause awhile? There was beauty in pauses, lulls, interludes. I'd experienced that before, if only for a short spell, but alone time was beckoning me again.

While I was at it, why not go for broke divesting myself of all reference points? Proximity to friends, neighborhood, church, meditation center, gym, dry cleaner, my favorite pizza joint. As I worked up my courage, I considered that my real friends, my true friends, would surface and remain, whether I stayed or not. So again, what did I have to be afraid of? And if more loss occurred, well, I was no stranger to loss.

Where are you moving to? It was of course the most rational and logical of questions for anyone to ask, despite the underlying assumption selling my house required me to decide then and there where I was going to settle next, sign a lease, commit. Mom was understandably concerned I had no concrete plans, though knowing me I wasn't sure why. A few others who registered alarm irked me. More than *where* they seemed to be asking *why*. That hit the familiar defensive nerve in me that lawyers and judges had primed so well, although the button wasn't as raw as it had once been. I did not want to provide reasons. *Is it your fear or mine?*

I wanted to toss back. Doesn't moving out of the shadow of your own fear tend to highlight the presence of it in others? Put the question back in their court? But that sounded confrontational, and I was invigorated, with no stomach for conflict. Somewhere in the mix I knew, too, there was genuine, even if misguided and unwarranted, concern.

Maybe I'd fought for too long to be myself—thinking I'd lost the opportunity—that I was fearful of slipping away again. I kept my response to a minimum, at least to certain folks. I wondered how I might distill my reply to its barest bones, stripped of explanation altogether. Even "because" was a reason.

My children were the only people to whom I owed anything more. But I couldn't live my life laser-focused on them, nor was it necessary. I'd raised them, and they were off. Their lives no longer required my physical proximity. Still, my daughters' opinions mattered and deserved the courtesy of a second thought. But Nicki and Ella both gave me a thumbs up.

"I'm so proud of you," Nicki said. "It's such an exciting thing to do. It's just what you should do."

"You'd probably fall back into the same old patterns if you stayed in New York right now," she added. "I'm so proud of you!" she said a second time, and it did my heart good to receive her endorsement. She seemed to understand me better than some of my girlfriends.

And how did I know that leaving town was the right move? Because it simply felt right, the way that honoring truth does.

I wasn't becoming homeless, not in the sense of today's use of the term. Far from it. With the sale of the house, I had means. I didn't feel lost either. To the contrary. But I wasn't afraid to let go of what I'd clung to without having the trappings of a new life laid out and some illusory golden ring to grab onto next.

Yet homeless is the word others used to describe my soon-to-be status. "You've decided to become homeless," people said. I shrugged.

Near the end of his life, while studying the ancient teachings of Shantideva, Thomas Merton wrote that true homelessness was something altogether different from how we've come to define it: "To be 'homeless' is to abandon one's attachment to a particular ego—and yet to care for one's own life (in the highest sense) in the service of others. A deep and beautiful idea."

Many years ago, right after my husband left, a friend gave me a card with a quote by a famous Sufi mystic and poet, Rumi. It said: "Try something different. Surrender." That's what I was trying to do.

Living without adequate shelter, of course, is a crushing hardship no person should ever endure. Everyone deserves a home. And Maslow had of course placed shelter at the bottom of his hierarchy of needs, without which progression to a better existence is often impossible. In that sense I was far from homeless. My house had provided stability when I needed it. A strong outer nest that allowed me to rebuild an inner one. Mothers know this from instinct. It's why I fought for our home.

In the United States alone, homelessness afflicts millions. In 2017, HUD's annual single night Point-in-Time tally showed more than 550,000 homeless people, an increase of the homeless population in America for the first time since 2010, including the number of homeless veterans. Single, adult, middle-aged, minority males are the most prevalent contingent. The leading causes cited are lack of affordable housing and unemployment, and after that, mental illness, substance abuse, prison reentry, domestic violence, and poverty.

After I left New York, I learned that during my final year there, the number of homeless individuals using the City's shelter system hit record numbers, including a record high for the amount of children needing access to shelter. The average length of shelter stay for singles and families was also the highest ever recorded.

When Nicki was a teen, she volunteered at a soup kitchen one evening. When she returned home, she said, without qualification, "That was the best night of my life." A fine girl from a fine home.

"Will you come back?" my friends asked.

"I can't know until I'm gone," I said. First, I wanted to observe my life from the vantage point of not home. A prism of not New York.

During my tenure, Brooklyn had become the writer's capital and unofficial hippest place on the planet. I decided to forgo it. I'd often done things backwards, or forward, depending on your thinking. When I first settled there, Manhattan was hot, not Brooklyn. I wore leather skirts to my law jobs while other women continued to wear man suits and silk blouses with bows tied around their necks. I'd studied Buddhism well before it became hot to meditate. My decisions weren't calculated to be trendy. I'd simply gone where intuition led, before divorce had me questioning my instincts.

Now I was leaving for the South, the Deep South, for Georgia. Savannah, Georgia, to be exact. After my marriage blew up, I told Anders I didn't trust my intuition anymore. Slowly though trust flowed back, and it pointed to Savannah, my instinct as natural now as it had once felt inaccessible.

I'd been to Savannah several times, a few instances alone and a couple of occasions with the children. I felt content there. The downtown was walkable, and the ocean wasn't far. Indeed, I couldn't imagine being landlocked. Inside the silence, when I closed my eyes, sand and a rocking chair and lemonade beckoned to me. Perhaps I'd travel and visit those friends and strangers who asked me to visit, but now I wanted to sit on a porch somewhere. Love myself into total well-being.

Quinnie mailed me a magazine article on the best places for older women to live in terms of weather, jobs, cost of living, and single men. I placed it in a folder for the future, not ready to contemplate permanency.

But I knew where to find a porch. I emailed a couple in Savannah from whom I'd rented an apartment, a floor in their house, during a previous trip. It had a porch overlooking a koi pond and was available for November and December. My hosts said not to worry if I decided to stay on; they'd help me find a place to land next. I trusted them to keep their word, imagine that. For now, I'd have a soft landing, a roof over my hand, and a place for Ella to come for Christmas.

I'd be lying if I said I didn't have to shut Frank Sinatra up occasionally. He crooned in the back of my head. *If you can't make it here, you won't*

235

make it anywhere, his mocking parody. As a New Yorker, Frank often climbs under your skin, bestowing or withholding his blessing. Doing his best to convince you that New York City is the only town capable of nourishment, with everywhere else second-best or worse. But Brooklyn no longer made me feel as hopeful as it once had, and that was no way to live. Leaving felt like one of the smartest decisions I'd ever made. I'd already made it once, even though my life had fallen apart. This time maybe I could do something even better. Maybe I could be happy too, no matter what the circumstances.

It's tougher to go AWOL than you might imagine. Perhaps if I was young without the trappings that come with age and family and planting roots or didn't have children or weren't a recovering responsible-to-the-extreme, vow-keeping perfectionist it would have been easier to ship off to Bali years before. Still, I cut my affairs to the bone, eager to leave town, even if it had taken me time to catch up.

I modified my bills to paperless settings and had other mail forwarded to a family member. I made sure my car was highway-worthy, coordinated the payment of taxes with my accountant, and opened a safe deposit box for valuables. I told Quinnie and another friend where I'd stored what remained of my possessions and legal files. I'd revoked my will so that only my children could touch my assets. I gave Quinnie the original document for safekeeping.

And then it was done, or would be, after hauling what remained to storage and signing the closing papers.

The price of freedom. I'd paid dearly for it. That phrase had been running through my head for months as I edged closer to what had once been a dream and, before that, my worst nightmare: Selling my house and leaving Brooklyn.

28

Moving Day

Roughly forty million Americans move each year, about 14 percent of the population. In 2013, I joined the exodus.

Instead of pricey corporate outfits, I hired Moving Man. It was a local move from my house to a storage facility in Queens. He'd been indispensable to me many times; I returned the favor.

John, aka Moving Man, and three of his workers, Jeremy, Kevin, and Jamal, came by two days beforehand to wrap furniture and other fragile pieces. They also carted boxes down from the third and second floors and up from the cellar, stacking as many as possible on the parlor floor to ease the procession on moving day. Except for Jamal, none of the men seemed particularly muscular. Yet, in the hands of pros the same boxes I had trouble scooting from one side of the room to the other appeared weightless, the men lifting them overhead and easily navigating the stairs.

Let go of control, I said to myself as I tried keeping up with them to make sure the boxes were on my master list and labeled. I had no idea how long my things would remain in storage so I segregated those I might need access to—additional clothes for me and Ella, some papers—for loading in the truck and storage unit last.

"You don't need to call me 'ma'am,'" I kept saying, most often to Kevin. "Call me 'Beverly.'"

"Yes, ma'am," Kevin said.

"You're so organized," he added. "I never saw anyone this organized. You pack your things so careful."

"You're calm too" Kevin repeated several times. "Most people are stressed out." He hadn't seen me a few days earlier, on Sunday morning, when John and Jeremy stopped by to pick up the overstuffed chair and ottoman someone had bought off Craigslist. The woman, well-spoken and well-dressed and in her early twenties, came by to inspect the chair more than a week before and said her friends would pick it up. But she kept stalling. She left my house before handing me a deposit too, and I forgot to ask.

"Do you want the chair or not?" I pressed, tracking her down by phone. She did, but had no movers, so I suggested Moving Man.

"You can pay me when they pick up the chair," I said.

On Sunday morning, John and Jeremy rang my doorbell precisely on schedule. Forty-five minutes later, no Tabitha. Meanwhile, John began constructing a box to house my glass table.

"You're not on my clock yet," I told him.

"It's a couple of minutes," John said, waving off my concerns. "It'll save me time later." I grabbed my phone and called Tabitha.

"Where are you?" I asked. Her voice told me I'd woken her up.

"Oh, I," she said floundering for words. "I got home late last night." As she spoke, I pictured her yawning and stretching.

"Just have the guy bring me the chair and I'll give him the money and he can pay you." What did she say? For fifty dollars Moving Man and I, and his helper, were supposed to be her servants for the day? John was supposed to make another half hour trip back from her place to mine to deliver the money? Was she reliable enough to pay John when he showed up?

"Get over here now!" I said.

"Oh, okay. Yes. Uh huh," I heard before hanging up, the woman stumbling toward speech, uncertain now whether she'd bother coming.

Forty-five minutes later, Tabitha rang my doorbell. As she stepped into the foyer, she opened her purse and pulled out her checkbook and pen, poised to write.

"Who should I make the check out to?" she asked, looking up at me.

I took her gently by the shoulders and swiveled her to face the door.

"I never said anything about a check. Cash," I said, giving her directions to the nearest ATM. "And get cash for Moving Man too." I could imagine her trying to hand John a check after he lugged the heavy chair across town and installed it in her apartment.

"Now go," I said, closing the door behind her.

John shook his head, unfazed.

When Tabitha returned, she handed me cash. I counted it to be sure. She'd given me one hundred dollars instead of fifty. I told her it was too much.

"Go for it," she said, staring at me, no hint of a smile, no articulation of an apology. If she'd behaved otherwise, I'd have given her the chair. I took the cash.

"We'll see you in a few days," John said, as he and Jeremy carried the chair outside.

Two days later, I laughed when Kevin remarked on my self-control. I had no compunction now about speaking up for myself, and perhaps I was projecting how calm I felt. Tabitha had irked me, but I hadn't lost my temper in a situation that cried out for me to lose it. With the other changes in my life, maybe I should also start giving myself credit.

"Some of my clients are crazy! But I like what I do," John said, finding an errant hair clip with a butterfly on it I'd forgotten to pack and fastening it to his thinning hair.

In the midst of this, people around me faced greater challenges. The same week Laura passed so had a woman I'd known from the Buddhist center. The chiropractor down the street who I'd gone to for my bad back also died. Another friend had stage three breast cancer. And my ex-husband's secretary had been diagnosed with spinal cancer. She'd been canned several years earlier and called to tell me how devastated and betrayed she felt too. I periodically sent her links to job opportunities, but nothing ever panned out. She was in her late sixties, had few family members, and none close by, wasn't married, and never had children.

"When I run out of money and can no longer afford my apartment in New York, I'm going to kill myself," she told me. I understood; I'd been there. But I'd turned the corner and tried to help her. I told her how talented she was and encouraged her to write, like she'd done early in her career. Over the last year she'd been in better spirits, before an abrupt cancer diagnosis.

I was about thirty when my mother had started calling me regularly with news of the latest funeral she'd attended. Now I was entering that phase in my own life.

"How long have you been working with John?" I asked Kevin.

"About five years," he said. "But I want to be a chef." His dream was to own a restaurant. He was already thirty. I told him how a decade—or two—could slip by.

"Is one of your guys free to help me tomorrow for a few hours?" I asked John as he was about to leave. I still had some fragile items to wrap and heavy clothes on hangers to lower into a wardrobe box. John said he'd send Jamal by in the morning.

"Will you take a check for today?" I asked in a sweet, high-pitched tone, winking as I handed John cash.

"Relax, doll," he said. "We've got you covered."

Around ten that night I climbed the stairs for bed.

"Will you have time to pack that up on Thursday morning?" I had asked Kevin and Jamal earlier that day when they began to disassemble my bed. Closing was set for the morning after Halloween and though I wouldn't be leaving the house until a few days after that, I wanted a bed to sleep in as long as possible. After Halloween, I'd be sleeping on the floor atop a cushion and sleeping bag until I left.

"Sure, no problem," they said. "Whatever you want." It went like that all day. Would there come a juncture when such simple displays of kindness would not elicit a lump in my throat?

I started crying the instant I stepped into my bedroom that night. The room was empty except for my bed. No dressers, nightstand, lamps, or books. Nothing on the walls. My bed looked forlorn. Even the rug in front of it had been rolled up and carted downstairs. It was scary, the jolt of austerity. I hadn't been ready for it. Was this how nuns and monks felt the first time they laid eyes on their new accommodations, realizing this is what they'd signed onto for life? I wandered how many ran for the hills. And how many stayed.

I nodded off and woke up the next morning sick as a dog. Diarrhea, nausea, fever, and chills: they hit me all at once. I could not afford to be sick, so I made coffee and talked myself out of it and somehow that worked. Jamal showed up around 11:00.

"Sorry I'm late," he said, when I answered the door. "My son's mother asked me if I could take him to school." Jamal was twenty-nine and had two children with two different women, neither of whom he had married. He said that one mother wouldn't allow him to see his nine-year-old daughter, but that he saw his son regularly and wanted to be an involved father.

Jamal helped me finish packing some boxes on the parlor floor, and then I headed to the kitchen, where John and his guys had placed a few plastic bins they'd brought up from the basement. I'd set them aside after the cartage cleanup, but hadn't opened them.

The day before Kevin had been thrilled with my offer of a video camera. I asked Jamal if he wanted the computer stand. I was taking the desk from upstairs but hadn't been able to sell the computer table. Jamal said he had no place for it so I asked him to carry it outside and place a "free" sign on it.

While he was gone, I opened the bins. Inside were the hospital blankets, outfits, bonnets, and booties I'd dressed Nicki and Ella in to bring them home from the hospital. Along with the standard issue white flannel blankets with pink and blue stripes each had been swaddled in moments after I gave birth. I'd carefully folded each item and wrapped it in white tissue paper and they looked brand-new. Underneath the clothes and blankets was the pair of nursery curtains on which I'd embroidered pink and green palm trees. The crib was gone, but I'd preserved all this for my daughters. One bin for Ella; the other for Nicki.

"You okay?" Jamal asked after he came back inside, seeing me crying in the kitchen.

He walked over, stood behind me, and started massaging my neck. It wasn't a come-on, instead, a great kindness. Another one. An hour before, he'd told me the story of his life. The abusive stepfather. His conclusion at fourteen that his only escape was to earn enough money to leave, selling drugs his avenue to funds. And then the wild car chase with cops in pursuit while he drove the luxury vehicle he'd purchased for which he had no driver's license. The high-speed chase ending in handcuffs and a seven-year jail sentence.

"I was so angry and causing fights so they threw me into solitary," Jamal said. "And it changed my life. I loved solitary. When they took me out, I picked another fight so I could go back." Finding his way back to himself in silence had become his way out.

"I used to be rich," Jamal said. "But I'm starting at the bottom again."

Later on I realized I'd spent the better part of a day alone in my house with an ex-con. I'd never thought twice about my safety. It was strange, this stage I was in, relying on instinct and trust.

The following morning I rose at six. John had another engagement so he sent his second-in-command, Malcolm. Malcolm arrived at nine with Jamal and Kevin. They parked in front of the house in the space Teddy and I had cordoned off with garbage cans. The men strode in and out of the house, their loading of the truck like a synchronized assembling of a puzzle. I slipped in beside them and took sandwich orders at lunchtime.

The truck was small and as it began to fill, it became apparent we'd have to make two trips to the storage facility in Queens. Midafternoon we made the first trip, the men in the truck and me in my car. I signed the lease for the storage unit; the woman at the desk was helpful, finding dollies. I was still the methodical, organized woman I'd been, making check marks on my packing list. But I also found myself laughing as we zoomed dollies down the hall.

When we arrived back in Brooklyn, school had let out and my neighborhood was a madhouse of trick-or-treaters. It was a balmy October day, and thousands of children and parents had poured onto the sidewalks and into the streets to begin the festivities that made Halloween one of the largest celebrations of the year. The parking spaces on my street were gone so Malcolm double parked around the corner. This extended the trek to load the truck with the men steering boxes around throngs of costumed youngsters.

"Boo!" a voice said, coming up behind me while I was walking up the stoop. I jumped and turned around. It was Jamal, wearing a hideous mask with red eyes and large white teeth. His gloves had fake blood stains. He'd bought a mask at the corner pharmacy for Kevin too, and they asked if they could hand out candy to the kids streaming up my stoop. I gave them bags I'd looked forward to distributing later that evening. But Jamal and Kevin were having so much fun there was no way I could deprive them of the pleasure.

Sometime after 6:15 I got behind the wheel of my car, and Malcolm bolted the door on the moving truck for our final trip. It had been an exhilarating day despite my worry that with rush hour, nightfall, and the drizzle that had started coming down, I couldn't see how we'd make it to Queens before the warehouse closed at seven. Once we arrived we had to unload the truck. One wrong turn or traffic gridlock and we'd be done for. Due to weight restrictions for trucks, Malcolm had to take a slightly longer route, as he had earlier in the day during our first trip. The plan was for me to lead the way and for us to keep in touch by phone.

I put on my driving glasses, squinted through the rain, and drove. *I'm not going to make it*, I said to myself. At intervals, my GPS updated later arrival times. And then, *I'm not perfect*, which was a huge admission for me. I still needed a plan B if we arrived after the facility closed. Could I leave everything in the truck overnight? Would my belongings be safe? Would Moving Man need the truck empty for a move the next day and were his men free to help me? The buyer was coming in the morning for a final walk-through, and I had the house to clean. Afterwards I was due at the closing. When did the storage facility open in the morning anyway? And how could I be in two places at once? No, three—I'd also have to go to the bank and get more cash for the additional moving costs. When did the bank open? I was attempting to stay on task while my mind leapt ahead to fix problems that hadn't yet occurred.

"I can't do this anymore," I said aloud. *Yes you can,* another voice announced. *Mother Tara can accomplish anything.*

And the next words out of my mouth, "God, please let me have your grace."

And that was it. In an instant the oxygen in the car changed. I felt myself sitting up taller in my seat. I dialed the storage facility while traffic stalled again, told them I was on my way, and pleaded with them to remain open. I said we'd unload super-fast. Every few minutes I redialed to make sure, but the man answering the phone continued to say he'd wait. The world was full of such kindness, the natural order of things. I needed to get used to it.

At 6:58 p.m. traffic halted again. Two minutes later I made a right turn, two blocks away from the storage facility. Malcolm arrived five or ten minutes later. Shortly after nine o'clock I stood with the guys on the deserted street, our work completed. Malcolm wrote out a bill; I handed him cash and generous tips.

Jamal opened his arms wide for a hug. Followed by Kevin, and then Malcolm.

"You're handling this so well," Kevin said.

"Start cooking," I said. I loved these men.

They waited to leave until I reached my car and drove off.

After I got home, I walked up and down each floor, staring at the void, assessing my cleaning tasks for the morning.

"Goodnight walls, goodnight doors, goodnight windows, goodnight stairs," I said, listening to the echoes throughout my house, nothing left to absorb the sound. I'd heard those same reverberations once before, in the summer of 2003. I'd called my husband at his nearby apartment after I'd gotten back from dropping the children off at camp. He was exiting Brooklyn for Manhattan and moving in with his girlfriend. I hadn't known that then and had been puzzled by the sound I heard in the background while he and I were on the phone. It was the same sound I heard in my house ten years later, the night before I sold it: The sound of empty rooms.

The first time I heard the sound it had been the echo of my husband's new life. The second time, it was the echo of mine.

29

Closing Day

I woke up, mopped floors, sprayed windows, and swished out tubs and toilets. I was a basket of nerves, but the final walk-through proceeded smoothly. After it was over, I caught a cab to the closing.

I arrived last, real estate agents, lawyers, the guy from the title insurance company, and Kenton and Colleen, the buyers, already seated when I got there. The buyers made a handsome pair, both in their thirties. I detected a whiff of the Irish in Colleen, like me.

"I have this for you," I said to them, passing a thick folder across the table. I'd gathered up appliance manuals, the warranty for the hot water heater, and take-out menus, and compiled a list of neighborhood resources and phone numbers. The couple thanked me. They said they'd lived in various places all over the world, and in New York, and had settled on my neighborhood as the ideal place to raise a family.

"Please feel free to stop by and see your house whenever you want," Colleen said. We traded Q&A about our children and then Colleen shared her news.

"We're expecting another baby," she said, glancing at Kenton. The conference table erupted in smiles. A new baby in my house. It was an auspicious omen.

"What's this other amount?" I asked Ziporah, as we went back to reviewing papers, pointing to another item on the closing statement that fell into the minus column. Ziporah whispered that it was the transfer tax imposed for the privilege of selling a house in New York.

Papers passed back and forth among the players. I sensed an urgency to escape.

"Where's the bathroom?" I asked. Ziporah followed me into the restroom, where I slammed my hand into the stall door. There was more purging to be done, and my pent-up emotions had welled up, so much to absorb. I blew my nose and wiped my face and asked Ziporah whether anyone would notice I'd been crying.

"No, you're good," she said. Was she lying? I craved her reassurance anyway.

"I feel like a fool. The buyers are so nice." Swallow, accept, repeat. My thoughts rattled out. Splitting myself into so many pieces for so long, I yearned with all my soul to be an integrated whole.

"You're good," Ziporah said again, grabbing my shoulders. "Life is going to be better for you now."

It was happening, real. And for the moment I had grasped hold of fear again.

Ziporah and I walked back to the conference room. "Where are you moving, by the way?" she asked.

"Nowhere for now. I'm taking whatever fits in my car and driving south."

"You're a rock star," Ziporah said, hugging me, her brown eyes sparkling. "Come on. Let's go get you some checks."

When the closing was over, I went straight to the bank. Afterwards I bought Champagne and wine and pastries from Monteleone's Bakery on Court Street. Mini cannolis and éclairs, fruit tarts, lemon and raspberry bars, a rum baba, and assorted chocolate treats. Later that night my girlfriends would be joining me at the house for a celebration. Like my husband, some of my girlfriends had abandoned me. Others had stayed, and new friends had also come into my life. The main course for the evening would be takeout from my favorite Thai restaurant on Smith Street.

At home, I draped a faded Provence-like tablecloth over a long folding table I planned on leaving for the buyers, set the table with paper plates, silverware, and wine glasses, and placed a large vanilla-scented candle in the middle.

Lola, the friend I'd gone to Florida with the morning the bathroom spigot came off in my hands, arrived on my doorstep from a Buddhist empowerment in Portugal. She'd asked whether she could crash with me for a few days before heading onto Los Angeles, where she now lived. I told her the only sleeping arrangement I could offer was a cushion beside me on the floor.

"Oh Bev-ee-la, a slumber party!" Lola squealed, eager to camp out. Actually, her presence was my good fortune. Years before, when Nicki and Ella were teens, Lola rang from the airport to say that her travel arrangements had fallen through. I invited her to sleep in the comfy extra bed in Ella's room for the next few days before going on to California. Before Lola arrived, Nicki and I were in the middle of a mother-daughter squabble. Minutes later, Lola descended like Athena in our midst, clearing the air as if the house had gotten a sage cleaning. She'd just spent four months in silence in a remote part of Scotland in the dead of winter. And although she hadn't said anything particularly profound, Lola glowed and her fairy dust rubbed off on each one of us after she walked through the door, enticing me to continue my own investigations into silence. I was eager to have her infectious good karma pervade my abode once more.

After Lola arrived, she helped me carry a hodgepodge of chairs in from the garden.

Quinnie hadn't completed her move back to New York so she wouldn't be there. But what a treat to have Lola and six more of my girlfriends ring my doorbell.

"Why don't we go around the table and tell how we met Beverly," someone suggested, I can't remember who. A few of my friends had met, but most hadn't. I hadn't traveled in a girl pack before; the thread connecting us ran through me.

Amy and I had been friends for twelve years, ever since our daughters bonded in first grade. Ruth and I met through our husbands, who had known each other before they married us.

Pat's son and Ella attended school together. "But mostly I've gotten to know Bev through her boxes," Pat said, laughing. She'd seen papers no one else at the table had.

"And I'm Bev's writing partner," Ethel chimed in. "We met in a writing class seven years ago."

"I have always found Beverly to be suspicious, too—I mean superstitious!" Ethel added, alluding to my proclivity to perceive signs. Ethel's observation received the heartiest laughter of the night.

"Well, Bevy and I met at the Buddhist Center," Lola said.

"And Bev and I met at the Episcopal Church!" Sandra added.

"And what about you?" someone asked Colletta, my friend from the neighborhood, who was from Italy, where she had also studied law.

"Beverly and I met in, what do you call it, a fulfillment house?" she said. People placed orders for holiday merchandise, and for a couple of months Colletta and I and our team of coworkers had processed them, from inputting the orders to packing boxes, affixing postage, and delivering the parcels to the loading dock. It was right after my divorce, and this was the only job I had found. I'd written about it for the "Lives" column of *The New York Times*. Except for a few articles, it was my first job after the divorce.

The labyrinth of paths that had brought us to my parlor from all over New York City, the U.S., and beyond, a medley of different faiths and backgrounds, all breaking bread together at the same card table in Brooklyn, fascinated me. Could this only happen in the City? I hoped not. The melting pot was one of the things I loved about New York most.

"I have to get something upstairs," I said, pushing my chair back from the table. I told my friends to look at the items I'd held back from the stoop as party favors and choose something to take home.

Upstairs, I grabbed a blue garment bag from Nicki's closet. Except for a few minor odds and ends I planned to leave on the stoop, it was the final item to dispose of. I'd come across it again and again while hauling out, stymied each time about its fate. The answer eventually came with the call of intuition I'd been learning to trust again.

I carried the bag downstairs, unzipped it, and asked my friends to gather on the floor in a circle.

"Ethel, can you grab the scissors from the countertop?" I asked.

I removed my wedding gown and fanned it out on the floor. It was magnificent, still snow white, a fitted bodice of lace and seed pearls with a low, rounded neckline, a full billowing skirt of soft lace and netting.

I had bought the dress the instant after I stepped into it. Once I'd been that certain about the groom.

My friends knelt with me on the floor, except for Sandra and Amy, who continued to stand on the sidelines, and Pat, who had headed toward the door. When I offered scissors, Sandra shook her head and folded her arms in front of her. Amy crossed her arms and took a step back.

"You don't want to help?" I asked, continuing to pass out scissors to the others.

"It's wrong," Amy said. Sandra was silent, but shook her head.

By then Pat had put on her jacket and grabbed her bag.

"You're wrong to cut the dress," she snapped, turning to face me. "And you're wrong to leave New York."

"Please don't go," I said.

"You're going to regret everything you're doing," Pat said, her pitch rising.

"I know what I'm doing," I said, starting to cry. "I've thought a lot about it." More reflection on this than probably anything else.

"It's a beautiful dress. You should donate it to some girl who can't afford one," Pat said, yelling by now. "That's what I did with mine."

"But I'm not you," I said. Not you, not my ex-husband, not my children.

"You're wrong," Pat repeated before storming out. But I knew my heart. I'd inspected it up and down, and there was further cleansing to be done. If I was making a mistake, it was mine to own.

Neither of my daughters wanted my wedding gown. I didn't ask why. Perhaps they wanted to choose their own dresses one day. Perhaps wearing it would remind them of the divorce, as I knew it would me, on occasions when the focus should be on them.

I didn't want the dress either, although I believed in marriage as much as I ever had. Maybe more. Not my marriage, of course. I had accepted that was over. Each time I assessed whether to donate the dress, however, I envisioned a hopeful yet unsuspecting woman walking down the aisle in my tainted gown. She wouldn't be the wiser, but I could not bear the thought of passing on a symbol of my failed marriage to a woman just starting hers.

Yet I couldn't toss my dress in the garbage either. That too felt wrong, cavalier. It would have been easy for me to donate the dress or leave it on the stoop. It was far tougher to face it down, to transform my act into an opportunity for growth. A full-blown declaration of independence. I knew cutting the dress was the wisest choice because it had been the toughest option to choose.

I'd told Ethel about my plan and had assumed my other friends would view the decision through my lens as well. The evening had flowed so fast, the year even, and I'd been on my feet most of the week. I hadn't stopped to consider what others might think. But my choice wasn't theirs to make.

Colletta walked me through my thoughts as I shared what had been stirring in my head.

"How do you feel?" she asked, drawing me back within the circle. Amy and Sandra looked on.

"I feel right doing this," I said, opening my scissors and making the first incision, starting at the hem. No grand high, no gloomy low. Just blissfully in the middle.

"And why do you need to do this?" she continued. While I spoke, other friends opened their scissors and began adding their own mark.

"Because I need to heal, to finish healing," I said. I'd been a fixer of so much for so long, turning my concerted attention to what was broken. Now the concentration had to be on me.

I smiled and cried all at the same time, certain of the massive restoration pouring through the pathway inside of me I'd pried open. I'd found the entry point, where it had started, at the beginning of my marriage, a fitting place to close up the wound and end the pain.

As my possessions dwindled, I had realized that my dress symbolized the final shield between the girl who stood at the altar and the one who existed before. I'd shed the bulk of what I owned in an attempt to resurrect that earlier girl, the hopeful one I began to rediscover while hauling out my house, petrified that she too, more than anything else, had disappeared.

Ten years before, I had reached for the phone one day and heard my high school friend Walt on the other line phoning from Iraq. During our conversation he had alluded to the possibility of this day.

"Oh my gosh, I can't believe it's you!" I'd said when I heard his voice. "What time is it there?"

"Night. We're eight hours ahead," he said. "So how are you?"

"I have court again tomorrow," I'd told him, filling him in on what had been happening.

"You're still giving your husband power over you."

"I know, but it's not easy," I said.

"My prediction is that one day you will rise from the ashes in glory like a beautiful phoenix," Walt said. In addition to my Good Fridays, Walt said he foresaw the coming of Easter too. I'd preserved those images in my head for a decade and was retrieving the power I'd given away. Rising from the ashes, letting go of loss itself, and celebrating my own Easter Sunday as I emerged toward my own rebirth.

"It's not about the dress," I said to my girlfriends. "And it's not about hate. This is about love. And forgiveness. And my way to move on." My slashing the dress a symbol of cutting the cord of my own attachment and depriving the gnarliest root tangled up inside of me of any more air. Symbols and rituals help us absorb and acknowledge the truth of our decisions and then seal them within our hearts.

The more I cut my dress the more the pain dissipated, the more I returned to myself, like a jar refilling itself with joy. A decade before, the day I'd come home from speaking with my meditation teacher, I'd envisaged a raging fire that consumed everything I owned. At the last minute, I'd stepped away, giving myself time to heal and to grieve and regain my balance. Now it was time to step forward into it. Buried within the symbol of what had once brought joy I had discovered the source of my pain.

"Your gesture was too strong for Pat to deal with," Colletta said to me the following summer. "But it was not about the dress; it was something deeper she saw inside of herself that night. Forgive her, but never question what you did." And I had forgiven, though Pat ignored my entreaties. So I let it go. She'd been a solid friend when I needed one. I wouldn't erase that. But I'd abandoned the role of fixer to become the maestro of my own life again.

Is it a sacrilege to destroy something sacred? I had asked myself that question and found no anger in my intention.

The most difficult and painful acts can produce the greatest beauty. In fact, I was scared the first time I gave birth. I didn't deal well with pain, though my mother said I'd have permanent amnesia once I held my child in my arms. I found it impossible to believe I'd forget the sensation of expelling another human from my own body and prayed for a Caesarian.

But I did forget. Right after my water broke with Nicki, Jake drove me straight to the hospital, where I begged for an epidural. *Ask for it before you need it,* my friends advised. Labor progressed slowly, before I rapidly dilated from three to ten centimeters. By then the effects of my epidural had worn off, and I cried for another one. It was too late. A nurse told me to start pushing. No matter how hard I bore down, Nicki refused to come out.

"One more push and we'll prep you for a Caesarian," my doctor said. Mad as a hornet to go through so much agony with nothing to show for it, I pushed with all my might and, with my next exhale, Nicki slid out.

It's like those events happened yesterday instead of decades ago, except for the pain, which had evaporated like my mother predicted. So a few years later I was eager to begin the process again with Ella.

But just as the joy of birth magically severs a mother's memory of her own distress, so too does the experience of being born erase the child's memory of its first scream. And what of life inside the womb, the growing child at first stretched and then compressed, utterly dependent, whatever the mother experiences or ingests filtering down into the fetus? That remembrance too is erased in the instant the mother's memory ceases. For both mother and child pain becomes the passage to the greatest gift of all: a precious new human life.

Ten years earlier, on Valentine's Day, a couple of months after my husband left, I'd applied my scissors to the sheer white nightgown he'd once given me, bowled over by grief.

That same year, I threw myself a heart mending party to cheer myself up. At the end of the evening, I stood at the front door and handed out party favors I'd created that afternoon—a handful of Hershey's kisses placed in the middle of a piece of netting from my bridal veil, tied up with a pink satin ribbon. My first baby step toward healing.

A decade later my wedding gown completed the cycle. A funeral followed by a resurrection. My period of mourning was over.

After my friends left, Lola and I crawled under the covers on the parlor floor and fell asleep. The next morning, I puzzled over the vestiges of my dress. My friends and I had cut part of the skirt and severed the bodice, but large ungainly pieces remained. It seemed a desecration to lump them with the garbage, mixed in with my coffee grounds, Thai food scraps, and pastry crumbs. So Lola and I transformed the skirt further, cutting it into hundreds of irregular shaped rectangles. The remnants filled a small white garbage bag as light as if it held no more than a puff of smoke.

I'd planned to roll up my Oriental rug and leave it on the sidewalk, but Lola convinced me to keep it, pointing out the expense of replace ment. Was I that attached to it anymore? Would it remind me of my marriage? No.

Lola helped me hoist the rug into the trunk of my car and off we went with it and my bag of netting and lace to the storage unit in Queens. Time would tell me what to do with them next.

30

Leap

Saturday night Lola and I attended the church auction, where so many of my possessions were on display. It had been less than two weeks since my church friends had carried them off. I'd lived with those belongings for decades and was amused at how unattached I felt. All sense of longing gone as if my things had belonged to someone else.

"Oh Bevy, you've got to see what I bid on!" Lola said, coming up behind me while I was browsing, giddy. I walked with her to a table where she pointed out a Whittall & Javits vintage hat, circa early 1980s, covered in white sequins and trimmed in soft wispy white fur.

"Isn't it beautiful?" Lola purred.

"Oh yes. And it used to be mine!" I said. We giggled. I'd worn it once with those fake lavender eyelashes. Lola's bid outstripped the others and at the end of the evening, I snapped a photo of her posing in the vestibule of the fellowship hall, the hat perched on the side of her head, her hands folded beneath her chin.

After Lola left for the airport the following morning, I cleaned house, then continued saying my goodbyes to Nicki and my neighbors.

Before I turned in, I placed the last items on the stoop—a single wine glass, the tablecloth from Friday night's celebration, a missed pepper grinder found at the back of the spice cabinet, and a few odds and ends my girlfriends hadn't selected at the party.

And then I wrote a letter to Kenton and Colleen.

"Dear Colleen and Kenton," I began. "When it came time to place my home on the market I wanted to leave it in good hands. When I read the letter that accompanied your offer, I cried. I knew you were the right family for my home and that I would be leaving it in good hands.

"Once this house was my dream house too," I continued. "It wasn't everything I imagined it would be, but there is an enormous amount of love and laughter baked into these walls."

Somehow I felt invested in the success of their family and marriage, and for them to fulfill the dreams for the house I hadn't been able to. I sealed the letter, closed my eyes, and prayed for them. And I prayed for my house. It too deserved a second chance, like me.

After I woke up Monday morning I made a beeline for the front door. The items I'd set out the night before had disappeared. I'd once likened myself to Hansel and Gretel; now I felt more akin to Johnny Appleseed, no longer lost, or frightened of becoming so.

I cleaned out the refrigerator, swept the floors, and took my final shower, bagging up the mildewed shower curtain, sheets, and pillows for the garbage. I had one final errand to run—to return the internet modem to the cable company. I walked down the stoop, but something drew me back, nearly making me trip. I'd caught the swirling hem of my dress in the door while locking it. I tugged at it softly, and the dress broke free.

Traffic on my side of the roadway was headed toward Sunset Park, deeper into Brooklyn. In the opposite lane, heavier traffic was bound for downtown Brooklyn and Manhattan. From a few blocks away, I spotted a truck with the letters MACK on its front grill barreling toward me, straddling the center line.

My mind returned to 2008.

"I'm going to run over you like a Mack truck," Jake's attorney said, opening the courtroom door for me. Trial was about to start and my attorney lagged several paces behind, out of earshot. My husband's lawyer obviously intended to unnerve me. And he had.

The truck sped toward me now. I assessed my escape route options; there weren't any. Cars were parked in the lane to my right, and there was no turn off before the truck would reach me. I considered stopping but worried about being rear-ended. In a small Jeep, I was no match for the truck hurtling toward me. If I focused my attention, might I slip between the truck on my left and cars on my right with an inch to spare? I couldn't see how but trusting in the near impossible seemed the sole possibility. So I galvanized my concentration and kept driving.

At the last second, the driver swerved and righted the truck back on its side of the center line, whizzing past me while I merrily motored on.

When I returned home, a parking spot waited nearby. I'd whittled stuff down to what would fit in the back seat and trunk of my car. Three suitcases, a few hanging bags, a bin with more of Ella's things, a plastic container of toiletries, a shopping bag of nonperishables, a plastic bin with writing supplies and tax papers, another filled with books, my computer, shoes, and a couple of purses. I mailed my printer to Georgia.

"You leaving, miss?" a man asked, pulling his car alongside mine.

"Not yet," I said.

Back inside I placed a bottle of Champagne inside the refrigerator for Colleen and Kenton. On the counter I set a metal tin of loose change leftover from coins my kids had once collected, along with a plastic container filled with duplicate keys to the house, all labeled and separated in plastic bags. Next to the bin of keys I laid the letter I'd written the night before. I admired the care and orderliness of my mind.

"The backyard is a perfect size to plant a few seeds in," the owners had written in their letter to me. In November, I couldn't find any seeds in Brooklyn, but in my letter I promised to send some once I arrived in the South.

While I waited for Colleen, I packed up the last few things into my briefcase, coming across the notes Madison and I had made when she and I had begun counting the stairs in the house. We hadn't finished. So I decided to.

I opened the kitchen door and counted off eleven steps from the deck down to the garden. Eleven more steps from the front stoop to the sidewalk, and then two more to the ground floor, below the wrought iron gate.

That left the spiral staircase that led from Ella's bedroom to the kitchen. While I walked down those stairs on the morning of my departure, I saw what Ella must have seen nearly eleven years to the day earlier on another November morning. I saw myself, Ella's mother, crying, broken. Like Ella, the woman Ella saw had also been frightened. But when my daughter asked me if everything was alright that day, I had lied. "I'm fine, honey," I'd said. Seconds before Ella appeared at the top of her stairs I'd been sitting at the kitchen table listening to love messages to her father from the girlfriend I didn't know he had. And in those few seconds, my life, Ella's, and Nicki's, had changed forever.

Fear exploded in my chest that day. And now an explosion of calm. In-between I'd accomplished what I'd set out to. To try and save my marriage, stand up for myself, and save the house, allowing my children to grow up there. I had collapsed decades' worth of stuff and sold my house to provide for my own next step in the world. Loss had miraculously brought unforeseen gain.

One, two, three. I counted off each step, all the way to step number sixteen, descending the stairs from Ella's room to the kitchen on a wave of tranquility. And then it was done, behind me.

The doorbell rang. It was Colleen come to collect the keys.

"I'll finish packing my car while you walk through and make sure everything's okay," I said. We both smiled. "And I also left you a few things in the kitchen."

"Thank you," Colleen said.

When I returned, Colleen stood in the kitchen holding my letter. She looked up, strode across the parlor floor, and hugged me.

"Be happy," I said before taking the one remaining key off my key ring and handing it to her. I always kept my car keys on the fob from the dealership and hadn't realized I would have no keys left on my ring once I handed the last house key to Colleen. A former boss had given me the key ring for Christmas close to thirty years before, a beautiful sterling silver loop in the shape of a heart. A heart charm containing my initials hung from it. I stared at the ring and then put my heart in my purse to carry with me wherever I went.

I said goodbye to Colleen, walked to the corner, and got in my car. And then I drove south where I had no home, no job, no family, no friends, and no plan. I had imagined that leaping into uncertainty would feel like the ziplining I'd done in Costa Rica years before, like floating or gliding in the air, only without the harness. My feet dangling with nothing beneath me. But that's not anything like how it felt.

Instead I sensed a definite foundation beneath me, deep and tangible. Strong and supportive, though not hard or rigid. An undercurrent of peace flowing below the surface.

Kierkegaard believed that all we go through in life has its end point at the crossroads of faith. To reach that juncture, we must shed the illusory armor we erect for self-protection. Only by leaping can we transcend anxiety.

I expected to be crying when I fired up the engine to leave Brooklyn. But my eyes were dry. The work I'd done not only led to this inevitable place, it would have been incomplete—and wasted—without it.

Fear and anxiety had overtaken me so many times in the past. I had wanted my life back so desperately that I'd held on more tightly than ever to what I had left after my marriage fell apart. I'd fought against the natural laws of change and acceptance. Once I anchored myself and regained my footing, however, though many years later, I began to declutter my house—and then my life—letting go of the loss holding me back. There was only one step more to continue moving forward and that was to leap.

And so, although I got the house, I let it go. Liberation had been a long time coming. But I was ready to begin, again.

Epilogue

Two months after I left Brooklyn, Ella came to Savannah for Christmas. As with Nicki before her, and my mother with me, I welcomed Ella back from college by leaving little presents in the middle of her bed—chocolate candy, hair ties, magazines.

As we sat down to breakfast one morning, Ella looked up at the gallery of needlepoint framed artwork on the wall next to the breakfast table in my vacation rental: ABC samplers, a couple of Santas, an angel, four skaters.

"What's this?" she asked.

"The owner's mom made them," I said. "And see the one that says 'Home'?"

Ella rolled her eyes.

"Now I suppose you're going to tell me that home is where the heart is," she said.

We laughed. I didn't need to.

~ ~ ~

AFTER CHRISTMAS, I SPENT EIGHT MONTHS hopping from one short-term furnished rental to the next with no more than the belongings I'd packed in the back seat and trunk of my car. Even that turned out to be far more than I used or needed. I sat on porches, rocked, and drank lemonade. I wrote, walked in the sand, and listened to the birds because I could finally hear them. The things I'd let go of eventually floated back to me—a new home, neighborhood, friends, church—and it was effortless. That room of my own in which to write appeared one day too, like Quinnie had predicted. I was happy and whenever I spoke to my mother, she said my voice had changed and she could hear the happiness in it.

I was still alone, single, and building a new career at midlife. The ceiling in the condo I moved into leaked. No one could replace Arman, but another fine handyman fixed it. New chairs and couch swapped places with each other several times. Nothing had changed that much—except for the shoveling of snow—and yet everything had.

Before moving into the condo, summer approached, and I wondered what to do after Ella returned from her first year at college. One night I asked my heart and it said: *I want to be with my daughter for the summer.* A teenage girl coming home from college, who had gone through what we had, needs her mother whether she thinks so or not. And sometimes her mother needs her.

I'd flown back to New York during the winter to celebrate Nicki's birthday and mine, and I longed to see her again too. But where would Ella and I live affordably in New York for the summer?

Point your heart in the right direction, pray, and there will be an opening. It may take years, maybe a lifetime. I trusted an answer would come. About a week later, Ethel called to say her friend had a one-bedroom inexpensive rent-controlled apartment smack dab in the middle of Greenwich Village available to sublet for the summer. "Do you want it?" Ethel asked.

Ella and Nicki and I had several Girls' Nights Out while I was in New York. One day I rode the subway to Brooklyn and walked around my old neighborhood. I passed by my house and when I looked up at it, I felt no longing. Not one tear to push back. Not even a few years later when I returned to visit my kids again, and Colleen and Kenton invited me in to see what they'd done with the place and to meet their new baby.

Teddy still lived next door, but by then Donna had died. My mother had passed away too. If I thought I'd faced loss before, losing my mother opened a fresh door of grief, yet another reference point gone. I cried harder than I ever had, but this time I did not lose my way.

By then the world had opened itself back up in my heart. I hoped no amount of loss would ever make me clude its embrace again.

At the end of the summer of 2014, Ella returned to college, and I drove back to Savannah. This time a moving truck followed me. Change your frame of reference, and your life will change. Mine had.

Despite what I'd gotten rid of, I would forever carry one thing with me. Wherever I went, I would take the strong, brave woman my seven-year-old had once seen, at a time when I could not recognize her, but needed her most.

THE END

Acknowledgments

So many people have contributed to this book, some assisting with its craft and publication, others supporting me in friendship.

Thanks first to my daughters who have given me more joy than I ever thought earthly possible. You have been my finest teachers. Being your mother has been my greatest honor. Thank you for your endless patience. I worship you, I truly do.

My deepest gratitude to my NYC writing partner, Lise Vogel, who has been by my side since 2007, reading each word, even after I settled in Savannah. I appreciate your steadfastness, advice, and careful and thoughtful edits. Our dinners in the early days of our writing were marvelous. Thank you for your enduring friendship.

To Sadie, who knows the inside of my soul. You have been with me every step of the way, during the worst suffering of my life. When I think of you, I see your face and hear your laughter. Thank you for never giving up your faith in me and for inspiring me to have faith in myself.

To Denise, Adele, Vicki, Lou, MJ, April, and Norman, my new Savannah family. When you lose so much in life, you don't expect everything to return, let alone sevenfold. I could never have seen this project through without your hugs, love, and cheerleading.

I am indebted to Susan Shapiro, Peter Trachtenberg, and Marian Landew, my early mentors and writing teachers, whose wise counsel has meant so much. Thank you for encouraging me to always dig deeper. Likewise, I am grateful to the many editors at newspapers and magazines it has been my pleasure to learn from. And to the readers who wrote to me—I think of you when I sit at the computer.

Thank you to Courtney Hargrave, Ann Hood, Jesse Kornbluth, Caroline Leavitt, and Melanie Bowden Simon for your blurbs. You are my literary rock stars. I'm lucky you sprinkled me with your fairy dust.

To the members of Wednesday Writers, Helen Bradley, Susan Earl, the late Kimberly Evans, and our newest member, Judy Bean. Your smiles and reassurance every Wednesday morning at The Foundry kept me going. Thank you for help with certain gnarly chapters as I neared the finish line.

Drew, Bliem, and Lisa, your friendship has withstood the test of time. Please keep making me laugh—it's good for my soul.

To my other NYC friends. Thank you for being there during the difficult days and the celebratory ones! It's impossible to name all my new Savannah friends and friends from afar, but special shout outs to my fellow Mint Julep Queens, members of the Peacock Guild Writers Salon at the Flannery O'Connor Childhood Home, Hilary Towers, and Dan Rizzo. Thank you Donna Shannon and Michael Hogan for giving me a porch to sit on and inviting me to share Thanksgiving my first year in Savannah when I knew no one.

To Vivian and Lillian: You may not be blood, but you will always be family to me.

To my Phi Mu sisters and in particular my life-long true blue buddy, Jeannine: WE ARE!

Deep gratitude to my Buddhist teacher and my Brooklyn priest, guardians of my spiritual life, for your guidance, wisdom, and prayers. To the sangha at Kadampa Meditation Center and parishioners of St. Paul's, Brooklyn, thank you for your spiritual friendship over so many years. Also to the members of Christ Church Episcopal for literally welcoming me with open arms when I arrived in Savannah!

I am eternally grateful to the team at Post Hill Press for giving my memoir a home. Thank you Anthony Ziccardi for your honesty, sharp advice, and belief in me and this book. My appreciation to editor Maddie

Sturgeon for your guidance, sure-handed shepherding of this book, editing, and kindness in calming my writerly nerves; to Devon Brown for your astute advice, cheerful emails, and reassuring spirit; to Rachel Shuster for your eagle-eyed editing; and to Cody Corcoran for wowing me with the most incredible cover design. Suzanne Venker, thank you for the introduction to Anthony!

To my friend Linda. I miss you. But you'll be at my book party in spirit.

To "Walt," my friend forever. You were right; Easter Sunday came. XO

Dear Mom and Dad, I miss you every day. Thank you for giving me a fine home and teaching me the importance of home, family, and commitment. You were wiser than I knew. I will forever carry you in my heart.

About the Author

Beverly Willett has written for *The New York Times*, *USA Today*, *The Washington Post*, *The New York Post*, *Family Circle*, *Woman's Day*, and many more. A former entertainment lawyer in New York City, she now lives in Savannah, Georgia, and serves on the boards of the homeless authority and the Flannery O'Connor Childhood Home. To learn more, watch her Tedx Talk "How to Begin Again."

www.beverlywillett.com